# God's Words to His Children

SERMONS SPOKEN AND UNSPOKEN

George MacDonald

**REGENT COLLEGE PUBLISHING**
Vancouver, British Columbia

First published 1887 by Funk & Wagnalis, New York

Reprinted 2006 by
Regent College Publishing
5800 University Blvd.
Vancouver, BC V6T 2E4 Canada
www.regentpubllishing.com

Regent College Publishing is an imprint of the Regent College Bookstore. Views expressed in works published by Regent College Publishing are those of the author and do not necessarily represent the official position of Regent College <www.regent-college.edu>.

ISBN 1-57383-388-6

## PREFACE.

Dr. George Mac Donald, the British author, was born in Huntly, Aberdeenshire, in 1824. His father a descendant of the Mac Donalds of Glencoe, was the proprietor of the Huntly Mills. This son graduated at the University of Aberdeen, studied theology in Owens College, Manchester, and for several years was a preacher of the Independent or Congregational church in Surrey and Sussex. He finally left the pulpit, with the view of devoting himself more directly to literature, as his books were multiplying upon his hands, and his fame was extending over the English-speaking world. Subsequently he became a lays member of the Church of England, and for a while was principal of a Seminary iu London. From time to time ever since, he has appeared occasionally in the metropolitan pulpits, where he is always welcome. His sermons are generally delivered entirely without notes, and so we are dependent largely upon the reports of stenographers for their preservation.

The purpose had in view, in the present attempt to group together some of these various discourses, has been to bring them within the reach of the readers who are not supposed to be possessed of the volumes or the periodicals in which Dr. Mac Donald's more serious work might be expected to appear. Indeed, it has been a task of some care and research in this country to gather these from the scat-

*tered sources indicated in the Table of Contents, and present them in a form sufficiently compact in order to secure a welcome. Sermons that have never been preached are not to be limited to regulation length in all cases. Something will have to be omitted, if they are to be rendered serviceable (as in this compilation it is devoutly hoped they will be) in vacant churches, where the pulpit is supplied by lay-readers.*

*There is a magnetism in this author's writings which fascinates at the moment of giving instruction. One may not, especially at the first perusal, accept his teaching; but even then, every suggestion is sure to start wholesome thought. And the unmistakable piety of each utterance is elevating and stimulating to spiritual devotion.*

*Of course, it is understood that the prayers added at the close of some chapters are none of them the composition of Dr. Mac Donald. Most of them will be recognized as belonging to some of the modern liturgies in use among the various churches.*

## TABLE OF CONTENTS.

|  |  | PAGE |
|---|---|---|
| I. | ALONE WITH GOD, Psalm 4:4.................... | 1 |
|  | [From "The Christian World Pulpit."] |  |
| II. | "HE SAW THEM TOILING," Mark 6:48........... | 13 |
|  | [From "The Seaboard Parish."] |  |
| III. | THE ONLY FREEDOM, Romans 1:1............... | 23 |
|  | [From "The English Pulpit of To-day."] |  |
| IV. | SIMON'S WIFE'S MOTHER, Luke 4:38............. | 36 |
|  | [From "The Miracles of Our Lord."] |  |
| V. | THE RESURRECTION HARVEST, Philippians 3:11, 12. | 46 |
|  | [From "The Seaboard Parish."] |  |
| VI. | LOVE THY NEIGHBOR, Matthew 22:39............. | 57 |
|  | [From "Unspoken Sermons": Series I.] |  |
| VII. | LOVE THINE ENEMY, Matthew 5:44............... | 68 |
|  | [From "Unspoken Sermons": Series I.] |  |
| VIII. | A CHRISTMAS LESSON, Matthew 6:24, 25......... | 80 |
|  | [From "Annals of a Quiet Neighborhood."] |  |
| IX. | TAKE NO THOUGHT, Matthew 6:31-33............. | 91 |
|  | [From "Annals of a Quiet Neighborhood."] |  |
| X. | THE CHILD IN THE MIDST, Mark 9:36, 37......... | 99 |
|  | [From "Unspoken Sermons"; Series I.] |  |
| XI. | FAITH THE PROOF OF THE UNSEEN, Hebrews 11:1.. | 113 |
|  | [From "The Christian World Pulpit."] |  |
| XII. | DIVINE AND HUMAN RELATIONSHIP, Matthew 12, 50. | 124 |
|  | [From "The Christian World Pulpit."] |  |
| XIII. | THE SLEEP OF LAZARUS, John 11:11............. | 134 |
|  | [From "The Seaboard Parish."] |  |

|       |                                                                 | PAGE |
|-------|-----------------------------------------------------------------|------|
| XIV.  | THE NEW NAME, Revelation 2:27................................... | 146  |
|       | [From "Unspoken Sermons": Series I.]                            |      |
| XV.   | THE GOD OF THE LIVING, Luke 20:38............................... | 157  |
|       | [From "Unspoken Sermons": Series I.]                            |      |
| XVI.  | THE TEMPTATION IN THE WILDERNESS, Matthew 4:4.................. | 165  |
|       | [From "Unspoken Sermons": Series I.]                            |      |
| XVII. | THE SECOND AND THIRD TEMPTATIONS, Matthew 4:10................. | 177  |
|       | [From "Unspoken Sermons": Series I.]                            |      |
| XVIII.| THE CRY, "ELOI, ELOI," Matthew 27:46........................... | 188  |
|       | [From "Unspoken Sermons": Series I.]                            |      |
| XIX.  | THE WAY, Matthew 19:21......................................... | 198  |
|       | [From "Unspoken Sermons": Series II.]                           |      |
| XX.   | THE HARDNESS OF THE WAY, Mark 10:24............................ | 215  |
|       | [From "Unspoken Sermons": Series II.]                           |      |
| XXI.  | THE BEGINNING OF MIRACLES, John 2:11........................... | 228  |
|       | [From "The Miracles of Our Lord."]                              |      |
| XXII. | MIRACLES OF HEALING UNSOLICITED, John 14:10.                    | 239  |
|       | [From "The Miracles of Our Lord."]                              |      |
| XXIII.| MIRACLES OF HEALING SOLICITED, Matthew 9:29.                    | 260  |
|       | [From "The Miracles of Our Lord."]                              |      |
| XXIV. | OTHER MIRACLES OF HEALING, Luke 17:13.......................... | 273  |
|       | [From "The Miracles of Our Lord."]                              |      |

# GOD'S WORDS

# TO HIS CHILDREN.

## I.

### ALONE WITH GOD.

"Stand in awe, and sin not: commune with your own heart upon your bed, and be still."—Psalm 4: 4.

It is a great sight to see a multitude of human faces around one, but the whole thing I would rather forget. Even when I stand before an assembly to speak to it, I would forget the gathering, and meet the individuals gathered; I would speak to the single heart and soul of the individual; to move the mass, as we say, I have no ambition.

The true power of life lies in the one soul; nay, the whole gathered mass is but a heap of human sand, except in proportion to the thing—the true thing awakened in the hearts of the individuals. There is no religion, no praise, no worship, but of the individual. And then, in proportion as the individual worships, there is something that rises from all the hearts and combines them into one before the face of their Father in heaven. But if the individuals know not God no gathering of multitudes brings them any nearer to the throne.

And, therefore, I choose to think of myself as speaking to one man or woman. You see, my text is just what must be said to every single, solitary person. It addresses him in the most solitary, silent time--when his day's work is done, and he is going to sleep. O friends! it is little of this kind of thing we are ready to think about in the heart of the city, and in all the tumultuous goings on of life—all this eager pursuit, whether of pleasure or wealth, or of bare livelihood; but if we make an end of anything else than the kingdom of God, we are of those who "lift up their souls to vanity," and who "swear deceitfully." The tumult of the day goes by, the pleasures of the evening pass, the last meal is taken, the "good-night" is said; as if we were preparing for our grave we put aside our garments in which we do the work of the day; we lay out ourselves straight in our bed; and there we lie, and God spreads the curtain of darkness round about us, just that he may shut himself in with his child. It is God and his child then, or God and somebody else— I mean, or God is left aside, shut out from his own child, and the man is with something else than God.

Now David knew all about the storms of the world; for be sure that a man learns quite as much in going about the wilderness and fighting for his life, as he does in a metropolitan counting-house; and be sure that when you have to protect yourselves on all sides and carry out your schemes in the face of multitudes of enemies, you learn to know man pretty well. And David, calm and solemn, Eastern as he was, without any sense of humor, or much of it, at least, if he had lived in the present day, would have understood us; and he could not have said a better word to any of us, even those of us who think the world everything, than "Commune with your own heart upon your bed, and be still."

"Still!" Ah, it is not bodily stillness alone; that is compelled. Little as we think of it, God has us in his hands far more than any mother has her little child of a week old. You cannot help going to sleep; he makes you. You do not know what sleep is a bit, with all the philosophy you can bring to bear upon it; you, so busy all the day, are still, when asleep—like death, and anybody might kill you. There you lie, passive, helpless, but not forgotten. If it were not for this sleep—that is, the bodily silence—we should all go mad. You know that sleeplessness is the first step to madness. If there never be a silence in the soul, and a man goes on always with his own thoughts and schemes and endeavors, it brings about a moral and a spiritual madness. That is tenfold worse than mere madness of the brain, when a man judges of everything by false ways, puts a wrong value upon everything, thinks little of great things and much of little things—that is a common way with all of us, more or less, only, thank God, with some of us it is growing less.

There comes a silence every now and then; and God makes it, just to put a stop to this kind of thing, and give himself a chance of speaking. Do you not believe, or can you believe, that there is all about us, and in us, an infinite thought; that the atmosphere in which we live and breathe, as the fishes live and breathe in the sea, is thought, and that thought is the thought of One, and that One is the thought whence we came—that is, the thinking God, thinking always? God's thoughts are power; they are like our thoughts, with this difference, that they are self-made, and ours are received from him. You cannot tell a moment before it comes what thought you are going to think. You cannot think at all in a certain sense; your thoughts are only the shadows of God's thoughts; but God is the living, original thought, and this is the atmosphere in which we poor little human creatures live.

Poor—do I say? To live in such an atmosphere, to live by it and breathe it, and be unable to exist without it, and yet do I say we are poor? Ah, poor if we do not know it! Ah, poor indeed if we value it as little and think about it as little as the fishes that swim in the sea think about the sea they swim in!

Friend, you are close to God, infinitely closer than your imagination can represent to you; and if you do not know it, you are in the very essence a poor, foolish thing—whom God has not forgotten, though.

But it is not in the midst of the tumult of life that a man first of all is able to hear God. We have not got up to Jesus Christ yet; God was always with him; he was never alone. So he is with us; but then Jesus knew it and felt it. "I know that thou hearest me always; I am not alone, for the Father is with me." Even he, when night came—and, I suppose, partly because there was not the retirement in the poor little houses that he wanted—went out into the great temple of God, the house of God—out to the mountains, that there might be nothing between him and God. In his love to us he had consented to a kind of vail being drawn between him and some of the aspects of God. When he took our human form the form was his own, but the kind of form was ours. Christ took his own shape when he took ours, but he did not need to be just made, as we are. A kind of vail came between him and God, which was something like another kind of faith—namely, shadowy human faith; I mean shadowy compared with what he had been before. The Son always has faith in the Father. That is an immortal faith, but now he has human faith as well; and, therefore, somehow it was better for him to go out and be alone, with nothing between his heart and the heart of the Father, just that he might lie still and let God and him be, and nothing else. The only name that will do for our God is, "I am that I am." There is no describing it: "I am." And for us, friends, when we are nearest God, it is just when we are in the knowledge that he *is*.

This is what David felt. When the tumult of the day was over, he lay down in his bed, and then God was and David was; there was nothing else for the time. That is the fountain of life to which we have to go to draw life, just to be at peace and let God let us know that he is there; it is just to let all the rest go away, all the troubles and anxieties of life, and let God say to our hearts, "Here I am, and here you are; you are in my charge, and nothing can hurt you; everything is well; I am here in peace, and I am leading you through these dreams of the daytime with all those troubles and pains; I am leading you up to my eternal peace, no dull existence, but with a sense of joy such as I have in my own heart, such joy that compelled me to create in you such joy as you have in the sense that you are my child."

Something like that it is, friends, between God and the man who knows how to be still. Let God speak to him. And this is what he wants to bring us to even by means of the tumult of life. I think God has sometimes great trouble in separating us far enough from himself that he can look round and know us. A mother will take her child and set it just as far as her arms can reach and draw back a little, so that the child may turn and run back to her. That is the first and most important lesson—the richest lesson that is given us in all our lives—just to run back to our mothers. And that is what God has been doing all the time through all the ages. My Father has taken the trouble to get me just far enough from him in order to let me know and choose him. Then am I of his kind when I know him, and choose him, and go back to him. This thing is what he wants us to know.

Oh, let the work of the day tire us! When the work of the day does not tire us, and we keep going on with it, there is no peace when we go to sleep. We dream about rubbish, and we know nothing about God at all. But sometimes we lie down and think with ourselves: "Oh, how stupid I have been! I have been forgetting my high calling, I have been fretful and distrustful, I have been unkind, I was not fair to that man; I have been cross to my own flesh and blood; it has not been a good shiny day with me." We think like that, and lift up our cry to the heart of our being, to the living, pure, loving Father, who cannot bear to see a spot on his child, and who has patience for a thousand years to get rid of that spot. Ah, that is a father indeed! The best of fathers are but little windows compared with God; and some fathers are very smoky windows, and have made a very wavy distorting glass for the child through them to see the path to eternal life. If we cry to God so, then sometimes there comes down upon us a peace, a rest, and an awareness of what he is and what we are; we get strength and hope; we may even be able to sleep. And often because we cannot get it in any other way, or cannot get enough of it in any other way, he gets us ill and sends us to bed; this is just another way to bring about that peace, that quiet of heart in which God can speak.

I do not believe in miracles in the sense that there is anything done against the laws of nature; when I say laws of nature, I mean the nature of God—God is he who made nature. I believe everything is done by the nature of God, and therefore I can believe anything the most wonderful if it be according to the nature of God. I find in the New Testament no miracle that I cannot believe; they seem to me just the right thing, just the natural, simple thing. I do not know how, but there is a good deal to be learned yet before we can venture to say it cannot be, of any one of those wonders which our Saviour wrought.

It seems, then, I was about to say, the most natural thing that God and man should thus meet, and know and understand each other; that there should be the meeting together of the thought of the one with the thought of the other. That is the simplest, most reasonable, common way; and therefore, I would say to some who get doubtful, whether it can be God that is speaking to them, because it seems to come in such a natural manner, just out of their own hearts—I would say to them: "God is so near you that he cannot speak into the deepest of you, and you become conscious of it, without its coming through the most reasonable natural channel, for all that you do not know of your own being joins on to what you do not know about God's." Our best thoughts come to us just simply up in our souls like our bad ones, only they come from a much deeper source. Bad ones are not half so deep as good ones, and it seems, "Can this be? am I not thinking this myself?" Yes; you are thinking it yourself, because God has thought it before you. And then you do think it yourself, for there is no possibility of dividing you from God. God thinks you out of himself, and you live because he lives; you have no independent existence at all. God has set us to choose the right thing and do the right thing, and then we are willing, and then we are like God—willing from ourselves, but those selves are of his making. They are not only rooted in him, but their very existence springs out of his existence, and so we live and cannot be parted from him. We are the heirs of him, our Father; we are the heirs of eternal life, and partakers of the divine nature, as soon as ever we give in to the real natural law of things, and say, "Thou art my Father, I am doing thy will."

And this is all that Jesus wants of us. But we are so hard to bring to this that, I say, he makes us ill, sends us to bed, and we have to lie still, and, perhaps, we are not able to think much, only able to feel, and so he makes a quiet around about us.

Upon others he brings sudden poverty. There comes a great shock, and then a silence; and then the man begins to think: "What have I been about? If I were to fill myself with this money that I have been seeking, if it filled every pocket, and every box at my banker's, where should I have been? Without life, without hope; a hollow, empty, miserable thing; sending my God-born being out to inhabit the forms of sovereigns and bank-notes, descending from my calling into this worship of the miserable."

O friends! commune with your own hearts, with your own body, and be still, and know that there is a Power that made you, made your money, too, and does not care much about it. It is not a sign of God's favor to give much money to people; and most heartily do I believe, not only because Christ said it, but because I see, that it is hard for a rich man to enter the kingdom of heaven, and I find it hard enough, being a poor man. It is not easy, but it is worth doing. It may not be easy to banish from your soul the things of the day in order that you may be still and hear God; but, oh, is God worth nothing? Is the presence closer than that of husband, or wife, or child, or brother? Is the presence of this loving power that loves you out and out—is it nothing to you? Do you prefer to write so many figures as your possessions to having God yourself? It is awful folly, friends, and yet you and I are always in danger of it, and every time we are miserable about what may happen to-morrow, we are denying God, and saying he is not enough for us. It is just as you have seen an ungracious child or an ungracious beggar sometimes snatch your gift from you. You see an ungracious dog do it sometimes, but not often. If you loved God, his gift to you would be a living gift, and you would use it for him. Reaping and keeping to one's self is altogether against the heart and thought, the very being of God, who lives in giving, from whom there is always a going out, and out, and out.

Friends, if we do not do the will of God in the day, it is not likely that we will be still upon our beds that he may come and visit us. We need not be without him during the day. Though not a business man myself, I sympathize with you who have so many things to think about, and who have to go out and do the work in the great city that you have got to do. A thousand things pressing in upon you, it must be so difficult for you to remember God; and I know it is such poverty, such wretchedness, not to remember him. But if you commune with your hearts on your bed, and are still, and God comes to you there, there will be a moment, even in the midst of your business, when a quiet will drop down upon you like a little bit of heaven covering your head, as it were, for an instant, and you will think, "Oh, there is God! and if God is there, how well all this is!"

Only, what an awful thing it is then, if you do not, from that thought, go up like a very priest of God in his temple, dispensing righteousness in truth—I do not mean in talking; I do not mean speaking about the Bible; but I mean in buying and selling, and in common speech, and in the common things of the day; for there is nothing in this world to be done that is not honorable in itself, and may not be, and ought not to be, a service—a service in the temple of the living God. Ah, it is indeed serving God if a man can make his counter the very altar of the living God! The goods he puts down upon it are holy before God, because they are placed there in honor and in service. I believe, friends, that the true temple, and the true worship, is an every-day-of-the-week worship. That is what our Lord would have. You do not hear him talk what we commonly call religious talk. He did not talk the religious talk of his day. But when he does talk to us now, it is as deep as the foundations of the universe; it is God and man, and that is real religion. It is not this observation and that observation; it is my soul and his soul, and then my hands to do his will. That is real religion.

There are those, and I suppose they are few compared with the rest, who, under religious service, under music, under preaching, and such like, feel very strongly this uplifting. O friends! it is the deed that stirs the man; it is the thing you do, and not what you feel. I have heard one of the best of men lamenting to me that sometimes it seemed to him as if he had no feeling at all; that he inherited a dull temperament from his poor father, who had no feeling, or next to none; but his hands and his heart were busy for his fellow-creatures from morning to night, and his prayer ascended to the God of his salvation. We were not meant to be creatures of feeling; we were meant to be creatures of conscience, first of all, and then of consciousness towards God—a sense of his presence; and if we go on, the feeling will come all right. Our feelings will blossom as a rose just from the very necessity of things. And blessed is the man whose highest, deepest feelings come to him when he is alone on his bed and still. But if even that man does not go out and carry with him the principle that God is all in all, he will be the worse. To know God, and not to do his will—that is eternal damnation.

I am getting into depths that I shrink from dealing with. I must stay my speech, and not weary you. At length we go to sleep. Thank God, he is with us still; but if we do not sleep when such times come, we are in great danger of falling. Let us be careful, above all things, if God has given any insight into the reality of his being, and our relation to him, and let us be tenfold careful about our fellow-man, that we do him no wrong.

"Lord, who shall abide in thy tabernacle? who shall dwell in thy holy hill? He that walketh uprightly, and worketh righteousness, and speaketh the truth in his heart." Some of us lead homely lives, and have not the temptations that others have. We have our own temptations. It is so easy to be rough in the house, so easy to lay aside our good manners to our wives and children. Ah, who shall know the eternal Father, and come forth, and not be a gentle father himself?

O friends, let us be jealous over ourselves! God will be readier to come to his child the next night, if during the day that child has been living childlike, walking in the steps of his father, holding fast by him. If he has been good to his fellow-children, to his brothers and sisters, wherever they are, God will be readier to meet him, readier to say, "My child, here I am." The one, eternal, original, infinite blessing of the human soul, is when in stillness, the Father comes and says, "My child, I am here."

ALMIGHTY GOD, the fountain of all wisdom, who knowest our necessities before we ask, and our ignorance in asking; we beseech thee to have compassion upon our infirmities; and those things, which for our unworthiness we dare not, and for our blindness we cannot, ask, vouchsafe to give us, for the worthiness of thy Son JESUS CHRIST our Lord. *Amen.*

## II.

## "HE SAW THEM TOILING."

"HE SAW THEM TOILING IN ROWING."—Mark 6; 48.

Once upon a time a man went up a mountain and staid there until it was dark, and staid on. Now a man who finds himself on a mountain as the sun is going down, especially if he is alone, makes haste to get down before it is dark. But this man went up when the sun was going down, and, as I say, continued there for a good long while after it was dark. You will want to know why. I will tell you. He wished to be alone. He had not a house of his own. He never had, all the time he lived. He had not even a room of his own into which he could go and bolt the door of it. True, he had kind friends, who gave him a bed; but they were all poor people, and their houses were small, and very likely they had large families, and he could not always find a quiet place to go into. And I dare say, if he had had a room, he would have been a little troubled with the children constantly coming to find him; for however much he loved them—and no man was ever so fond of children as he was—he needed to be left quiet sometimes.

So upon this occasion, he went up the mountain just to be quiet. He had been all day with a crowd of people, and he felt that it was time to be alone. For he had been talking with men all day, which tires and sometimes confuses a man's thoughts; and now he wanted to talk with God—for that makes a man strong, and puts all the confusion in order again, and lets a man know what he is about. So he went to the top of the hill. That was his secret chamber. It had no door; but that did not matter—no one could see him but God. There he staid for hours—sometimes, I suppose, kneeling in his prayer to God; sometimes, tired with his own thinking, sitting on a stone; sometimes walking about, looking forward to what would come next—not anxious about it, but contemplating it. For, just before he came up here, some of the people who had been with him wanted to make him a king; and this would not do—this was not what God wanted of him, and therefore he got rid of them, and came up here to talk to God.

It was so quiet up here! The earth had almost vanished. He could see just the bare hill-top beneath him, a glimmer below, and the sky and the stars over his head. The people had all gone away to their own homes, and perhaps next day would hardly think about him at all, busy catching fish, or digging their gardens, or making things for their houses. But he knew that God would not forget him the next day any more than this day, and that God had sent him not to be the king that these people wanted him to be, but their servant. So, to make his heart strong, I say, he went up into the mountain alone to have a talk with his Father. How noisy it had been down there a little while ago! But God had been in the noise then as much as he was in the quiet now—the only difference being that he could not then be alone with him. I need

## HE SAW THEM TOILING. 15

not tell you who this man was—it was the king of men, the Lord Jesus Christ, the everlasting Son of our Father in heaven.

Now this mountain on which he was praying had a small lake at the foot of it—that is, about thirteen miles long, and five miles broad. Not wanting his usual companions to be with him this evening—partly, I presume, because they were of the same mind as those who desired to make him a king—he had sent them away in their boat, to go across this water to the other side, where were their homes and their families. Now, it was not pitch dark either on the mountain-top or on the water down below; yet I doubt if any other man than he would have been keen-eyed enough to discover that little boat down in the middle of the lake, much distressed by the west wind that blew right in their teeth. But he loved every man in it so much, that I think even as he was talking to his Father his eyes would now and then go looking for and finding it— watching it on its way across to the other side. You must remember it was a little boat; and there are often tremendous storms upon these little lakes with great mountains about them. For the wind will come all at once, rushing down through the clefts in as sudden a squall as ever overtook a sailor at sea. And then, you know, there is no sea room. If the wind get the better of them, they are on the shore in a few minutes, whichever way the wind may blow. He saw them worn out at the oar, toiling in rowing, for the wind was contrary unto them.

So the time for loneliness and prayer was over, and the time to go down out of his secret chamber and help his brethren was come. He did not need to turn and say good-bye to his Father, as if he dwelt on that mountain-top alone: his Father was down there on the lake as well. He went straight down. Could not his Father, if he too was down on the lake, help them without him? Yes. But he wanted him to do it, that they might see that he did it. Otherwise they could only have thought that the wind fell and the waves lay down, without supposing for a moment that their Master or his Father had had anything to do with it. They would have done just as people do nowadays: they think that the help comes of itself instead of by the will of him who determined from the first that men should be helped. So the Master went down the hill. When he reached the border of the lake, the wind being from the other side, he must have found the waves breaking furiously upon the rocks, but that made no difference to him. He looked out as he stood alone on the edge, amidst the rushing wind and the noise of the water, out over the waves under the clear starry sky, saw where the tiny boat was tossed about like a nutshell, and set out.

The companions of our Lord had not been willing to go away and leave him behind. Now, I dare say, they wished more than ever that he had been with them— not that they thought he could do anything with a storm, only that somehow they would have been less afraid with his face to look at. They had seen him cure men of dreadful diseases; they had seen him turn water into wine—some of them; they had seen him feed five thousand people the day before with five loaves and two small fishes: but had one of their number suggested that if he had been with them they would have been safe from the storm, they would not have talked any nonsense about the laws of nature, not having learned that kind of nonsense, but they would

## HE SAW THEM TOILING. 17

have said that was quite a different thing—altogether too much to expect or believe; *nobody* could make the wind mind what it was about, or keep the water from drowning you if you fell into it and could not swim; or such like.

At length, when they were nearly worn out, taking feebler and feebler strokes, sometimes missing the water altogether, at other times burying their oars in it up to the handles—as they rose on the crest of a huge wave, one of them gave a cry, and they all stopped rowing and stared, leaning forward to peer through the darkness. And through the spray which the wind tore from the tops of the waves and scattered before it like dust, they saw, perhaps a hundred yards or so from the boat, something standing up from the surface of the water. It seemed to move towards them. It was a shape like a man. They all cried out with fear, as was natural, for they thought that it must be a ghost.

But then, over the noise of the wind and the waters, came the voice they knew so well. It said, "Be of good cheer; it is I. Be not afraid." I should think, between wonder and gladness, they hardly knew for some moments where or what they were about. Peter was the first to recover himself apparently. In the first flush of his delight he felt strong and full of courage. "Lord, if it be thou," he said, "bid me come unto thee on the water." Jesus just said, "Come," and Peter unshipped his oar, and scrambled over the gunwale on to the sea. But when he let go his hold of the boat, and began to look about him, and saw how the wind was tearing the water, and how it tossed and raved between him and Jesus, he began to be afraid. And as soon as he began to be afraid he began to sink. But he had, notwithstanding his fear, just sense enough to do the one sensible thing. He cried out, "Lord! save me." And Jesus put out his hand and took hold of him, and lifted him out of the water, and said to him, "O thou of little faith, wherefore didst thou doubt?" And then they got into the boat, and the wind fell all at once and altogether.

Now, you will not think that Peter was a coward, will you? It was not that he had not courage, but that he had not enough of it. And why was it that he had not enough of it? Because he had not faith enough. Peter was always very easily impressed with the look of things. It was not at all likely that a man should be able to walk on the water: and yet Peter found himself standing on the water. You would have thought that when he once found himself standing on the water, he need not have been afraid of the winds and the waves that lay between him and Jesus. But they looked so ugly that the fearfulness of them took hold of his heart, and his courage went. You would have thought that the greatest trial of his courage was over when he got out of the boat, and that there was comparatively little more ahead of him. Yet the sight of the waves, and the blast of the boisterous wind, were too much for him.

I will tell you how I fancy it was, and I think there are several instances of the same kind of thing in Peter's life. When he got out of the boat, and found himself standing on the water, he began to think much of himself for being able to do so, and fancy himself better and greater than his companions, and an especial favorite of God above them. Now, there is nothing that kills faith sooner than pride. The two are directly against each other. The moment that Peter grew proud, and began to think about himself instead of about his Master, he began to lose faith, and then

## HE SAW THEM TOILING. 19

he grew afraid, and then he began to sink—and that brought him to his senses. Then he forgot himself and remembered his Master, and then the hand of the Lord caught him, and the voice of the Lord gently rebuked him for the smallness of his faith, asking, "Wherefore didst thou doubt?" I wonder if Peter was able to read his own heart sufficiently well to answer that *wherefore?* I do not think it likely at this period of his history. But God has immeasurable patience, and before he had done teaching Peter, even in this life, he had made him know quite well that pride and conceit were at the root of all his failures. Jesus did not point it out to him now. Faith was the only thing that would reveal that to him, as well as cure him of it; and was, therefore, the only thing he required of him in his rebuke.

I suspect Peter was helped back into the boat by the eager hands of his companions already in an humbler state of mind than when he left it, but before his pride would be quite overcome, it would need that same voice of loving-kindness to call him Satan, and the voice of the cock to bring to his mind his loud boast, and his sneaking denial: nay, even the voice of one who had never seen the Lord till after his death, but was yet a readier disciple than he—the voice of St. Paul, to rebuke him because he dissembled, and was not downright honest. But at the last even he gained the crown of martyrdom, enduring all extremes, nailed to the cross like his Master, rather than deny his name. This should teach us to distrust ourselves, and yet have great hope for ourselves, and endless patience with other people. But to return to the story, and what the story itself teaches us.

If the disciples had known that Jesus saw them

from the top of the mountain, and was watching them all the time, would they have been frightened at the storm (as I have little doubt they were, for they were only fresh-water fishermen, you know)? Well, to answer my own question, I do not know that, as they then were, it would have made so much difference to them, for none of them had risen much above the look of the things nearest them yet. But supposing you, who know something about him, were alone on the sea, and expecting your boat to be swamped every moment—if you found out all at once that he was looking down at you from some lofty hill-top, and seeing all round about you in time and space too, would you be afraid? He might mean you to go to the bottom, you know. Would you mind going to the bottom with him looking at you? I do not think I should mind it myself. But I must take care lest I be boastful like Peter.

Why should we be afraid of anything with him looking at us, who is the Saviour of men? But we are afraid of him instead, because we do not believe that he is what he says he is—the Saviour of men. We do not believe what he offers us is salvation. We think it is slavery, and therefore continue slaves. Friends, I will speak to you who think you do believe in him. I am not going to say that you do not believe in him, but I hope I am going to make you say to yourselves that you too deserve to have those words of the Saviour spoken to you that were spoken to Peter, "O ye of little faith!" Floating on the sea of your troubles, all kinds of fears and anxieties assailing you, is he not on the mountain-top? Sees he not the little boat of your fortunes tossed with the waves and the contrary wind? Assuredly he will come to you walking on the waters.

It may not be in the way you wish, but if not, you will say at last, "This is better." It may be he will come in a form that will make you cry out for fear in the weakness of your faith, as the disciples cried out— not believing any more than they did that it can be he. But will not each of you arouse your courage, that to you also he may say, as to the woman with the sick daughter, whose confidence he so sorely tried, "Great is thy faith." Will you not arouse yourself, I say, that you may do him justice, and cast off the slavery of your own dread? O ye of little faith, wherefore will ye doubt? Do not think that the Lord sees and will not come. Down the mountain assuredly he will come; and you are now safe in your troubles as the disciples were in theirs with Jesus looking on. They did not know it, but it was so; the Lord was watching them. And when you look back upon your past lives, cannot you see some instance of the same kind—when you felt and acted as if the Lord had forgotten you, and found afterwards that he had been watching you all the time?

But the reason why you do not trust him more is that you obey him so little. If you would only ask what God would have you to do, you would soon find your confidence growing. It is because you are proud and envious and greedy after gain that you do not trust him more. Ah! trust him if it were only to get rid of these evil things, and be clean and beautiful in heart.

O sailors with me on the ocean of life, will you, knowing that he is watching you from his mountain-top, do and say the things that hurt, and wrong, and disappoint him? Sailors on the waters that surround this globe, though there be no great mountain that overlooks the little lake on which you float, not the less does he behold you, and care for you, and watch over you. Will you do that which is unpleasant, distressful to him? Will you be irreverent, cruel, coarse? Will you say evil things, lie, and delight in vile stories and reports, with his eye on you, watching your ship on its watery ways, ever ready to come over the waves to help you? It is a fine thing to fear nothing, but it would be far finer to fear nothing *because* he is above all, and over all, and in you all. For his sake and for his love, give up everything bad, and take him for your captain. He will be both captain and pilot to you, and steer you safe into the port of glory.

ALMIGHTY God, who hast promised to hear the petitions of those who ask in thy Son's name; we beseech thee mercifully to incline thine ears to us who have now made our prayers and supplications unto thee; and grant that those things which we have faithfully asked according to thy will, may effectually be obtained, to the relief of our necessity, and to the setting forth of thy glory; through JESUS CHRIST our Lord. *Amen.*

## III.

## THE ONLY FREEDOM.

"PAUL, A SERVANT OF JESUS CHRIST."—Rom. I: I.

St. Paul, in addressing the Romans, begins thus: "Paul, a servant of Jesus Christ." Well, you all know that it is more than that that he says. I do not know why they put the word "bondservant" in the margin. For my part, I should translate it just as it stands, "Paul, a slave of Jesus Christ." And again—for he does not want to be exclusive even in this humility—when he is writing to the Philippians, he joins another with him, namely, Timothy, his young friend, and he says, "Paul and Timothy, slaves of Jesus Christ." But the word does mean just that. It is not what we call a servant in our day, for they could not come and go as they pleased. They were not even servants who were slaves taken in war, but it means even more than the bondslave. It means a born slave, and there we have it—" a born slave of Jesus Christ."

It is a figure, you know; but the plague of it is that most people, who deal with the figures in the New Testament, make them to mean less because they are figures. That is the way in which the commonplace devil that possesses many men and women makes them treat all the high and holy things. Where there is a figure used in the New Testament, it means more than it can say; and more than any word that man can utter did St. Paul mean when he said that he was a born slave of Jesus Christ. No doubt there is in the word an element which St. Paul did not mean—did not feel. You know how a mother will sometimes, just out of tenderness to her child, call it bad names. So St. Paul here, just in the despair of faith, takes delight in belonging to Christ utterly, altogether, inconceivably, saved by Christ himself, for he could not tell or feel— he knew that he could not even feel—how much he belonged to Christ; and he used a word that indicates in it something which is not real, not true. He says, "I am the slave of Jesus Christ," and yet, if any man in this world was free besides the Lord himself, that man was St. Paul. As for us, as soon as we begin to say high things in our human speech, we immediately begin to say them wrong. There is no help for it. Whatever of high things can be put into words is not right; it is not correct. We are only trying after what language is unequal to. It cannot do all, and therefore sometimes we just go wrong the other way, and use, as it were, the wrong word in a kind of agony of outreaching after the true.

"But St. Paul was an enthusiast." Yes, I believe that he was an enthusiast; and, if he had not been an enthusiast about such a thing as this, he would not have been worthy to be a slave to the lowest of Christ's people. There is no reality in the relation of things that are high, if we be not enthusiastic about them, if they do not possess us, hold us, fill us, lead us, drive us, teach us, feed us, live in us, and make us live in them. No good can be done without enthusiasm. There is no reality of love without enthusiasm. What! shall I know anything at all that is genuine about Jesus Christ? Am I a fool capable of believing that that man came from the bosom of the Father to be to me my loving Brother and my Saviour; to take me, at his own torture, out of my misery, out of myself, which is my torture, into the life of his Father in heaven? Shall I believe that—shall I even believe that he had not a selfish thought in him, and not be enthusiastic about him? Have I the faculty of enthusiasm in me? Is it possible for me to give myself away—to do anything that is not urged and suggested by the lower self? Am I capable of these things at all? Then, if I am not enthusiastic about Jesus Christ, this whole faculty of my nature lies useless, rotting in me, for there is nothing else in the universe to call it out, or capable of calling it out. The poor enthusiasms that one sees in the world for things that are less than the truth, or that are small passing facts of our condition here—look how they last when a man is vigorous, and how they wither when he grows older! But you will find that St. Paul, at the very last of his life, was more a slave of Jesus Christ than ever before—far more his slave than when he lay struck blind and helpless by the light of his appearing.

For my part, it seems to me a grand proof—and we can have no external proof better, though we may have better proof in ourselves, for the least feeling of these things in ourselves is a higher and better proof than anything brought from the outside—I say that the fact that a man like St. Paul, (brought up as he was, with such a brain and such a heart, and turned the wrong way at first,) should be capable of burning with such enthusiasm for a man of whose history he knew very little that was real or true until he saw him in heavenly glory—that after that he should live to be the rejoicing slave of Jesus Christ—is it a wonder that such a fact should weigh with me ten times more than the denial of the highest intellect of this world who gives me by the very terms that he uses, concerning what he thinks my faith, the conviction that he knows nothing about what I believe? He talks as if he did, but he knows nothing about it. St. Paul knew the Lord Christ; and, therefore, heart and soul, mind, body, and brain. he belonged to Jesus Christ, even as his born slave.

But let us try to understand a little what is meant by a slavery which is a liberty. One of the first feelings of the noble-minded youth is a love of liberty. In our history he has been taught it from his earliest thought, and he feels that the grand thing is that he shall be free and the slave of no man. As a rule he has a very low notion of what liberty is, and in most cases it does not grow very much better as he gets older; but still there is, at the root of it, a something genuine and real, which is capable of being interpreted into a high and holy thing. But is it, as the boy thinks about it? Well, it is just to do as he likes; or, if he carries it a little higher, and thinks of political liberty, it is that nobody may meddle with him, that he is to stand without any weight, or bond, or command upon him. And for the sake of this kind of liberty, too often, he will bind his soul in chains of misery. Sometimes, for instance, he will run away from school; he will run away from home; he will shirk doing the things that his parents tell him; and, in order that his feet may be free to wander where they will, he ties up his inner man in a sense of wrath, in garments of pain, in a feeling of bondage; and because he would be free he makes himself a slave far deeper than any outward law could make him.

Suppose, however, that there was no law of parent, or teacher, or magistrate, or ruler of any kind whatever, laid upon us, and suppose that the man has plenty of money and all kinds of what he calls freedom to go and do what he pleases. Suppose that, outside, he is aware of no bondage whatever. That cannot last long. As soon as there comes a touch of pain, the least sense of weakness—as soon as the first white begins to come on the hair—well, perhaps not quite so soon as that, but when he has the first feeling, "I am not quite capable of what I used to do,"—as soon as any of these merest touches come on the consciousness of a man, the sense of freedom begins to go. But suppose that in the heyday of a man's strength, in the heartiness of ripe youth, before middle age has begun to come, he can move as he pleases and do as he wills, and suppose that there is no one to say nay to him, is he free? Young man, would you think that that was all right? Would you think that this was your calling? Would you say, "For this end came I into the world, that I might do whatever I liked"? And would you feel that you were grand and free? If you do feel so, you will not believe me, but I tell you—and one day you will believe me if you remember it, which is not likely—I tell you that, to me and to every man who has had the experience of any effort of true liberty, you are a most wretched slave, for your very ideal is slavery; your very high notion is mean and despicable. You cannot see it; I know that, but you do not see everything yet; and the time is coming when you will be compelled to see it, and can no more help seeing it than now you can help—or, rather, I should say, will help not seeing it. For what is it that drives you on? There is a devil who has whispered to you—affected, perhaps, a certain convolution of your brain, touched you at some certain spot; and you say that you are free, and all the time you are the real sport of temptation. You call it liberty. You stay till the point of the arrow that directs you turns against you and pierces you to the centre. You stay till the devil that tempted you mocks you, and you gaze at him and get no help; for there is no such thing in the world as liberty, except under the law of liberty; that is, the acting according to the essential laws of our own being—not our feelings which go and come. The man that will rage one hour and be cold the next—what a fool he is if he supposes that he is to walk either by his rage or by his coldness! It is a law that he is to obey. He is to follow the lines upon which this being of his is constructed, this central, original, heart-emotion of his existence. Why, as soon might a man attempt to drive some great engine backward—as soon might he lay hold of its centre pinion and try to stop it, as you can think to make it go well with your being if you live contrary to the very essence of your being; for, let me tell you, you are not bad, or, if you are bad, you are damnably bad. You are not made bad. God forbid; for God made us, and he made nothing bad, and if you will be bad that is fearful indeed. The lines of our being are laid, I will not even say by the hand of the living God, they were laid in his heart. The idea of every one of us was known and thought over in that heart; and, out of his heart we have gone. He has set before us a way that we may turn, and, of our own free will, run back to him, embrace the Father's knees, and be lifted to the Father's heart.

There is no liberty but in doing right. There is no freedom but in living out of the deeps of our nature—not out of the surface. Why, look at you. You lose your temper. You think that you are free when you go into a rage. Half-an-hour after you are ashamed.

## THE ONLY FREEDOM.    29

God grant that you may be sorry. That is something more. But you are ashamed of yourself; and yet you think that you are a free man. You acted out the mere surface of your nature—a something which it needed but half-an-hour to make you ashamed of. That is not liberty. That is acting out of your poor, mean, despicable self, which we have all got, and not out of the divine self, the deepest in us, for the deepest in us is God. We did not come into this world because we willed it. We did not say what we should be. It is God in every man that enables that man even to stretch out his hand. The moment may come when he can lift it no more. Let him will, and will to do it with an agony of willing; yet he cannot raise his hand any more. He cannot do it. It is God; none else.

But I am talking about liberty, and what I want to impress upon those who will be impressed is this—that the one only liberty lies in obedience. Can you lay hold of it? Do you think that Jesus Christ—and he will let me put it so because it is for the sake of the truth—do you think that Jesus Christ would have felt free one moment if he had not been absolutely devoted to the will of his Father in heaven? Suppose it had been possible, which, thank the Lord Christ and his Father, it was not, else we were now in the darkness of helplessness—suppose it had been possible that Jesus Christ should have been less devoted to his Father, for he might have said in the same high, figurative sense that he was the slave of his Father; for, look you, he cares for nothing but his Father's will. There is nothing else that he has anything to do with. The very reason for which he came into the world was "that the world may know that I am of the Father." "As the Father has given me commandment," he says, "so I do;" and then he says, "Arise, let us go hence"—away to the death, because the Father willed it. Oh, if Jesus had been less the slave of his Father, do you think that he would have felt that he was a free man? Do you not think that that was what made the devil? He had a notion of being free. "Here I am. I will be the slave of no man—not even of the God that made me." And so all goes wrong, and he is the devil—no archangel any longer—and a mean devil, too, who tries to pull all down into the same abyss with himself well knowing that he cannot even give them his pride to uphold them. If, friends, it should be slavery to obey the very source of our being, think what mean creatures we are that, having come from that source, to follow the law of our life is a slavery.

Well, then, we are the born slaves—ah, thank God, we are the born slaves of Christ! But then he is liberty himself, and all his desire is that we should be such noble, true, right creatures that we never can possibly do or think a thing that shall bind a thread round our spirits and make us feel as if we were bound anywhere. He wants us to be free—not as the winds—not to be free as the man who owns no law, but to be free by being law, by being right, by being truth. When you know that the law goes in one way, is it freedom to bring your will against that law, or to avoid it, and go another way, when the very essence of your existence means that you do not oppose, but yield to the conditions—I do not mean arbitrary conditions, but the essential conditions—of your being, those conditions that make your being divine, for God has made us after his own fashion, and when we do as God would do, as God delights to do—when we act according to the divine mind and nature, we are acting according to our own deepest self, which is the law and will of God. Jesus Christ might have said, "I am the slave of my Father in heaven." He has nowhere used the phrase, but it was in that sense that St. Paul said, "I am the slave of Jesus Christ." Oh, I appeal to you women— I mean those of you that love Jesus Christ—what would you not do to show him that you love him? Then when I say the words there comes a painful thought, whether some of you may not be like children who indulge in all kinds of tender caresses, but who, when told to do something, begin to pout and refuse to obey. Oh, to think that you should love with all your feeling—that you should love the Lord so much, and yet take so little trouble to know from the story left behind what he really now at this moment wants you to do! That is the way to show your love to him. But, I put it to you again, what would you not do to show that you love him? There were two women who seem to have gone as far as women could go to show their love to him. You know the story—something that one cannot speak. You know the story. Some of you would do that, oh, how rejoicingly! And when you say "Master," you would like to say with St. Paul, just because you have no other word strong enough, "Lord, I am thy bondslave." That was St. Paul's feeling when he used the word. But then St. Paul spent his whole life, all his thoughts, all his energies, simply to obey this Lord and Master; and so he was the one free man —not the only free man; there were some more amongst the apostles, and, by his preaching, here and there and everywhere, there started up free men, or, at least, men who were beginning to grow free by beginning to be the slaves of Jesus Christ.

But let me show you a little more. I do not say that the moment you begin to obey the Lord Jesus Christ, and to be his slave, then you are free. I do not say that then you know what is meant by liberty. I will show you. There are many things that we know are right, and we are not inclined to do them. There are many things that we know are wrong, and we are inclined to do them. But when the law of liberty comes, the will of Jesus Christ, we begin to try to do the things we do not like to do, and not to do the things that we do like to do. But do you not see that here is a strife? So long as we are in this condition, so long as we know that we have to do the things that we do not like, and that we must not do the things we would like, we are not free. We are only fighting for freedom, but we are not free. We do not know liberty yet; and yet, on the other hand (try to follow me), if we liked the good things, and did not like the bad thing, and without any thought or effort of our own, just went to the good thing and not to the bad thing, we should not be free either, because we should be going just by the impulse in us. So there comes a contradiction which it is not easy to explain or understand. But, you know, God could not be satisfied to make us like the animals. A good dog does not bite, because he is not inclined to bite. He loves you, but you do not say that he is high morally because he is not inclined to do anything bad. But if we, choosing, against our liking, to do the right, go on so until we are enabled by doing it to see into the very loveliness and essence of the right, and know it to be altogether beautiful, and then at last never think of doing evil, but delight with our whole souls in doing the will of God, why then, do you not see, we combine the two, and we are free indeed, because we are acting like God out of the essence of our nature, knowing good and evil, and choosing the good with our whole hearts and delighting in it?

It is not enough to love because we cannot help it. We must love, too, because we will it with our whole nature, and then, do you not see, when we come to love one another perfectly, we do not need to be told, "Thou shalt not steal; thou shalt not kill; thou shalt not bear false witness," because the thing is absolutely abhorrent to us, if the thought would come up at all? But, when we have learned to love our neighbor as ourselves the thought of killing and stealing never comes out, or of defrauding or of doing ignoble things and calling them "business." Nothing of that kind. We positively love our neighbor, and to hurt him would be to hurt ourselves worse. That is liberty, but we can come to that only by willing it, the root of our being is that will. We must fall in with it. We must will it ourselves, and then, at last, the lovely will of God will possess us from head to feet and fingers, and we shall live in the very breath of God and act like God himself, free like the Living One, because we are one with the source of our life and our being.

So, friends, you see how all through, as far as the words go, we have got to deal with something like contradictions, but in the meaning of the thing your own hearts tell you—the hearts of many of you, at least, tell you—what it is, and you will see that there is no contradiction in it at all. Though it might be exceedingly difficult to lay it out all plain in logical language, your hearts can understand it. Nay, they witness to it because they have grown hungry. You want to be such children of God as this. You want to be free from the oppression of evil in every way. Nay, the time will come when you will lay down the arms of your battle, fighting for the truth. You will have to lay them down even because you have conquered. How conquered? Because you are perfectly satisfied with God, one with his will, rejoicing in his joy, living in his life, having no fear, no ambition, no anxiety, but a constant strength of life that death and hell cannot touch. You would not be afraid then if you were cast into the middle of hell fire. The flames could not touch you. If you had a body that they could scorch and burn, yet the soul within you would rise superior even to that torture, because, being of the very nature of God, partakers of the divine nature, you would be able to bear pain in triumph, and with a sense of freedom in the midst of it, and slavery would be far from you.

But I have just a word to say now to those specially who think that they have belonged to Christ for many years. Are you in any sense, can you say it out of your heart and meaning it, "I am a slave of Christ?" Object to the term, and I say, are you the free man of Christ? for they mean the same thing. His slave is his free brother. Is there anything that you do now? And we cannot divide our lives, we cannot say that the private gentleman will be saved when the man of business will be condemned; we are either all Christ's, or not at all, for he has told us that no man can serve two masters. Are you doing anything now that is not just all that you would like, suppose the thing were to come to be laid open to the purest eyes of those who know you? If there is such a thing as you would not like seen, does the Master see it, or does he not? If he does not, he is no Master; we want a greater. If you think he will let it slip, God forbid that I should serve that Master! I want a Master that will not pass over

## THE ONLY FREEDOM. 35

a farthing, a Master who will not let me go from his cleansing hand even if that hand be washing me with fire so long as there is any spot of defilement on my spirit; and the least shadow of dishonesty is the deepest defilement. Are you not sometimes content with saying, "I do as my neighbor would do to me"? You cannot say, "I do as I would like my neighbor to do to me," perhaps. I wonder whether you could say, then, what the Lord said; for remember he never said, "Thou shalt love thy neighbor as thyself." That was not what he taught. That was taught long before. The spirit of God taught it, but not by Jesus Christ. What Christ taught was, "Love one another as I have loved you." Do we behave to our fellow-men as Christ has behaved to us? If we do not, we are not his slaves. We may be even following in the track of his triumph— I do not say that we shall not get in, but I am clear upon this—that we never shall enter until we have passed through what ordeal is needful to make us clean as God himself. We have got to be good, and if we will not willingly of ourselves, he will make us. It is what he made us for, and it ought to be the business of our lives.

O LORD, raise up, we pray thee, thy power, and come among us, and with great might succor us; that whereas, through our sins and wickedness, we are sore let and hindered in running the race that is set before us, thy bountiful grace and mercy may speedily help and deliver us through the satisfaction of thy Son our Lord, to whom, with thee, and the HOLY GHOST, be honor and glory, world without end. *Amen.*

## IV.

## SIMON'S WIFE'S MOTHER.

"AND SIMON'S WIFE'S MOTHER WAS TAKEN WITH A GREAT FEVER; AND THEY BESOUGHT HIM FOR HER."—Luke 4: 38.

There are some, I think, who would perhaps find it more possible to accept the New Testament story if the miracles did not stand in the way. But perhaps, again, it would be easier for them to accept both if they could once look into the true heart of these miracles. So long as they regard only the surface of them, they will, most likely, see in them only a violation of the laws of nature: when they behold the heart of them, they will recognize there at least a possible fulfilment of her deepest laws. With such, however, is not my main business now, any more than with those who cannot believe in a God at all, and therefore to whom a miracle is an absurdity.

It seems to me that it needs no great power of faith to believe in the miracles, for true faith is a power, not a mere yielding. There are far harder things to believe than the miracles. For a man is not required to believe in them save as believing in Jesus. If a man can believe that there is a God, he may well believe that, having made creatures capable of hungering and thirsting for him, he must be capable of speaking a word to guide them in their feeling after him. And if he is a grand God, a God worthy of being God, yea (his metaphysics even may show the seeker), if he is a God capable of being God, he will speak the clearest, grandest word of guidance which he can utter intelligibly to his creatures. For us that word must simply be the gathering of all the expressions of his visible works into an infinite human face, lighted up by an infinite human soul behind it—namely, that potential essence of man, if I may use a word of my own, which was in the beginning with God. If God should *thus* hear the cry of the noblest of his creatures—for such are all they who do cry after him—and in very deed show them his face, it is but natural to expect that the deeds of the great Messenger should be just the works of the Father done in little. If he came to reveal his Father in miniature, as it were (for in those unspeakable things we can but use figures, and the homeliest may be the holiest), to tone down his great voice—which, too loud for men to hear aright, could but sound to them as an inarticulate thundering—into such a still small voice as might enter their human ears in welcome human speech, then the works that his Father does so widely, so grandly, that they transcend the vision of men, the Son must do briefly and sharply before their very eyes.

Let us then recognize the works of the Father as epitomized in the miracles of the Son. What in the hands of the Father are the mighty motions and progresses and conquests of life, in the hands of the Son are miracles. I do not myself believe that he valued the working of these miracles as he valued the utterance of the truth in words: but all that he did had the one root, *obedience*, in which alone can any son can be free. And what is the highest obedience? Simply a following of the Father—a doing of what the Father does. Every true father wills that his child should be as he is in his deepest love, in his highest hope. All that Jesus does is of his Father. What we see in the Son is of the Father. What his works mean concerning him, they mean concerning the Father. That men might see the will of God, Jesus did the works of his Father thus.

For my subject now I choose the story of the cure of St. Peter's mother-in-law. Bare as the narrative is, the events it records have elements which might have been moulded with artistic effect—on the one hand, the Woman tossing in the folds of the fever, on the other, the entering Life. But it is not from this side that I care to view it.

Neither do I wish to look at it from the point of view of the by-standers, although it would appear that we had the testimony of three of them in the three Gospels which contain the story. We might almost determine the position occupied by each of the three, in the group about the bed, from the differences between their testimonies. One says Jesus stood over her; another, he touched her hand: the third, he lifted her up: they agree that the fever left her, and she ministered unto them. In the present case, I mean to regard the miracle from the point of view of the person healed.

Pain, sickness, delirium, madness, as great infringements of the laws of nature as the miracles themselves, are such veritable presences to the human experience, that what bears no relation to their existence, cannot be the God of the human race. And the man who cannot find his God in the fog of suffering, no less than he who forgets his God in the sunshine of health, has learned little either of St. Paul or of St. John. The religion, whose light renders no dimmest glow across

## SIMON'S WIFE'S MOTHER.

this evil air, cannot be more than a dull reflex of the true. And who will mourn to find this out? There are, perhaps, some so anxious about themselves that, rather than say, "I have it not; it is a better thing than I ever possessed;" they would say, "I have the precious thing, but in the hour of trial it is of little avail." Let us rejoice that the glory is great, even if we dare not say, "It is mine." Then shall we try the more earnestly to lay hold upon it.

So long as men must toss in weary fancies all the dark night, crying, "Would God it were morning!" to find, it may be, when morning arrives, but little comfort in the gray dawn, so long must we regard God as one to be seen or believed in—cried unto, at least—across all the dreary flats of distress or dark mountains of pain; and therefore those who would help their fellows must sometimes look for him, as it were, through the eyes of those who suffer, and try to help them to think, not from ours, but from their own point of vision. I shall now write, therefore, almost entirely for those to whom suffering is familiar, or at least well known.

And, first, I would remind them that all suffering is against the ideal order of things. No man can love pain. It is an unlovely, an ugly, an abhorrent thing. The more true and delicate the bodily and mental constitution, the more must it recoil from pain. No one, I think, could dislike pain so much as the Saviour must have disliked it. God dislikes it. He is, then, on our side in the matter. He knows it is grievous to be borne, a thing he would cast out of his blessed universe, save for reasons.

But one will say—How can this help me when the agony racks me, and the weariness rests on me like a grave stone? Is it nothing, I answer, to be reminded that suffering is in its nature transitory—that it is against the first and final will of God—that it is a means only, not an end? Is it nothing to be told that it will pass away? Is not that what you would desire? God made man for lovely skies, great sunshine, gay colors, free winds, and delicate odors; and however the fogs may be needful for the soul, right gladly does he send them away, and cause the dayspring from on high to revisit his children. While they suffer, he is brooding over them an eternal day, suffering with them, but rejoicing in their future. He is the God of the individual man, or he could be no God of the race.

I believe it is possible—and that some have achieved it—so to believe in and rest upon the immutable Health —so to regard one's own sickness as a kind of passing aberration—that the soul is thereby sustained, even as sometimes in a weary dream the man is comforted by telling himself it is but a dream, and that waking is sure. God would have us reasonable and strong. Every effort of his children to rise above the invasion of evil, in body or in mind, is a pleasure to him. Few, I suppose, attain to this; but there is a better thing—which to many, I trust, is easier—to say, "Thy will be done."

But now let us look at the miracle as received by the woman.

She had "a great fever." She was tossing from side to side in vain attempts to ease a nameless misery. Her head ached, and forms dreary, even in their terror, kept rising before her in miserable and aimless dreams; senseless words went on repeating themselves till her very brain was sick of them; she was destitute, afflicted, tormented; now the centre for the convergence of innumerable atoms, now driven along in an uproar of hideous globes; faces grinned and mocked at her; her mind ever strove to recover itself, and was ever borne away in the

## SIMON'S WIFE'S MOTHER. 41

rush of invading fancies; but through it all was the nameless unrest, not an aching, nor a burning, nor a stinging, but a bodily grief, dark, drear, and nameless. How could they have borne such before Christ had come?

A sudden ceasing of motions uncontrolled; a coolness gliding through the burning skin; a sense of waking into repose; a consciousness of all-pervading well-being, of strength conquering weakness, of light displacing darkness, of urging life at the heart; and, behold! she is sitting up in bed, a hand clasping hers, a face looking in hers! Jesus Christ has judged the evil thing, and it is gone. He has saved her out of her distresses; they fold away from her like the cerements of death. She is new-born, new-made; all things are new-born with her; and he who makes all things new is there. From him, she knows, has the healing flowed. He has given of his life to her. Away, afar behind her, floats the cloud of her suffering; she almost forgets it in her grateful joy. She is herself now. She rises. The sun is shining. It has been shining all the time—waiting for her. The lake of Galilee is glittering joyously. That too sets forth the law of life. But the fulfilling of the law is love: she rises and ministers.

I am tempted to remark in passing, although I shall have better opportunity of dealing with the matter involved, that there is no sign of those whom our Lord cures desiring to retain the privileges of the invalid. The joy of health is labor. He who is restored must be fellow-worker with God. This woman, lifted out of the whelming sand of the fever, and set upon her feet, hastens to her ministrations. She has been used to hard work. It is all right now; she must to it again.

But who was he who had thus lifted her up? She saw a young man by her side. Is it the young man,

Jesus, of whom she has heard? For Capernaum is not far from Nazareth, and the report of his wisdom and goodness must have spread; he had grown in favor with man as well as with God. Is it he, to whom God has given such power, or is it John, of whom she has also heard? Whether he was a prophet or a son of a prophet, whether he was Jesus or John, she waits not to question; for here are guests; here is something to be done. Questions will keep; work must be despatched. It is the day, and the night is at hand: "she rose and ministered unto them."

But if we ask who he is, this is the answer: He is the Son of God, come to do the works of his Father. Where, then, is the healing of the Father? All the world over, in every man's life and knowledge, almost in every man's personal experience, although it may not be recognized as such. For, just as in certain moods of selfishness our hearts are insensible to the tenderest love of our surrounding families, so the degrading spirit of the commonplace *enables* us to live in the midst of ministrations—so far from knowing them as such, that it is hard for us to believe that the very heart of God would care to do that which his hand alone can do, and is doing every moment. I remind my reader that I have taken it for granted that he confesses there is a God, or at least hopes there may be a God.

If any one interposes, saying that science nowadays will not permit him to believe in such a Being, I answer it is not for him I am at this instant writing, but for such as have gone through a different course of thought and experience from his. To him I may be honored to say a word some day: I do not think of him now. But to the reader of my choice I do say that I see no middle course between believing that every alleviation of pain, every dawning of hope across the troubled atmosphere of the spirit, every case of growing well again, is the doing of God, or that there is no God at all—none at least in whom *I* could believe. Had Christians been believing in God better, more grandly, the present phase of unbelief, which no doubt is needful, and must appear some time in the world's history, would not have appeared in our day. No doubt it has come when it must, and will vanish when it must; but those who do believe are more to blame for it, I think, than those who do not believe. The common kind of belief in God is rationally untenable. Half to an insensate nature, half to a living God, is a worship that cannot stand. God is all in all, or no God at all. The man, who goes to church every Sunday, and yet trembles before chance, is a Christian only because Christ has claimed him; is not a Christian as having believed in him. I would not be hard. There are so many degrees in faith! A man may be on the right track, may be learning of Christ, and be very poor and weak. But I say there is no standing-room, no reality of reason, between absolute faith and absolute unbelief. Either not a sparrow falls to the ground without him, or there is no God, and we are fatherless children. Those who attempt to live in such a limbo as lies between the two, are only driven of the wind and tossed.

Has my reader ever known the weariness of suffering, the clouding of the inner sky, the haunting of spectral shapes, the misery of disordered laws, when nature is wrong within him, and her music is out of tune and harsh, when he is shot through with varied griefs and pains, and it seems as if there were no more life in the world, save of misery—" pain, pain ever, pain forever?" Then, surely, he has also known the turn of the tide, when the pain begins to abate, when the sweet sleep falls upon soul and body, when a faint hope doubtfully glimmers across the gloom! Or has he known the sudden waking from sleep and from fever at once, the consciousness that life is life, that life is the law of things, the coolness and the gladness, when the garments of pain, which, like that fabled garment of Dejanira, enwrapped and ate into his being, have folded back from head and heart, and he looks out again once more new-born? It is God. This is his will, his law of life conquering the law of death. Tell me not of natural laws, as if I were ignorant of them, or meant to deny them. The question is whether these laws go wheeling on of themselves in a symmetry of mathematical shapes, or whether their perfect order, their unbroken certainty of movement, is not the expression of a perfect intellect informed by a perfect heart. Law is truth: has it a soul of thought, or has it not? If not, then farewell hope and love and possible perfection. But for me, I will hope on, strive on, fight with the invading unbelief; for the horror of being the sport of insensate law, the more perfect the more terrible, is hell and utter perdition. If a man tells me that science says God is not a likely Being, I answer, Probably not—such as you, who have given your keen, admirable, enviable powers to the observation of outer things only, are capable of supposing him; but that the God I mean may not be the very heart of the lovely order you see so much better than I, you have given me no reason to fear. My God may be above and beyond and in all that.

In this matter of healing, then, as in all the miracles, we find Jesus doing the works of the Father. God is our Saviour: the Son of God comes healing the sick—doing that, I repeat, before our eyes, which the Father, for his own reasons, some of which I think I can see well enough, does from behind the vail of his creation and its laws. The cure comes by law, comes by the physician who brings the law to bear upon us; we awake, and lo! it is God the Saviour. Every recovery is as much his work as the birth of a child; as much the work of the Father as if it had been wrought by the word of the Son before the eyes of the multitude.

Need I, in order to combat again the vulgar notion that the essence of the miracles lies in their power, dwell upon this miracle further? Surely no one who honors the Saviour will for a moment imagine him, as he entered the chamber where the woman lay tormented, saying to himself, "Here is an opportunity of showing how mighty my Father is!" No: there was suffering; here was healing. What I could imagine him saying to himself would be, "Here I can help! Here my Father will let me put forth my healing, and give her back to her people." What should we think of a rich man, who, suddenly brought into contact with the starving upon his own estate, should think within himself, "Here is a chance for me! Now I can let them see how rich I am!" and so plunge his hands in his pockets, and lay gold upon the bare table? The receivers might well be grateful; but the arm of the poor neighbor put under the head of the dying man, would gather a deeper gratitude, a return of tenderer love. It is heart alone that can satisfy heart. It is the love of God alone that can gather to itself the love of his children. To believe in an almighty being, and that only, is hardly to believe in a God at all. To believe in a being, who, in his weakness and poverty, if such could be, would die for his creatures, would be to believe in a God indeed.

## V.

## THE RESURRECTION HARVEST.

"IF BY ANY MEANS I MIGHT ATTAIN UNTO THE RESURRECTION OF THE DEAD. NOT AS THOUGH I HAD ALREADY ATTAINED, EITHER WERE ALREADY PERFECT."—Philippians 3 : 11, 12.

The world, my friends, is full of resurrections, and it is not always of the same resurrection that St. Paul speaks. Every night that folds us up in darkness is a death; and those of you that have been out early and have seen the first of the dawn, will know it—the day rises out of the night like a being that has burst its tomb and escaped into life. That you may feel that the sunrise is a resurrection—the word resurrection just means a rising again—I will read you a little description of it from a sermon by a great writer and great preacher called Jeremy Taylor. Listen:

"But as when the sun approaching towards the gates of the morning, he first opens a little eye of heaven and sends away the spirits of darkness, and gives light to a cock, and calls up the lark to matins, and by and by gilds the fringes of a cloud, and peeps over the eastern hills, thrusting out his golden horns like those which decked the brows of Moses, when he was forced to wear a vail, because himself had seen the face of God; and still while a man tells the story, the sun gets up higher, till he shows a fair face and a full light, and then he shines one whole day, under a cloud often, and sometimes weeping great and little showers, and sets quickly; so is a man's reason and his life."

## THE RESURRECTION HARVEST.

Is not this a resurrection of the day out of the night? Or hear how Milton makes his Adam and Eve praise God in the morning :—

> "Ye mists and exhalations, that now rise
> From hill or steaming lake, dusky or gray,
> Till the sun paint your fleecy skirts with gold,
> In honor to the world's great Author rise ;
> Whether to deck with clouds the uncolored sky,
> Or wet the thirsty earth with falling showers,
> Rising or falling, still advance his praise."

But it is yet more of a resurrection to you. Think of your own condition through the night and in the morning. You die, as it were, every night. The death of darkness comes down over the earth; but a deeper death, the death of sleep, descends on you. A power overshadows you; your eyelids close, you cannot keep them open if you would; your limbs lie moveless; the day is gone ; your whole life is gone; you have forgotten everything; an evil man might come and do with your goods as he pleased; you are helpless. But the God of the Resurrection is awake all the time, watching his sleeping men and women, even as a mother who watches her sleeping baby, only with larger eyes and more full of love than hers ; and so, you know not how, all at once you know that you are what you are ; that there is a world that wants you outside of you, and a God that wants you inside of you; you rise from the death of sleep, not by your own power, for you know nothing about it; God put his hand over your eyes, and you were dead; he lifted his hand and breathed light on you, and you rose from the dead, thanked the God that raised you up, and went forth to do your work. From darkness to light; from blindness to seeing; from knowing nothing to looking abroad on the mighty world; from helpless submission to willing obedience—is not this a resurrection indeed?

That St. Paul saw it to be such may be shown from his using the two things with the same meaning when he says, "Awake, thou that sleepest, and arise from the dead, and Christ shall give thee light." No doubt he meant a great deal more. No man who understands what he is speaking about can well mean only one thing at a time.

But to return to the resurrections we see around us in nature. Look at the death that falls upon the world in winter. And look how it revives when the sun draws near enough in the spring to wile the life in it once more out of its grave. See how the pale, meek snowdrops come up with their bowed heads, as if full of the memory of the fierce winds they encountered last spring, and yet ready in the strength of their weakness to encounter them again. Up comes the crocus, bringing its gold safe from the dark of its colorless grave into the light of its parent gold. Primroses, and anemones, and blue-bells, and a thousand other children of the spring, hear the resurrection-trumpet of the wind from the west and south, obey, and leave their graves behind to breathe the air of the sweet heavens. Up and up they come till the year is glorious with the rose and lily, till the trees are not only clothed upon with new garments of loveliest green, but the fruit-tree bringeth forth its fruit, and the little children of men are made glad with apples, and cherries, and hazelnuts. The earth laughs out in green and gold. The sky shares in the grand resurrection. The garments of its mourning, wherewith it made men sad, its clouds of snow and hail and stormy vapors, are swept away,

## THE RESURRECTION HARVEST. 49

have sunk indeed to the earth, and are now humbly feeding the roots of the flowers whose dead stalks they beat upon all the winter long. Instead, the sky has put on the garments of praise. Her blue, colored after the sapphire-floor on which stands the throne of him who is the Resurrection and the Life, is dashed and glorified with the pure white of sailing clouds, and at morning and evening prayer, puts on colors in which the human heart drowns itself with delight—green and gold and purple and rose. Even the icebergs, floating about in the lonely summer seas of the north, are flashing all the glories of the rainbow. But, indeed, is not this whole world itself a monument of the Resurrection? The earth was without form and void. The wind of God moved on the face of the waters, and up arose this fair world. Darkness was on the face of the deep: God said, "Let there be light," and there was light.

In the animal world, as well, you behold the goings of the Resurrection. Plainest of all, look at the story of the butterfly—so plain that the pagan Greeks called it and the soul by one name—Psyche. Psyche meant with them a butterfly or the soul, either. Look how the creeping thing, ugly to our eyes, so that we can hardly handle it without a shudder, finding itself growing sick with age, straightway falls a-spinning and weaving at its own shroud, coffin, and grave, all in one —to prepare, in fact, for its resurrection; for it is for the sake of the resurrection that death exists. Patiently it spins its strength, but not its life, away, folds itself up decently, that its body may rest in quiet till the new body is formed within it; and at length when the appointed hour has arrived, out of the body of this crawling thing breaks forth the winged splendor of the butterfly—not the same body—a new built out of the ruins of the old—even as St. Paul tells us that it is not the same body *we* have in the resurrection, but a nobler body like ourselves, with all the imperfect and evil thing taken away. No more creeping for the butterfly; wings of splendor now. Neither yet has it lost the feet wherewith to alight on all that is lovely and sweet. Think of it—up from the toilsome journey over the low ground, exposed to the foot of every passer-by destroying the lovely leaves upon which it fed, and the fruit which they should shelter, up to the path at will through the air, and a gathering of food which hurts not the source of it, a food which is but as a tribute from the loveliness of the flowers to the yet higher loveliness of the flower-angel; is not this a resurrection? Its children too shall pass through the same process, to wing the air of a summer noon, and rejoice in the ethereal and the pure.

I come now naturally to speak of what we commonly call the Resurrection. Some say: "How can the same dust be raised again, when it may be scattered to the winds of heaven?" It is a question I hardly care to answer. The mere difficulty can in reason stand for nothing with God; but the apparent worthlessness of the supposition renders the question uninteresting to me. What is of import is, that I should stand clothed upon, with a body which is *my* body because it serves my ends, justifies my consciousness of identity by being, in all that was good in it, like that which I had before, while now it is tenfold capable of expressing the thoughts and feelings that move within me. How can I care whether the atoms that form a certain inch of bone should be the same as those which formed that bone when I died? All my lifetime I never felt or thought of the existence of such a bone! On the other hand, I object to having the same worn muscles, the same shriveled skin, with which I may happen to die. Why give me the same body as that? Why not rather my youthful body, which was strong, and facile, and capable? The matter in the muscle of my arm at death would not serve to make half the muscle I had when young.

But I thank God St. Paul says it will *not* be the same body. That body dies—up springs another body. I suspect myself that those are right who say that this body being the seed, the moment it dies in the soil of this world, that moment is the resurrection of the new body. The life in it rises out of it in a new body. This is not after it is put in the mere earth; for it is dead then, and the germ of life gone out of it. If a seed rots, no new body comes of it. The seed dies into a new life, and so does man. Dying and rotting are two very different things. But I am not sure by any means. As I say, the whole question is rather uninteresting to me. What do I care about my old clothes after I have done with them? What is it to me to know what becomes of an old coat or an old pulpit-gown? I have no such clinging to the flesh. It seems to me that people believe their bodies to be themselves, and are therefore very anxious about them—and no wonder then. Enough for me that I shall have eyes to see my friends, a face that they shall know me by, and a mouth to praise God withal. I leave the matter with one remark, that I am well content to rise as Jesus rose, however that was. For me the will of God is so good that I would rather have his will done than my own choice given me.

But I now come to the last, because infinitely the most important, part of my subject—the resurrection for the sake of which all the other resurrections exist —the resurrection unto Life. This is the one of which St. Paul speaks in my text. This is the one I am most anxious—indeed, the only one I am anxious to set forth, and impress upon you.

Think, then, of all the deaths you know; the death of the night, when the sun is gone, when friend says not a word to friend, but both lie drowned and parted in the sea of sleep; the death of the year, when winter lies heavy on the graves of the children of summer, when the leafless trees moan in the blasts from the ocean, when the beasts even look dull and oppressed, when the children go about shivering with cold, when the poor and improvident are miserable with suffering; or think of such a death of disease as befalls us at times, when the man who says, "Would God it were morning!" changes but his word, and not his tune, when the morning comes, crying, "Would God it were evening!" when what life is left is known to us only by suffering, and hope is among the things which were once and are no more—think of all these, think of them all together, and you will have but the dimmest, faintest picture of the death, from which the resurrection, of which I have now to speak, is the rising. I shrink from the attempt, knowing how weak words are to set forth *the* death, set forth *the* resurrection. Were I to sit down to yonder organ, and crash out the most horrible dissonances that ever took shape in sound, I should give you but a weak figure of this death; were I capable of drawing from many a row of pipes an exhalation of dulcet symphonies and voices sweet, such as Milton himself could have invaded our ears withal, I could give you but a faint figure of this resurrection. Nevertheless, I must try what I can do in my own way.

## THE RESURRECTION HARVEST.

If into the face of the dead body, lying on the bed, waiting for its burial, the soul of the man should begin to dawn again, drawing near from afar to look out once more at those eyes, to smile once again through those lips, the change on that face would be indeed great and wondrous, but nothing for marvel or greatness to that which passes on the countenance, the very outward bodily face of the man who wakes from his sleep, arises from the dead, and receives light from Christ.

Too often indeed, the reposeful look on the face of the dead body would be troubled, would vanish away at the revisiting of the restless ghost; but when a man's own right true mind, which God made in him, is restored to him again, and he wakes from the death of sin, then comes the repose without the death. It may take long for the new spirit to complete the visible change, but it begins at once, and will be perfected. The bloated look of self-indulgence passes away like the leprosy of Naaman, the cheek grows pure, the lips return to the smile of hope instead of the grin of greed, and the eyes that made innocence shrink and shudder with their yellow leer grow childlike and sweet and faithful. The mammon-eyes, hitherto fixed on the earth, are lifted to meet their kind; the lips that mumbled over figures and sums of gold learn to say words of grace and tenderness. The truculent, repellent, self-satisfied face begins to look thoughtful and wistful, as if searching for some treasure of whose whereabouts it had no certain sign. The face, anxious, wrinkled, peering, troubled, on whose line you read the dread of hunger, poverty and nakedness, thaws into a smile; the eyes reflect in courage the light of the Father's care; the back grows erect under its burden with the assurance that the hairs of its head are all numbered.

But the face can with all its changes set but dimly forth the rising from the dead which passes within. The heart, which cared but for itself, becomes aware of surrounding thousands like itself, in the love and care of which it feels a drawing blessedness undreamt of before. From selfishness to love—is not this a rising from the dead? The man whose ambition declares that his way in this world would be to subject everything to his desires, to bring every human care, affection, power, and aspiration to his feet—(such a world it would be, and such a king it would have, if individual ambition might work its will, if a man's opinion of himself could be made out in the world, degrading, compelling, oppressing, doing everything for his own glory, and such a glory)—but a pang of light strikes this man to the heart; an arrow of truth, feathered with suffering and loss and dismay, finds out—the open joint in his armor, I was going to say—no, finds out the joint in the coffin where his heart lies festering in a death so dead that itself calls it life. He trembles, he awakes, he rises from the dead. No more he seeks the slavery of all: where can he find whom to serve? how can he become if but a threshold in the temple of Christ, where all serve all, and no man thinks first of himself? He, to whom the mass of his fellows, as he massed them, was common and unclean, bows before every human sign of the presence of the creating God. The sun which was to him but a candle with which to search after his own ends, wealth, power, place, praise—the world, which was but the cavern where he thus searched—are now full of the mystery of the loveliness, full of the truth of which sun and wind and land and sea are symbols and signs. From a withered old age of unbelief, the dim eyes of which refuse the glory of things a passage to the heart, he is raised up a child full of admiration, surprise, and gladness. Everything is glorious to him; he can believe, and therefore he sees. It is from the grave into the sunshine, from the night into the morning, from death into life.

To come out of the ugly into the beautiful; out of the mean and selfish into the noble and loving; out of the paltry into the great; out of the false into the true; out of the filthy into the clean; out of the commonplace into the glorious; out of the corruption of disease into the fine vigor and gracious movements of health; in a word, out of evil into good—is not this a resurrection indeed—*the* resurrection of all, the resurrection of Life? God grant that with St. Paul we may attain to this resurrection of the dead!

This rising from the dead is often a long and a painful process. Even after he had preached the gospel to the Gentiles, and suffered much for the sake of his Master, Paul sees the resurrection of the dead towering grandly before him, not yet climbed, not yet attained unto—a mountainous splendor and marvel still shining aloft in the air of existence, still, thank God, to be attained, but ever growing in height and beauty as, forgetting those things that are behind, he presses towards the mark, if by any means he may attain to the resurrection of the dead. Every blessed moment, in which a man bethinks himself that he has been forgetting his high calling, and sends up to the Father a prayer for aid; every time a man resolves that what he has been doing he will do no more; every time that the love of God, or the feeling of the truth, rouses a man to look first up at the light, then down at the skirts of his own garments—that moment a divine resurrection is wrought in the earth. Yea, every time that a man passes from resentment to forgiveness, from cruelty to compassion, from harshness to tenderness, from indifference to carefulness, from selfishness to honesty, from honesty to generosity, from generosity to love,—a resurrection, the bursting of a fresh bud of life out of the grave of evil, gladdens the eye of the Father watching his children.

Awake, then, thou that sleepest, and arise from the dead, and Christ will give the light! As the harvest rises from the wintry earth, so rise thou up from the trials of this world, a full ear in the harvest of him who sowed thee in the soil that thou mightest rise above it. As the summer rises from the winter, so rise thou from the cares of eating, and drinking, and clothing into the fearless sunshine of confidence in the Father. As the morning rises out of the night, so rise thou from the darkness of ignorance to do the will of God in the daylight; and as a man feels that he is himself when he wakes from the troubled and grotesque visions of the night into the glory of the sunrise, even so wilt thou feel that then first thou knowest what thy life, the gladness of thy being, is. As from painful tossing in disease, rise into the health of well-being. As from the awful embrace of thy own dead body, burst forth in thy spiritual body. Arise thou, responsive to the indwelling will of the Father, even as thy body will resound to the indwelling soul.

> "White wings are crossing: glad waves are tossing;
> The earth flames out in crimson and green:
> Spring is appearing, summer is nearing—
> Where hast thou been?
>
> Down in some cavern, death's sleepy tavern,
> Housing, carousing with spectres of night?
> The trumpet is pealing sunshine and healing—
> Spring to the light!"

## VI.

## LOVE THY NEIGHBOR.

"THOU SHALT LOVE THY NEIGHBOR AS THYSELF."—Matthew 22: 39.

The passage here quoted by our Lord is to be found in the words of God to Moses: "Thou shalt not avenge, nor bear any grudge against the children of thy people, but thou shalt love thy neighbor as thyself: I am the Lord."—Lev. 19: 18. Our Lord never thought of being original. The older the saying the better, if it utters the truth he wants to utter. In him it becomes fact: the *Word* was made *flesh*. And so, in the wondrous meeting of extremes, the words he spoke were no more words, but spirit and life.

The same words are twice quoted by St. Paul, and once by St. James, always in a similar mode: love they represent as the fulfilling of the law. Is the converse true then? Is the fulfilling of the law love?

It *is* possible to love our neighbor as ourselves. Our Lord *never* spoke hyperbolically, although, indeed, that is the supposition on which many unconsciously interpret his words, in order to be able to persuade themselves that they believe them. We may see that it is possible before we attain to it; for our perceptions of truth are always in advance of our condition. True, no man can see it perfectly until he is it; but we must see it, that we may be it. A man who knows that he does not yet love his neighbor as himself may believe in such a condition, may even see that there is no other goal of human perfection, nothing else to which the universe is speeding, propelled by the Father's will. Let him labor on, and not faint at the thought that God's day is a thousand years: his millennium is likewise one day—yea, this day, for we have him, The Love, in us, working even now the far end.

But while it is true that only when a man loves God with all his heart, will he love his neighbor as himself, yet there are mingled processes in the attainment of this final result. Let us try to aid such operation of truth by looking farther. Let us suppose that the man who believes our Lord both meant what he said, and knew the truth of the matter, proceeds to endeavor obedience in this of loving his neighbor as himself.

He begins to think about his neighbors generally, and he tries to feel love towards them. He finds at once that they begin to classify themselves. With some he feels no difficulty, for he loves them already, not indeed because they *are*, but because they have, by friendly qualities, by showing themselves lovable, that is loving, already, moved his feelings as the wind moves the waters, that is, without any self-generated action on his part. And he feels that this is nothing much to the point; though, of course, he would be farther from the desired end if he had none such to love, and farther still if he loved none such. He recalls the words of our Lord: "If ye love them which love you, what reward have ye?" and his mind fixes upon—let us say—one of a second class, and he tries to love him. The man is no enemy—we have not come to that class of neighbors yet—but he is dull, uninteresting—in a negative way, he thinks, unlovable. What is he to do with him? With all his effort, he finds the goal as far off as ever.

## LOVE THY NEIGHBOR.

Naturally, in his failure, the question arises, "Is it my duty to love him who is unlovable?" Certainly not, if he is unlovable. But that is a begging of the question.

Thereupon the man falls back on the primary foundation of things, and asks: "How, then, is the man to be loved by me? Why should I love my neighbor as myself?" We must not answer "Because the Lord says so." It is because the Lord says so that the man is inquiring after some help to obey. No man can love his neighbor *merely* because the Lord says so. The Lord says so because it is right and necessary and natural, and the man wants to feel it thus right and necessary and natural. Although the Lord would be pleased with any man for doing a thing because he said it, he would show his pleasure by making the man more and more dissatisfied until he knew why the Lord had said it. He would make him see that he could not in the deepest sense—in the way the Lord loves—obey any command until he saw the reasonableness of it.

Observe I do not say the man ought to put off obeying the command until he see its reasonableness: that is another thing quite, and does not lie in the scope of my present supposition. It is a beautiful thing to obey the rightful source of a command: it is a more beautiful thing to worship the radiant source of our light, and it is for the sake of obedient vision that our Lord commands us. For then our heart meets his: we see God.

Let me represent in the form of a conversation what might pass in the man's mind on the opposing sides of the question. "Why should I love my neighbor?" "He is the same as I, and therefore I ought to love him." "Why? I am I. He is he." "He has the same thoughts, feelings, hopes, sorrows, joys, as I." "Yes; but why should I love him for that? He must mind his, I can only do with mine." "He has the same consciousness as I have. As things look to me, so things look to him." "Yes; but I cannot get into his consciousness, nor he into mine. I feel myself, I do not feel him. My life flows through my veins, not through his. The world shines into my consciousness, and I am not conscious of his consciousness. I wish I could love him, but I do not see why. I am an individual; he is an individual. My self must be closer to me than he can be. Two bodies keep me apart from his self. I am isolated with myself."

Now, here lies the mistake at last. While the thinker supposes a duality in himself which does not exist, he falsely judges the individuality a separation. On the contrary, it is the sole possibility and very bond of love. *Otherness* is the essential ground of affection. But in spiritual things, such a unity is pre-supposed in the very contemplation of them by the spirit of man, that wherever anything does not exist that ought to be there, the space it ought to occupy, even if but a blank, assumes the appearance of a separating gulf. The negative looks a positive. Where a man does not love, the not-loving must seem rational. For no one loves because he sees why, but because he loves. No human reason can be given for the highest necessity of divinely created existence. For reasons are always from above downwards. A man must feel this necessity, and then questioning is over. It justifies itself. But he who has not felt has it not to argue about. He has but its phantom, which he created himself in a vain effort to understand, and which he supposes to be it. Love cannot be argued about in its absence, for

## LOVE THY NEIGHBOR.

there is no reflex, no symbol of it near enough to the fact of it, to admit of just treatment by the algebra of the reason or imagination. Indeed, the very talking about it raises a mist between the mind and the vision of it. But let a man once love, and all these difficulties which appeared opposed to love, will just be so many arguments for loving.

Let a man once find another who has fallen among thieves; let him be a neighbor to him, pouring oil and wine into his wounds, and binding them up, and setting him on his own beast, and paying for him at the inn; let him do all this merely from a sense of duty; let him even, in the pride of his fancied, and the ignorance of his true calling, bate no jot of his Jewish superiority; let him condescend to the very baseness of his own lowest nature; yet such will be the virtue of obeying an eternal truth even to his poor measure, of putting in actuality what he has not even seen in theory, of doing the truth even without believing it, that even if the truth does not after the deed give the faintest glimmer as truth in the man, he will yet be ages nearer the truth than before, for he will go on his way loving that Samaritan neighbor a little more than his Jewish dignity will justify. Nor will he question the reasonableness of so doing, although he may not care to spend any logic upon its support.

How much more if he be a man who would love his neighbor if he could, will the higher condition unsought have been found in the action? For man is a whole; and so soon as he *unites himself* by obedient action, the truth that is in him makes itself known to him, shining from the new whole. For his action is his response to his Maker's design, his individual part in the creation of himself, his yielding to the All-in-all, to the tides of whose harmonious cosmoplastic life all his being thenceforward lies open for interpenetration and assimilation. When will once begins to aspire, it will soon find that action must precede feeling, that the man may know the foundation itself of feeling.

With those who recognize no authority as the ground of tentative action, a doubt, a suspicion of truth ought to be ground enough for putting it to the test.

The whole system of divine education as regards the relation of man and man, has for its end that a man should love his neighbor as himself. It is not a lesson that he can learn by itself, or a duty the obligation of which can be shown by argument, any more than the difference between right and wrong can be defined in other terms than their own.

"But that difference," it may be objected, "manifests itself of itself to every mind: it is self-evident; whereas the loving of one's neighbor is not seen to be a primary truth; so far from it, that far the greater number of those who hope for an eternity of blessedness through him who taught it, do not really believe it to be a truth; believe, on the contrary, that the paramount obligation is to take care of one's self at much risk of forgetting one's neighbor."

But the human race generally has got as far as the recognition of right and wrong; and therefore most men are born capable of making the distinction. The race has not yet lived long enough for its latest offspring to be born with the perception of the truth of love to the neighbor. It is to be seen by the present individual only after a long reception of and submission to the education of life. And once seen, it is believed.

The whole constitution of human society exists for

## LOVE THY NEIGHBOR.

the express end, I say, of teaching the two truths by which man lives, Love to God and Love to Man. I will say nothing more of the mysteries of the parental relation (because they belong to the teaching of the former truth) than that we come into the world as we do, to look up to the love over us, and see in it a symbol, poor and weak, yet the best we can have or receive of the divine love. This might be expressed after a deeper and truer fashion by saying that, God making human affairs after his own thoughts, they are therefore such as to be the best teachers of love to him and love to our neighbor. This is an immeasurably nobler and truer manner of regarding them than as a scheme or plan invented by the divine intellect. And thousands more would find it easy to love God if they had not such miserable types of him in the self-seeking, impulse-driven, purposeless, faithless beings who are all they have for father and mother, and to whom their children are no dearer than her litter is to the unthinking dam.

What I want to speak of now, with regard to the second great commandment, is the relation of brotherhood and sisterhood. Why does my brother come of the same father and mother? Why do I behold the helplessness and confidence of his infancy? Why is the infant laid on the knee of the child? Why do we grow up with the same nurture? Why do we behold the wonder of the sunset and the mystery of the growing moon together? Why do we share one bed, join in the same games, and attempt the same exploits? Why do we quarrel, vow revenge and silence and endless enmity, and, unable to resist the brotherhood within us, wind arm in arm and forget all within the hour? Is it not that Love may grow lord of all between him and me? Is it not that I may feel towards him what there are no words or forms of words to express—a love namely, in which the divine self rushes forth in utter self-forgetfulness to live in the contemplation of the brother—a love that is stronger than death,—glad and proud and satisfied? But if love stop there, what will be the result? Ruin to itself; loss of the brotherhood. He who loves not his brother for deeper reasons than those of a common parentage will cease to love him at all. The love that enlarges not its borders, that is not ever spreading and including, and deepening, will contract, shrivel, decay, die. I have had the sons of my mother that I may learn the universal brotherhood.

For there is a bond between me and the most wretched liar that ever died for the murder he would not even confess, closer infinitely than that which springs only from having one father and mother. That we are the sons and the daughters of God born from his heart, the outcoming offspring of his love, is a bond closer than all other bonds in one. No man ever loved his own child aright who did not love him for his humanity, for his divinity, to the utter forgetting of his origin from himself. The son of my mother is indeed my brother by this greater and closer bond as well; but if I recognize that bond between him and me at all, I recognize it for my race. True, and thank God! the greater excludes not the less; it makes all the weaker bonds stronger and truer, nor forbids that where all are brothers, some should be those of our bosom. Still my brother according to the flesh is my first neighbor, that we may be very nigh to each other, whether we will or no, while our hearts are tender, and so may learn brotherhood. For our love to each other

## LOVE THY NEIGHBOR.

is but the throbbing of the heart of the great brotherhood, and could come only from the eternal Father, not from our parents.

Then my second neighbor appears, and who is he? Whom I come in contact with soever. He with whom I have any transactions, any human dealings whatever; Not the man only with whom I dine; not the friend only with whom I share my thoughts; not the man only whom my compassion would lift from some slough but the man who makes my clothes; the man who prints my book; the man who drives me in his cab; the man who begs from me in the street, to whom, it may be, for brotherhood's sake, I must not give; yea, even the man who condescends to me. With all and each there is a chance of doing the part of a neighbor, if in no other way yet by speaking truly, acting justly, and thinking kindly. Even these deeds will help to that love which is born of righteousness. All true action clears the springs of right feeling, and lets their waters rise and flow. A man must not choose his neighbor: he must take the neighbor that God sends him. In him, whoever he be, lies, hidden or revealed, a beautiful brother. The neighbor is just the man who is next to you at the moment, the man with whom any business has brought you in contact.

Thus will love spread and spread in wider and stronger pulses till the whole human race will be to the man sacredly lovely. Drink-debased, vice-defeatured, pride-puffed, wealth-bollen, vanity-smeared, they will yet be brothers, yet be sisters, yet be God-born neighbors. Any rough-hewn semblance of humanity will at length be enough to move the man to reverence and affection. It is harder for some to learn thus than for others. There are those whose first impulse is ever to repel and not to receive. But learn they may, and learn they must. Even these may grow in this grace until a countenance unknown will awake in them a yearning of affection rising to pain, because there is for it no expression, and they can only give the man to God and be still.

And now will come in all the arguments out of which the man tried in vain before to build a stair up to the sunny heights of love. "Ah, brother! thou hast a soul like mine," he will say. "Out of thine eyes thou lookest, and sights and sounds and odors visit thy soul as mine, with wonder and tender comforting. Thou, too, lovest the faces of thy neighbors. Thou art oppressed with thy sorrows, uplifted with thy joys. Perhaps thou knowest not so well as I, that a region of gladness surrounds all thy grief, of light all thy darkness, of peace all thy tumult. O my brother! I will love thee. I cannot come very near thee: I will love thee the more. It may be thou dost not love thy neighbor; it may be thou thinkest only how to get from him, how to gain by him. How lonely then must thou be! how shut up in thy poverty-stricken room, with the bare walls of thy selfishness, and the hard couch of thy unsatisfaction! I will love thee the more. Thou shalt not be alone with thyself. Thou art not me; thou art another life—a second self; therefore I can, may, and will love thee."

One word more: this love of our neighbor is the only door out of the dungeon of self, where we mope and mow, striking sparks, and rubbing phosphorescences out of the walls, and blowing our own breath in our own nostrils, instead of issuing to the fair sunlight of God, the sweet winds of the universe. The man thinks his consciousness is himself; whereas his life

## LOVE THY NEIGHBOR.

consisteth in the inbreathing of God, and the consciousness of the universe of truth. To have himself, to know himself, to enjoy himself, he calls life; whereas, if he would forget himself, tenfold would be his life in God and his neighbors. The region of man's life is a spiritual region. God, his friends, his neighbors, his brothers all, is the wide world in which alone his spirit can find room. Himself is his dungeon. If he feels it not now, he will yet feel it one day—feel it as a living soul would feel being prisoned in a dead body, wrapped in sevenfold cerements, and buried in a stone-ribbed vault within the last ripple of the sound of the chanting people in the church above. His life is not in knowing that he lives, but in loving all forms of life. He is made for the All, for God, who is the All, is his life. And the essential joy of his life lies abroad in the liberty of the All. His delights, like those of the Ideal Wisdom, are with the sons of men. His health is in the body of which the Son of Man is the head. The whole region of life is open to him—nay, he must live in it or perish.

Nor thus shall a man lose the consciousness of well-being. Far deeper and more complete, God and his neighbor will flash it back upon him—pure as life. No more will he agonize "with sick assay" to generate it in the light of his own decadence. For he shall know the glory of his own being in the light of God and of his brother.

## VII.

## LOVE THINE ENEMY.

"LOVE YOUR ENEMIES, BLESS THEM THAT CURSE YOU, DO GOOD TO THEM THAT HATE YOU, AND PRAY FOR THEM WHICH DESPITEFULLY USE YOU, AND PERSECUTE YOU."—Matthew 5 : 44.

The apostle Paul has written: "Love worketh no ill to his neighbor, therefore love is the fulfilling of the law." Does it follow that *working no ill* is love? Love will fulfil the law: will the law fulfil love? No, verily. If a man keeps the law, I know he is a lover of his neighbor. But he is not a lover because he keeps the law: he keeps the law because he is a lover. No heart will be content with the law for love. The law cannot fulfil love.

"But, at least, the law will be able to fulfil itself, though it reaches not to love."

I do not believe it. I am certain that it is impossible to keep the law towards one's neighbor except one loves him. The law itself is infinite, reaching to such delicacies of action, that the man who tries most will be the man most aware of defeat. We are not made for law, but for love. Love is law, because it is infinitely more than law. It is of an altogether higher region than law—is, in fact, the creator of law. Had it not been for love, not one of the *shalt-nots* of the law would have been uttered. True, once uttered, they show themselves in the form of justice, yea, even in the inferior and worldly forms of prudence and self-preservation; but it was love that spoke them first. Were there no love in us, what sense of justice could we have? Would not each be filled with the sense of his own wants, and be forever tearing to himself? I do not say it is *conscious* love that breeds justice, but I do say that without love in our nature justice would never be born. For I do not call that justice which consists only in a sense of *our own* rights. True, there are poor and withered forms of love which are immeasurably below justice now; but even now they are of speechless worth, for they will grow into that which will supersede, because it will necessitate, justice.

Of what use then is the law? To lead us to Christ, the Truth,—to waken in our minds a sense of what our deepest nature, the presence, namely, of God *in* us, requires of us,—to let us know, in part by failure, that the purest effort of will of which we are capable cannot lift us up even to the abstaining from wrong to our neighbor.

What man, for instance, who loves not his neighbor and yet wishes to keep the law, will dare be confident that never by word, look, tone, gesture, silence, will he bear false witness against that neighbor? What man can judge his neighbor aright, save him whose love makes him refuse to judge him? Therefore are we told to love, and not judge. It is the sole justice of which we are capable, and that perfected will comprise all justice. Nay more, to refuse our neighbor love, is to do him the greatest wrong. But of this afterwards.

In order to fulfil the commonest law, I repeat, we must rise into a loftier region altogether, a region that is above law, because it is spirit and life and makes the law: in order to keep the law towards our neighbor we must love our neighbor. We are not made for law, but for grace—or for faith, to use another word so much misused. We are made on too large a scale altogether to have any pure relation to mere justice, if indeed we can say there is such a thing. It is but an abstract idea which, in reality, will not be abstracted. The law comes to make us long for the needful grace,—that is, for the divine condition, in which love is all, for God is love.

Though the fulfilling of the law is the practical form love will take, and the neglect of it is the conviction of lovelessness; though it is the mode in which a man's *will* must begin at once to be love to his neighbor, yet, that our Lord meant by the love of our neighbor not the fulfilling of the law towards him but that condition of being which results in the fulfilling of the law and more, is sufficiently clear from his story of the good Samaritan. "Who is my neighbor?" said the lawyer. And the Lord taught him that every one to whom he could be, or for whom he could do, anything was his neighbor; therefore, that each of the race, as he comes within the touch of one tentacle of our nature, is our neighbor. Which of the inhibitions of the law is illustrated in the tale? Not one. The love that is more than law, and renders its breach impossible, lives in the endless story, coming out in active kindness, that is, the recognition of kin, of *kind*, of nighness, of *neighborhood;* yea, in tenderness and loving-kindness—the Samaritan-heart akin to the Jew-heart, the Samaritan hands neighbors to the Jewish wounds.

"*Thou shalt love thy neighbor as thyself.*" So direct and complete is this parable of our Lord, that one becomes almost ashamed of further talk about it. Suppose a man of the company had put the same question to our Lord that we have been considering, had said: "But I may keep the law and yet not love my neighbor;" would he not have returned: "Keep thou the law thus, not in the letter, but in the spirit, that is, in the truth of action, and thou wilt soon find, O Jew, that thou lovest thy Samaritan"? And yet, when thoughts and questions arise in our minds, he desires that we should follow them. He will not check us with a word of heavenly wisdom scornfully uttered. He knows that not even *his* words will apply to every question of the willing soul; and we know that his Spirit will reply. When we want to know more, that more will be there for us. Not every man, for instance, finds his neighbor in need of help, and he would gladly hasten the slow results of opportunity by true thinking. Thus would we be ready for further teaching from that Spirit who is the Lord.

"But how," says a man, who is willing to recognize the universal neighborhead, but finds himself unable to fulfil the bare law towards the woman even whom he loves best—"how am I then to rise into that higher region, that empyrean of love?" And, beginning straightway to try to love his neighbor, he finds that the empyrean of which he spoke is no more to be reached in itself than the law was to be reached in itself. As he cannot keep the law without first rising into the love of his neighbor, so he cannot love his neighbor without first rising higher still. The whole system of the universe works upon this law—the driving of things upward towards the centre. The man who will love his neighbor can do so by no immediately operative exercise of the will. It is the man fulfilled of God from whom he came and by whom he is who alone can as himself love his neighbor, who came from God too and is by God too. The mystery of individuality and consequent relation is deep as the beginnings of humanity, and the questions thence arising can be solved only by him who has, practically at least, solved the holy necessities resulting from his origin. In God alone can man meet man. In him alone the converging lines of existence touch and cross not. When the mind of Christ, the life of the Head, courses through that atom which the man is of the slowly revivifying body, when he is alive too, then the love of the brothers is there as conscious life. From Christ through the neighbors comes the life that makes him a part of the body.

So we reach another word: " Love your enemies, bless them that curse you, do good to them that hate you, and pray for them which despitefully use you, and persecute you."

Is not this at length *too* much to expect? Will a man ever love his enemies? He may come to do good to them that hate him; but when will he pray for them that despitefully use him and persecute him? When? When he is the child of his Father in heaven. Then shall he love his neighbor as himself, even if that neighbor be his enemy. In the passage in Leviticus already referred to as quoted by our Lord and his apostles, we find the neighbor and the enemy are one. "Thou shalt not avenge, nor bear any grudge against the children of thy people, but thou shalt love thy neighbor as thyself: I am the Lord."

Look at the glorious way in which Jesus interprets the scripture that went before him. *"I am the Lord,"* —"That ye may be perfect, as your Father in heaven is perfect."

Is it then reasonable to love our enemies? God

## LOVE THINE ENEMY.

does; therefore it must be the highest reason. But is it reasonable to expect that man should become capable of doing so? Yes; on one ground: that the divine energy is at work in man, to render at length man's doing divine as his nature is. For this our Lord prayed when he said: "That they all may be one, as thou, Father, art in me, and I in thee, that they also may be one in us." Nothing could be less likely to human judgment: our Lord knows that one day it will come.

Why should we love our enemies? The deepest reason for this we cannot put in words, for it lies in the absolute reality of their being, where our enemies are of one nature with us, even of the divine nature. Into this we cannot see, save as into a dark abyss. But we can adumbrate something of the form of this deepest reason if we let the thoughts of our heart move upon the face of the dim profound.

"Are our enemies men like ourselves?" let me begin by asking. "Yes." "Upon what ground? The ground of their enmity? The ground of the wrong they do us?" "No." "In virtue of cruelty, heartlessness, injustice, disrespect, misrepresentation?" "Certainly not. *Humanum est errare*—to err is human—is a truism; but it possesses, like most truisms, a latent germ of worthy truth. The very word *errare* is a sign that there is a way so truly the human that, for a man to leave it, is to *wander*. If it be human to wander, yet the wandering is not humanity. The very words *humane* and *humanity* denote some shadow of that loving kindness which, when perfected after the divine fashion, shall include even our enemies. We do not call the offering of human sacrifices, the torturing of captives, cannibalism—humanity. Not because they do such deeds are they men. Their humanity must be deeper than those. It is in virtue of the divine essence which is in them, that pure essential humanity, that we call our enemies men and women. It is this humanity that we are to love—a something, I say, deeper altogether than and independent of the region of hate. It is the humanity that originates the claim of neighborhead; the neighborhead only determines the occasion of its exercise." "Is this humanity in every one of our enemies?" "Else there were nothing *to* love." "Is it there in very deed?—Then we *must* love it, come between us and it what may."

But how can we love a man or a woman who is cruel and unjust to us?—who sears with contempt, or cuts off with wrong every tendril we would put forth to embrace?—who is mean, unlovely, carping, uncertain, self-righteous, self-seeking, and self-admiring?—who can even sneer, the most inhuman of human faults, far worse in its essence than mere murder?

These things cannot be loved. The best man hates them most; the worst man cannot love them. But are these the man? Does a woman bear that form in virtue of these? Lies there not within the man and the woman a divine element of brotherhood, of sisterhood, a something lovely and lovable,—slowly fading it may be,—dying away under the fierce heat of vile passions, or the yet more fearful cold of sepulchral selfishness— but there? Shall that divine something, which, once awakened to be its own holy self in the man, will loathe these unlovely things tenfold more than we loathe them now—shall this divine thing have no recognition from us? It is the very presence of this fading humanity that makes it possible for us to hate. If it were an animal only, and not a man or a woman that did us hurt, we should not hate: we should only kill. We hate the man just because we are prevented from loving him. We push over the verge of the creation—*we damn*—just because we cannot embrace.

For to embrace is the necessity of our deepest being. That foiled, we hate. Instead of admonishing ourselves that there is our enchained brother, that there lies our enchanted, disfigured, scarce recognizable sister, captive of the devil, to break, how much sooner, from their bonds, that we love them!—we recoil into the hate which would fix them there! and the dearly lovable reality of them we sacrifice to the outer falsehood of Satan's incantations, thus leaving them to perish. Nay, we murder them to get rid of them: we *hate* them. Yet within the most obnoxious to our hate, lies that which, could it but show itself as it is, and as it will show itself one day, would compel from our hearts a devotion of love. It is not the unfriendly, the unlovely, that we are told to love, but the brother, the sister, who is unkind, who is unlovely. Shall we leave our brother to his desolate fate? Shall we not rather say, "With my love at least shalt thou be compassed about, for thou hast not thy own lovingness to infold thee; love shall come as near thee as it may; and when thine comes forth to meet mine, we shall be one in the indwelling God"?

Let no one say I have been speaking in a figure merely. That I have been so speaking I know. But many things which we see most vividly and certainly are more truly expressed by using a right figure than by attempting to give them a clear outline of logical expression. My figure means a truth.

If any one say, "Do not make such vague distinctions. There is the person. Can you deny that that person is unlovely? How then can you love him?" I answer, "That person, with the evil thing cast out of him, will be yet more the *person*, for he will be his real self. The thing that now makes you dislike him is separable from him, is therefore not he, makes himself so much less himself, for it is working death in him. Now he is in danger of ceasing to be a person at all. When he is clothed and in his right mind he will be a person indeed. You *could* not then go on hating him. Begin to love him now, and help him into the loveliness which is his. Do not hate him although you can. The personality, I say, though clouded, besmeared, defiled with the wrong, lies deeper than the wrong, and indeed, so far as the wrong has reached it, is by the wrong injured, yea, so far, it may be, destroyed.

But those who will not acknowledge the claim of love, may yet acknowledge the claim of justice. There are those who would shrink with horror from the idea of doing injustice to those, from the idea of loving whom they would shrink with equal horror. But if it is impossible, as I believe, without love to be just, much more cannot justice co-exist with hate. The pure eye for the true vision of another's claims can only go with the loving heart. The man who hates can hardly be delicate in doing justice, say to his neighbor's love, to his neighbor's predilections and peculiarities. It is hard enough to be just to our friends; and how shall our enemies fare with us? For justice demands that we shall think rightly of our neighbor as certainly as that we shall neither steal his goods nor bear false witness against him. Man is not made for justice from his fellow, but for love, which is greater than justice, and by including supersedes justice. *Mere* justice is an impossibility, a fiction of analysis. It does not exist between man and man, save relatively to human *law*. Justice to be justice must be much more than justice. Love is the law of our condition, without which we can no more render justice than a man can keep a straight line walking in the dark. The eye is not single, and the body is not full of light. No man who is even indifferent to his brother can recognize the claims which his humanity has upon him. Nay, the very indifference itself is an injustice.

I have taken for granted that the fault lies with the enemy so considered, for upon the primary rocks would I build my foundation. But the question must be put to each man by himself, "Is my neighbor indeed my enemy, or am I my neighbor's enemy, and so take him to be mine?—awful thought! Or, if he be mine, am not I his? Am I not refusing to acknowledge the child of the kingdom within his bosom, so killing the child of the kingdom within my own?" Let us claim for ourselves no more indulgence than we give to him. Such honesty will end in severity at home and clemency abroad. For we are accountable for the ill in ourselves, and have to kill it; for the good in our neighbor, and have to cherish it. He only, in the name and power of God, can kill the bad in him; we can cherish the good in him by being good to it across all the evil fog that comes between our love and his good.

Nor ought it to be forgotten that this fog is often the result of misapprehension and mistake, giving rise to all kinds of indignations, resentments, and regrets. Scarce anything about us is just as it seems, but at the core there is truth enough to dispel all falsehood and reveal life as unspeakably divine. O brother, sister, across this weary fog, dim-lighted by the faint torches of our truth-seeking, I call to the divine in thee, which is mine, not to rebuke thee, not to rouse thee, not to say, "Why hatest thou me?" but to say, "I love thee; in God's name I love thee." And I will wait until the true self looks out of thine eyes, and knows the true self in me.

But in the working of the Divine Love upon the race, my enemy is doomed to cease to be my enemy, and to become my friend. One flash of truth towards me would destroy my enmity at once; one hearty confession of wrong, and our enmity passes away; from each comes forth the brother who was inside the enemy all the time. For this the Truth is at work. In the faith of this, let us love the enemy now, accepting God's work in reversion, as it were; let us believe as seeing his yet invisible triumph, clasping and holding fast our brother, in defiance of the changeful wiles of the wicked enchantment which would persuade our eyes and hearts that he is not our brother, but some horrible thing, hateful and hating.

But again I must ask, What if *we* are in the wrong and do the wrong, and hate because we have injured? What then? Why, then, let us cry to God as from the throat of hell; struggle, as under the weight of a spiritual incubus; cry, as knowing the vile disease that cleaveth fast unto us; cry, as possessed of an evil spirit; cry, as one buried alive, from the sepulchre of our evil consciousness, that he would take pity upon us the chief of sinners, the most wretched and vile of men, and send some help to lift us from the fearful pit and the miry clay. Nothing will help but the Spirit proceeding from the Father and the Son, the spirit of the Father and the Brother casting out and revealing. It will be with tearing and foaming, with a terrible cry and a lying as one dead, that such a demon will go out. But what a vision will then arise in the depths of the purified soul!

"Be ye therefore perfect, even as your Father which is in heaven is perfect." "Love your enemies, and ye shall be the children of the Highest." It is the divine glory to forgive.

O Father, thou art All-in-all, perfect beyond the longing of thy children, and we are all and altogether thine. Thou wilt make us pure and loving and free. We shall stand fearless in thy presence, because perfect in thy love. Then shall thy children be of good cheer, infinite in the love of each other, and eternal in thy love. Lord Jesus, let the heart of a child be given to us, that so we may arise from the grave of our dead selves and die no more.

## VIII.

## A CHRISTMAS LESSON.

"YE CANNOT SERVE GOD AND MAMMON. THEREFORE I SAY UNTO YOU, TAKE NO THOUGHT FOR YOUR LIFE." Matthew 6 : 24, 25."

When the Child, whose birth we celebrate with glad hearts this day, grew up to be a man, he said this. Did he mean it—he never said what he did not mean. Did he mean it wholly? He meant it far beyond what the words could convey. He meant it altogether and entirely. When people do not understand what the Lord says, when it seems to them that his advice is impracticable, instead of searching deeper for a meaning which will be evidently true and wise, they comfort themselves by thinking he could not have meant it altogether, and so leave it. Or they think that if he did mean it, he could not expect them to carry it out. And in the fact that they could not do it perfectly if they were to try, they take refuge from the duty of trying to do it at all; or oftener, they do not think about it at all as anything that in the least concerns them.

The Son of our Father in heaven may have become a child, may have led the one life which belongs to every man to lead, may have suffered because we are sinners, may have died for our sakes, doing the will of his Father in heaven, and yet we have nothing to do with the words he spoke out of the midst of his true, perfect knowledge, feeling and action! Is it not strange that it should be so? Let it not be so with us this day.

## A CHRISTMAS LESSON.

Let us seek to find out what our Lord means, that we may do it; trying and failing and trying again—verily to be victorious at last—what matter *when*, so long as we are trying, and so coming nearer to our end.

*Mammon*, you know, means *riches*. Now, riches are meant to be the slave—not even the servant of man, and not to be the master. If a man serve his own servant, or, in a word, any one who has no just claim to be his master, he is a slave. But here he serves his own slave. On the other hand, to serve God, the source of our being, our own glorious Father, is freedom; in fact, is the only way to get rid of all bondage. So you see plainly enough that a man cannot serve God and Mammon. For how can a slave of his own slave, be the servant of the God of freedom, of him who can have no one to serve him but a free man? His service is freedom. Do not, I pray you, make any confusion between service and slavery. To serve is the highest, noblest calling in creation. For even the Son of Man came not to be ministered unto, but to minister, yea, with himself.

But how can a man *serve* riches? Why, when he says to riches, "Ye are my good." When he feels he cannot be happy without them. When he puts forth the energies of his nature to get them. When he schemes, and dreams, and lies awake about them. When he will not give to his neighbor for fear of becoming poor himself. When he wants to have more, and to know he has more, than he can need. When he wants to leave money behind him, not for the sake of his children or relatives, but for the name of the wealth. When he leaves his money, not to those who *need* it, even of his relations, but to those who are rich like himself, making them yet more the slaves to the overgrown monster

they worship for his size. When he honors those who
have money because they have money, irrespective of
their character; or when he honors in a rich man what
he would not honor in a poor man. Then he is the
slave of Mammon.

Still more is he Mammon's slave when his devotion
to his god makes him oppressive to those over whom
his wealth gives him power; or when he becomes unjust in order to add to his stores. How will it be with
such a man when on a sudden he finds that the world
has vanished and he is alone with God? There lies the
body in which he used to live, whose poor necessities
first made money of value to him, but with which itself
and its fictitious value are both left behind. He cannot
now even try to bribe God with a check. The angels
will not bow down to him because his property, as set
forth in his will, takes five or six figures to express its
amount. It makes no difference to them that he has
lost it, though; for they never respected him. And the
poor souls of Hades, who envied him the wealth they
had lost before, rise up as one man to welcome him, not
for love of him—no worshiper of Mammon loves another
—but rejoicing in the mischief that has befallen him,
and saying, "Art thou also become one of us?" And
Lazarus in Abraham's bosom, however sorry he may
be for him, however grateful he may feel to him for the
broken victuals and the penny, cannot with one drop
of the water of Paradise cool that man's parched
tongue.

Alas, poor Dives! poor server of Mammon, whose
vile god can pretend to deliver him no longer! Or
rather, for the blockish god never pretended anything
—it was the man's own doing—alas for the Mammon-worshiper! he can no longer deceive himself in his

## A CHRISTMAS LESSON.

riches. And so even in hell he is something nobler than he was on earth; for he worships his riches no longer. He cannot. He curses them.

Terrible things to say on Christmas-day! But if Christmas-day teaches us anything, it teaches us to worship God and not Mammon; to worship spirit and not matter; to worship love and not power.

Do I now hear any of my friends saying in their hearts: Let the rich take that! It does not apply to us. We are poor enough! Ah, my friends, I have known a light-hearted, liberal rich man lose his riches, and be liberal and light-hearted still. I knew a rich lady once, in giving a large gift of money to a poor man, say apologetically, "I hope it is no disgrace in me to be rich, as it is none in you to be poor." It is not the being rich that is wrong, but the serving of riches, instead of making them serve your neighbor and yourself—your neighbor for this life, yourself for the everlasting habitations. God knows it is hard for the rich man to enter into the kingdom of heaven; but the rich man does sometimes enter in; for God hath made it possible. And the greater the victory, when it is the rich man that overcometh the world. It is easier for the poor man to enter the kingdom, yet many of the poor have failed to enter in, and the greater is the disgrace of their defeat. For the poor have more done for them, as far as outward things go, in the way of salvation, than the rich, and have a beatitude all to themselves besides.

For in the making of this world as a school of salvation, the poor, as the necessary majority, have been more regarded than the rich. Do not think, my poor friend, that God will let you off. He lets nobody off. You, too, must pay the uttermost farthing. He loves you too well to let you serve Mammon a whit more than your rich neighbor. "Serve Mammon!" do you say? "How can I serve Mammon? I have no Mammon to serve." Would you like to have riches a moment sooner than God gives them? Would you serve Mammon if you had him? "Who can tell?" do you answer? "Leave those questions till I am tried." But is there no bitterness in the tone of that response? Does it not mean, "It will be a long time before I have a chance of trying *that?*"

But I am not driven to such questions for the chance of convicting some of you of Mammon-worship. Let us look to the text. Read it again. "Ye cannot serve God and Mammon. Therefore I say unto you, Take no thought for your life."

Why are you to take no thought? Because you cannot serve God and Mammon. Is taking, then, a serving of Mammon? Clearly. Where are you now, poor man? Brooding over the frost? Will it harden the ground, so that the God of the sparrows cannot find food for his sons? Where are you now, poor woman? Sleepless over the empty cupboard and to-morrow's dinner? "It is because we have no bread!" do you answer? Have you forgotten the five loaves among the five thousand, and the fragments that were left? Or do you know nothing of your Father in heaven, who clothes the lilies and feeds the birds? O ye of little faith? O ye poor-spirited Mammon-worshipers! who worship him not even because he has given you anything, but in the hope that he may some future day benignantly regard you.

But I may be too hard upon you. I know well that our Father sees a great difference between the man who is anxious about his children's dinner, or even about

## A CHRISTMAS LESSON.

his own, and the man who is only anxious to add another ten thousand to his much goods laid up for many years. But you ought to find it easy to trust in God for such a matter as your daily bread, whereas no man can by any possibility trust in God for ten thousand pounds. The former need is a God-ordained necessity; the latter desire a man-devised appetite at best —possibly swinish greed. Tell me, do you long to be rich? Then you worship Mammon. Tell me, do you think you would feel safer if you had money in the bank? Then you are Mammon-worshipers; for you would trust the barn of the rich man rather than the God who makes the corn to grow. Do you say—"What shall we eat? and what shall we drink? and wherewithal shall we be clothed?" Are ye thus of doubtful mind? Then you are Mammon-worshipers.

But how is the work of the world to be done if we take no thought? We are nowhere told not to take thought. We *must* take thought. The question is— What are we to take or not to take thought about? By some who do not know God, little work would be done if they were not driven by anxiety of some kind. But you, friends, are you content to go with the nations of the earth, or do you seek a better way—*the* way that the Father of nations would have you walk in?

*What* then are we to take thought about? Why, about our work. What are we not to take thought about? Why, about our life. The one is our business: the other is God's. But you turn it the other way. You take no thought of earnestness about the doing of your duty; but you take thought of care lest God should not fulfil his part in the goings on of the world. A man's business is just to do his duty. God takes upon himself the feeding and the clothing. Will the work of the world be neglected if a man thinks of his work, his duty, God's will to be done, instead of what he is to eat, what he is to drink, and wherewithal he is to be clothed? And remember all the needs of the world come back to these three. You will allow, I think, that the work of the world will be only so much the better done; that the very means of procuring the raiment or the food will be the more thoroughly used. What, then, is the only region on which the doubt can settle? Why, God. He alone remains to be doubted. Shall it be so with you? Shall the Son of Man, the baby now born, and forever with us, find no faith in you?

Ah, my poor friend, who canst not trust in God—I was going to say you *deserve*—but what do I know of you to condemn and judge you?—I was going to say, you deserve to be treated like the child who frets and comp'ains because his mother holds him on her knee and feeds him mouthful by mouthful with her own loving hand. I meant—you deserve to have your own way for a while; to be set down, told to help yourself, and see what it will come to; to have your mother open the cupboard door for you, and leave you alone to your pleasures. Alas! poor child! When the sweets begin to pall, and twilight begins to come duskily into the chamber, and you look about all at once and see no mother, how will your cupboard comfort you then? Ask it for a smile, for a stroke of the gentle hand, for a word of love. All the full-fed Mammon can give you is what your mother would have given you without the consequent loathing, with the light of her countenance upon it all, and the arm of her love around you. And this is what God does sometimes, I think, with the Mammon-worshipers amongst the poor. He says to them, Take your Mammon, and see what he is worth.

## A CHRISTMAS LESSON.

Ah, friends, the children of God can never be happy serving other than him. The prodigal might fill his belly with riotous living or with the husks that the swine ate. It was all one so long as he was not with his father. His soul was wretched. So would you be if you had wealth, for I fear you would only be worse Mammon-worshipers than now, and might well have to thank God for the misery of any swine-trough that could bring you to your senses.

"But we do see people die of starvation sometimes." Yes. But if you did your work in God's name, and left the rest to him, that would not trouble you. You would say, "If it be God's will that I should starve, I can starve as well as another." And your mind would be at ease. "Thou wilt keep him in perfect peace whose mind is stayed upon thee, because he trusteth in thee." Of that I am sure. It may be good for you to go hungry and barefoot; but it must be utter death to have no faith in God. It is not, however, in God's way of things that the man who does his work shall not live by it. We do not know why here and there a man may be left to die of hunger, but I do believe that they who wait upon the Lord shall not lack any good. What it may be good to deprive a man of till he knows and acknowledges whence it comes, it may be still better to give him when he has learned that every good and perfect gift is from above, and cometh down from the Father of lights.

I *should* like to know a man who just minded his duty and troubled himself about nothing; who did his own work and did not interfere with God's. How nobly he would work—working not for reward, but because it was the will of God! How happily he would receive his food and clothing, receiving them as the gifts of God!

What peace would be his! What a sober gayety! How hearty and infectious his laughter! What a friend he would be! How sweet his sympathy! And his mind would be so clear he would understand everything. His eye being single, his whole eye would be full of light. No fear of his ever doing a mean thing. He would die in a ditch rather. It is this fear of want that makes men do mean things. They are afraid to part with their precious lord—Mammon. He gives no safety against such a fear. One of the richest men in England is haunted with the dread of the workhouse. This man whom I should like to know, would be sure that God would have him liberal, and he would be what God would have him. Riches are not in the least necessary to that. Witness our Lord's admiration of the poor widow with her great farthing.

But I think I hear my troubled friend who does not love money, and yet cannot trust in God out and out, though she fain would—I think I hear her say, "I believe I could trust him for myself, or at least I should be ready to dare the worst for his sake; but my children—it is the thought of my children that is too much for me." Ah, woman! she whom the Saviour praised so pleasedly, was one who trusted him for her daughter. What an honor she had. "Be it unto thee even as thou wilt." Do you think you love your children better than he who made them? Is not your love what it is because he put it into your heart first? Have not you often been cross with them? Sometimes unjust to them? Whence came the returning love that rose from unknown depths in your being, and swept away the anger and the injustice? You did not create that love. Probably you were not good enough to send for it by prayer. But it came; God sent it. He makes you love your children; be sorry when you have been cross to them; ashamed when you have been unjust to them; and yet you will not trust him to give them food and clothes! Depend upon it, if he ever refused to give them food and clothes, and you knew all about it, the why and the wherefore, you would not dare to give them food or clothes either. He loves them a thousand times better than you do—be sure of that—and feels for their sufferings too, when he cannot give them just what he would like to give them—cannot for their good, I mean.

It has been well said that no man ever sank under the burden of the day. It is when to-morrow's burden is added to the burden of to-day, that the weight is more than a man can bear. Never load yourselves so, my friends. If you find yourselves so loaded, at least remember this: it is your own doing, not God's. He begs you to leave the future to him, and mind the present. What more or what else could he do to take the burden off you? Nothing else would do it. Money in the bank would not do it. He cannot do to-morow's business for you beforehand to save you from fear about it. That would derange everything. What else is there but to tell you to trust in him, irrespective of the fact that nothing else but such trust can put our hearts at peace from the very nature of our relation to him as well as the fact that we need these things.

We think that we come nearer to God than the lower animals do by our foresight. But there is another side to it. We are like to him with whom there is no past or future, with whom a day is as a thousand years, and a thousand years as one day, when we live with large bright spiritual eyes, doing our work in the great present, leaving both past and future to him, to whom they are ever present, and fearing nothing, because he is in our future, as much as he is in our past, as much as, and far more than, we can feel him to be in our present. Partakers thus of the divine nature, resting in that perfect All-in-all in whom our nature is eternal too, we walk without fear, full of hope and courage and strength to do his will, waiting for the endless good which he is always giving as fast as he can get us able to take it in.

Would not this be to be more of gods than Satan promised to Eve? To live carelessly-divine, duty-doing, fearless, loving, self-forgetting lives—is not that more than to know both good and evil—lives in which the good, like Aaron's rod, has swallowed up the evil, and turned it into good? For pain and hunger are evils: but if faith in God swallows them up, do they not so turn into good? I say they do. And I am glad to believe that I am not alone in the world in this conviction. I have never been too hungry, but I have had trouble which I would gladly have exchanged for hunger, and cold, and weariness. Some of you have known hunger, and cold, and weariness. Do you not join with me to say: It is well, and better than well—whatever helps us to know the love of him who is our God?

## IX.

## "TAKE NO THOUGHT."

"THEREFORE TAKE NO THOUGHT, SAYING, WHAT SHALL WE EAT? OR, WHAT SHALL WE DRINK? OR, WHEREWITHAL SHALL WE BE CLOTHED? (FOR AFTER ALL THESE THINGS DO THE GENTILES SEEK;) FOR YOUR HEAVENLY FATHER KNOWETH THAT YE HAVE NEED OF ALL THESE THINGS. BUT SEEK YE FIRST THE KINGDOM OF GOD, AND HIS RIGHTEOUSNESS; AND ALL THESE THINGS SHALL BE ADDED UNTO YOU.—Matthew 6:31-33.

When God comes to a man, man looks round for his neighbor. When man departed from God in the Garden of Eden, the only man in the world ceased to be the friend of the only woman in the world; and, instead of seeking to bear her burden, became her accuser to God, in whom he saw only the Judge, unable to perceive that the infinite love of the Father had come to punish him in tenderness and grace. But when God in Jesus comes back to men, brothers and sisters spread forth their arms to embrace each other, and so to embrace him. This is, when he is born again in our souls.

For, dear friends, what we all need is just to become little children like him; to cease to be careful about many things, and to trust in him, seeking only that he should rule, and that we should be made good like him. What else is meant by "Seek ye first the kingdom of God and his righteousness, and all these things shall be added unto you?" Instead of doing so, we seek the things God has promised to look after for us, and refuse to seek the thing he wants us to seek—a thing that cannot be given us except we seek it. We profess to think Jesus the grandest and most glorious of men, and yet hardly care to be like him; and so when we are offered his Spirit, that is, his very nature within us, for the asking, we will hardly take the trouble to ask for it.

But to-night, at least, let all unkind thoughts, all hard judgments of one another, all selfish desires after our own way, be put from us, that we may welcome the Babe into our very bosoms; that when he comes amongst us—for is he not a child still, meek and lowly of heart?—he may not be troubled to find that we are quarrelsome, and selfish, and unjust.

"No man can serve two masters: for either he will hate the one, and love the other; or else he will hold to the one, and despise the other. Ye cannot serve God and Mammon. Therefore I say unto you, Take no thought for your life, what ye shall eat, or what ye shall drink; nor yet for your body, what ye shall put on. Is not the life more than meat, and the body than raiment? Behold the fowls of the air: for they sow not, neither do they reap, nor gather into barns; yet your heavenly Father feedeth them. Are ye not much better than they?"

But as your mistrust will go further, I can go further to meet it. You will say, "Ah, yes!" In your feeling, I mean, not in words—you will say, "Ah! yes—food and clothing of a sort! Enough to keep life in and too much cold out! But I want my children to have plenty of *good* food and *nice* clothes."

"Which of you by taking thought can add one cubit unto his stature? And why take ye thought for raiment? Consider the lilies of the field how they grow; they toil not, neither do they spin; and yet I say unto you, That even Solomon in all his glory was not arrayed like one of these. Wherefore, if God so clothe the grass of the field, which to-day is, and to-morrow is cast into the oven, shall he not much more clothe you, O ye of little faith?"

Faithless mother! Consider the birds of the air. They have so much that at least they can sing. Consider the lilies—they were red lilies, those. Would you not trust him who delights in glorious colors—more at least than you, or he would never have created them and made us to delight in them? I do not say that your children shall be clothed in scarlet and fine linen; but if not, it is not because God despises scarlet and fine linen, or does not love your children. He loves them, I say, too much to give them every thing all at once. But he would make them such that they may have everything without being the worse, and without being the better for it. And if you cannot trust him yet, it begins to be a shame, I think.

"Therefore take no thought, saying, What shall we eat? or, What shall we drink? or, Wherewithal shall we be clothed? (for after all these things do the Gentiles seek:) for your heavenly Father knoweth that ye have need of all these things. But seek ye first the kingdom of God, and his righteousness, and all these things shall be added unto you."

Now there *has been* just one man who acted thus. And it is his Spirit in our hearts that makes us desire to know or to be another such—who would do the will of God for God, and let God do God's will for him. For his will is all. And this man is the baby whose birth we celebrate this day. Was this a condition to choose —that of a baby—by one who thought it part of a man's high calling to take care of the morrow? Did he not thus cast the whole matter at once upon the hands and heart of his Father? Sufficient unto the baby's day is the need thereof; he toils not, neither does he spin; and yet he is fed and clothed, and loved, and rejoiced in. Do you remind me that sometimes even his mother forgets him—a mother, most likely, to whose self-indulgence or weakness the child owes his birth as heirs. Ah! but he is not therefore forgotten, however like things it may look to our half-seeing eyes, by his Father in heaven. One of the highest benefits we can reap from understanding the way of God with ourselves is, that we become able thus to trust him for others with whom we do not understand his ways.

But let us look at what will be more easily shown —how, namely, he did the will of his Father, and took no thought for the morrow after he became a man. Remember how he forsook his trade when the time came for him to preach. Preaching was not a profession then. There were no monasteries, or vicarages, or stipends, then. Yet witness for the Father the garment woven throughout; the ministering of women, the purse in common! Hard-working men and rich ladies were ready to help him, and did help him with all that he needed. Did he then never want? Yes; once at least —for a little while only.

He was a-hungered in the wilderness. "Make bread," said Satan. "No," said our Lord. He could starve: but he could not eat bread that his Father did not give him, even though he could make it himself. He had come hither to be tried. But when the victory was secure, lo! the angels brought him food from his Father. Which was better? To feed himself, or be fed by his Father? Judge yourselves, anxious people. He sought the kingdom of God and his righteousness, and the bread was added unto him.

And this gives me occasion to remark that the same truth holds with regard to any portion of the future as well as the morrow. It is a principle, not a command, or an encouragement, or a promise merely. In respect of it there is no difference between next day and next year, next hour and next century. You will see at once the absurdity of taking no thought for the morrow, and taking thought for next year. But do you see likewise that it is equally reasonable to trust God for the next moment, and equally unreasonable not to trust him? The Lord was hungry and needed food now, though he could still go without for awhile. He left it to his Father. And so he told his disciples to do when they were called to answer before judges and rulers. "Take no thought: it shall be given you what to speak."

You have a disagreeable duty to do at twelve o'clock. Do not blacken nine and ten and eleven, and all between with the color of twelve. Do the work of each, and reap your reward in peace. So when the dreaded moment in the future becomes the present, you shall meet it walking in the light, and that light will overcome its darkness. How often do men who have made up their minds what to say and do under certain expected circumstances, forget the words and reverse the actions! The best preparation is the present well seen to, the last duty done. For this will keep the eye so clear and the body so full of light that the right action will be perceived at once, the right words will rush from the heart to the lips, and the man, full of the Spirit of God because he cares for nothing but the will of God will trample on the evil thing in love, and be sent, it may be, in a chariot of fire to the presence of his

Father, or stand unmoved among the cruel mockings of the men he loves.

Do you feel inclined to say in your hearts: "It was easy for him to take no thought, for he had the matter in his own hands?" But observe, there is nothing very noble in a man's taking no thought except it be from faith. If there were no God to take thought for us, we should have no right to blame any one for taking thought. You may fancy the Lord had his own power to fall back upon. But that would have been to him just the one dreadful thing. That his Father should forget him!—no power in himself could make up for that. He feared nothing for himself, and never once employed his divine power to save him from his human fate. Let God do that for him if he saw fit. He did not come into the world to take care of himself. That would not be in any way divine. To fall back on himself, God failing him—how could that make it easy for him to avoid care? The very idea would be torture. That would be to declare heaven void, and the world without a God. He would not even pray to his Father for what he knew he should have if he did ask it. He would just wait his will.

But see how the fact of his own power adds tenfold significance to the fact that he trusted in God. We see that this power would not serve his need—his need not being to be fed and clothed, but to be one with the Father, to be fed by his hand, clothed by his care. This was what the Lord wanted—and we need, alas! too often without wanting it. He never once, I repeat, used his power for himself. That was not his business. He did not care about it. His life was of no value to him but as his Father cared for it. God would mind all that was necessary for him, and he would mind the work his Father had given him to do. And, my friends, this is just the one secret of a blessed life, the one thing every man comes into this world to learn. With what authority it comes to us from the lips of him who knew all about it, and ever did as he said!

Now you see that he took no thought for the morrow. And, in the name of the holy child Jesus, I call upon you, this Christmas-day, to cast care to the winds and trust in God; to receive the message of peace and good will to men; to yield yourselves to the Spirit of God, that you may be taught what he wants you to know; to remember that the one gift promised without reserve to those who ask it—the one gift worth having —the gift which makes all other gifts a thousandfold in value, is the gift of the Holy Spirit, the spirit of the child Jesus, who will take of the things of Jesus, and show them to you—make you understand them, that is —so that you shall see them to be true, and love him with all your heart and soul, and your neighbor as yourself.

> "O man! thou image of thy Maker's good,
> What canst thou fear, when breathed into thy blood
> His Spirit is that built thee? What dull sense
> Makes thee suspect, in need, that Providence
> Who made the morning, and who placed the light,
> Guide to thy labors; who called up the night,
> And bid her fall upon thee like sweet showers,
> In hollow murmurs, to lock up thy powers;
> Who gave thee knowledge; who so trusted thee
> To let thee grow so near himself, the Tree?
> Must he then be distrusted? Shall his frame
> Discourse with him why thus and thus I am?
> He made the Angels thine, thy fellows all;
> Nay, even thy servants, when devotions call.
> Oh! canst thou be so stupid then, so dim,
> To seek a saving influence, and lose him?

Can stars protect thee? Or can poverty,
Which is the light to heaven. put out his eye?
He is my star; in him all truth I find,
All influence, all fate. And when my mind
Is furnished with his fulness, my poor story
Shall outlive all their age, and all their glory.
The hand of danger cannot fall amiss,
When I know what, and in whose power, it is,
Nor want, the curse of man, shall make me groan;
A holy hermit is a mind alone.
Affliction, when I know it, is but this,
A deep alloy whereby man tougher is
To bear the hammer; and the deeper still,
We still arise more image of his will;
Sickness, and humorous cloud 'twixt us and light;
And death, at longest, but another night."

O GOD, that despisest not the sighing of a broken heart, nor the desire of the sorrowful, mercifully assist our prayers that we make before thee in all our troubles, trials, and sorrows, whensoever they come upon us; and for the glory of thy name turn from us all those evils that we most justly have deserved; and grant that in all our anxiety sickness, or weakness we may put our whole trust in the kindness and faithfulness, and ever serve thee in holiness, patience, and pureness of living, to thy honor and glory, through Jesus Christ, our Lord. *Amen.*

## X.

## THE CHILD IN THE MIDST.

"AND HE TOOK A CHILD, AND SET HIM IN THE MIDST OF THEM: AND WHEN HE HAD TAKEN HIM IN HIS ARMS, HE SAID UNTO THEM, WHOSOEVER SHALL RECEIVE ONE OF SUCH CHILDREN IN MY NAME, RECEIVETH ME; AND WHOSOEVER SHALL RECEIVE ME, RECEIVETH NOT ME, BUT HIM THAT SENT ME."—Mark 9: 36, 37.

Of this passage in the life of our Lord the account given by St. Mark is the more complete. But it may be enriched and its lesson rendered yet more evident from the record of St. Matthew.

These passages record a lesson our Lord gave his disciples against ambition, against emulation. It is not for the sake of setting forth this lesson that I write about these words of our Lord, but for the sake of a truth, a revelation about God, in which his great argument reaches its height.

He took a little child—possibly a child of Peter; for St. Mark says that the incident fell at Capernaum, and "in the house,"—a child therefore with some of the characteristics of Peter, whose very faults were those of a childish nature. We might expect the child of such a father to possess the childlike countenance and bearing essential to the conveyance of the lesson which I now desire to set forth as contained in the passage.

For it must be confessed that there are children who are not childlike. One of the saddest and not least common sights in the world is the face of a child whose mind is so brimful of worldly wisdom that the human childishness has vanished from it, as well as the divine childlikeness. For the *childlike* is the divine, and the very word "marshals me the way that I was going." But I must delay my ascent to the final argument in order to remove a possible difficulty, which, in turning us towards one of the grandest truths, turns us away from the truth which the Lord had in view here.

The difficulty is this: Is it like the *Son of man* to pick out the beautiful child, and leave the common child unnoticed? What thank would he have in that? Do not even the publicans as much as that? And do not our hearts revolt against the thought of it? Shall the mother's heart cleave closest to the deformed of her little ones? and shall "Christ as we believe him" choose according to the sight of the eye? Would he turn away from the child born in sin and taught iniquity, on whose pinched face hunger and courage and love of praise have combined to stamp the cunning of avaricious age, and take to his arms the child of honest parents, such as Peter and his wife, who could not help looking more good than the other? That were not he who came to seek and to save that which was lost. Let the man who loves his brother say which, in his highest moments of love to God, which, when he is nearest to that ideal humanity whereby *a man* shall be a hiding-place from the wind, he would clasp to his bosom of refuge. Would it not be the evil-faced child, because he needed it most? Yes; in God's name, yes. For is not that the divine way? Who that has read of the lost sheep or the found prodigal, even if he had no Spirit bearing witness with his spirit, will dare to say that it is not the divine way? Often, no doubt, it will *appear* otherwise, for the childlike child is easier to save than

## THE CHILD IN THE MIDST. 101

the other, and may *come* first. But the rejoicing in heaven is greatest over the sheep that has wandered the farthest—perhaps was born on the wild hill-side, and not in the fold at all. For such a prodigal, the elder brother in heaven prays thus—" Lord, think about my poor brother more than about me, for I know thee, and am at rest in thee. I am with thee always."

Why, then, do I think it necessary to say that this child was probably Peter's child, and certainly a child that looked childlike because it was childlike? No amount of evil can *be* the child. No amount of evil, not to say in the face, but in the habits, or even in the heart of the child, can make it cease to be a child, can annihilate the divine idea of childhood which moved in the heart of God when he made that child after his own image. It is the essential of which God speaks, the real by which he judges, the undying of which he is the God.

Heartily I grant this. And if the object of our Lord in taking the child in his arms had been to teach love to our neighbor, love to humanity, the ugliest child he could have found, would, perhaps, have served his purpose best. The man who receives any, and more plainly he who receives the repulsive child, because he is the offspring of God, because he is his own brother born, must receive the Father in thus receiving the child. Whosoever gives a cup of cold water to a little one, refreshes the heart of the Father. To do as God does, is to receive God; to do a service to one of his children is to receive the Father. Hence, any human being, especially if wretched and woe-begone and outcast, would do as well as a child for the purpose of setting forth this love of God to the human being. Therefore something more is probably intended here. The lesson will be found to lie not in the *humanity*, but in the *childhood* of the child.

Again, if the disciples could have seen that the essential childhood was meant, and not a blurred and half-obliterated childhood, the most selfish child might have done as well, but could have done no better than the one we have supposed in whom the true childhood is more evident. But when the child was employed as a manifestation, utterance, and sign of the truth that lay in his childhood, in order that the eyes as well as the ears should be channels to the heart, it was essential—not that the child should be beautiful but—that the child should be childlike; that those qualities which wake in our hearts, at sight, the love peculiarly belonging to childhood, which is, indeed, but the perception of the childhood, should at least glimmer out upon the face of the *chosen type*. Would such an unchildlike child as we see sometimes, now in a great house, clothed in purple and lace, now in a squalid close, clothed in dirt and rags, have been fit for our Lord's purpose, when he had to say that his listeners must become like this child? when the lesson he had to present to them was that of the divine nature of the child, that of childlikeness? Would there not have been a contrast between the child and our Lord's words, ludicrous except for its horror, especially seeing he set forth the individuality of the child, by saying, "this little child," "one of such children," and "these little ones that believe in me?" Even the feelings of pity and of love that would arise in a good heart upon further contemplation of such a child, would have turned it quite away from the lesson our Lord intended to give.

That this lesson did lie, not in the humanity, but in

## THE CHILD IN THE MIDST. 103

the childhood of the child, let me now show more fully. The disciples had been disputing who should be the greatest, and the Lord wanted to show them that such a dispute had nothing whatever to do with the way things went in his kingdom. Therefore, as a specimen of his subjects, he took a child and set him before them. It was not, it could not be, in virtue of his humanity, it was in virtue of his childhood that this child was thus presented as representing a subject of the kingdom. It was not to show the scope but the nature of the kingdom. He told them they could not enter into the kingdom save by becoming little children —by humbling themselves. For the idea of ruling was excluded where childlikeness was the one essential quality. It was to be no more who should rule, but who should serve; no more who should look down upon his fellows from the conquered heights of authority, even of sacred authority, but who should look up honoring humanity, and ministering unto it, so that humanity itself might at length be persuaded of its own honor as a temple of the living God. It was to impress this lesson upon them that he showed them the child. Therefore, I repeat, the lesson lay in the *childhood* of the child.

But I now approach my especial object; for this lesson led to the enunciation of a yet higher truth, upon which it was founded, and from which indeed it sprung. Nothing is required of man that is not first in God. It is because God is perfect that we are required to be perfect. And it is for the revelation of God to all the human souls that they may be saved by knowing him, and so becoming like him, that this child is thus chosen and set before them in the gospel. He who, in giving the cup of water or the embrace, comes into contact with the essential childhood of the child—that is, embraces the *childish* humanity of it—(not he who embraces it out of love to humanity, or even love to God as the Father of it)—is partaker of the meaning, that is, the blessing of this passage. It is the recognition of the childhood as divine that will show the disciple how vain the strife is after relative place or honor in the great kingdom.

For it is *In my name*. This means *as representing me;* and, therefore, *as being like me*. Our Lord could not commission any one to be received in his name who could not more or less represent him; for there would be untruth and unreason. Moreover, he had just been telling the disciples that they must become like this child; and now, when he tells them to receive *such* a little child in his name, it must surely imply something in common between them all—something in which the child and Jesus meet—something in which the child and the disciples meet. What else can that be than the spiritual childhood? *In my name* does not mean *because I will it*. An arbitrary utterance of the will of our Lord would certainly find ten thousand to obey it, even to suffering, for one that will be able to receive such a vital truth of his character as is contained in the words; but it is not obedience alone that our Lord will have, but obedience to the *truth*, that is, to the Light of the World, truth beheld and known. *In my name*, if we take all we can find in it, the full meaning which alone will harmonize and make the passage a whole, involves a revelation from resemblance, from fitness to represent and so reveal.

He who receives a child, then, in the name of Jesus, does so, perceiving wherein Jesus and the child are one, what is common to them. He must not only see the

## THE CHILD IN THE MIDST.

*ideal* child in the child he receives—that reality of loveliness which constitutes true childhood—but must perceive that the child is like Jesus, or rather, that the Lord is like the child, and may be embraced, yea, is embraced, by every heart childlike enough to embrace a child for the sake of his childness. I do not therefore say that none but those who are thus conscious in the act partake of the blessing. But a special sense, a lofty knowledge of blessedness, belongs to the act of embracing a child as the visible likeness of the Lord himself. For the blessedness is the perceiving of the truth—the blessing is the truth itself—the God-known truth, that the Lord has the heart of a child. The man who perceives this knows in himself that he is blessed—blessed because that is true.

But the argument as to the meaning of our Lord's words, *in my name*, is incomplete, until we follow our Lord's enunciation to its second and higher stage: "He that receiveth me, receiveth him that sent me." It will be allowed that the connection between the first and second link of the chain will probably be the same as the connection between the second and third. I do not say it is necessarily so; for I aim at no logical certainty. I aim at showing, rather than at proving, by means of my sequences, the idea to which I am approaching. For if, (once a man beholds it,) he cannot receive it, if it does not show itself to him to be true, there would not only be little use in convincing him by logic, but I allow that he can easily suggest other possible connections in the chain, though, I assert, none so symmetrical. What, then, is the connection between the second and third? How is it that he who receives the Son receives the Father? Because the Son is as the Father; and he whose heart can perceive the essential in Christ, has the essence of the Father—that is, sees and holds to it by that recognition, and is one therewith by recognition and worship. What, then, next, is the connection between the first and second? I think the same. "He that sees the essential in this child, the pure childhood, sees that which is the essence of me," grace and truth—in a word, childlikeness. It follows not that the former is perfect as the latter, but it is the same in kind, and therefore, manifest in the child, reveals that which is in Jesus.

Then to receive a child in the name of Jesus is to receive Jesus; to receive Jesus is to receive God; therefore to receive the child is to receive God himself.

That such is the feeling of the words, and that such was the feeling in the heart of our Lord when he spoke them, I may show from another golden thread that may be traced through the shining web of his golden words.

What is the kingdom of Christ? A rule of love, of truth—a rule of service. The king is the chief servant in it. "The kings of the earth have dominion: it shall not be so among you." "The Son of Man came to minister." "My Father worketh hitherto, and I work." The great Workman is the great King, laboring for his own. So he that would be greatest among them, and come nearest to the King himself, must be the servant of all. It is *like king, like subject,* in the kingdom of heaven. No rule of force, as of one kind over another kind. It is the rule of *kind,* of *nature,* of deepest nature—of *God.* If, then, to enter into this kingdom, we must become children, the spirit of children must be its pervading spirit throughout, from lowly subject

THE CHILD IN THE MIDST. 107

to lowliest king. The lesson added by St. Luke to the presentation of the child is: "For he that is least among you all, the same shall be great." And St. Matthew says: "Whosoever shall humble himself as this little child, the same is greatest in the kingdom of heaven." Hence the sign that passes between king and subject. The subject kneels in homage to the kings of the earth: the heavenly king takes his subject in his arms. This is the sign of the kingdom between them. This is the all-pervading relation of the kingdom.

To give one glance backward then:—To receive the child because God receives it or for its humanity, is one thing; to receive it because it is like God, or for its childhood, is another. The former will do little to destroy ambition. Alone it might argue only a wider scope to it, because it admits all men to the arena of the strife. But the latter strikes at the very root of emulation. As soon as even service is done for the honor and not for the service-sake, the doer is that moment outside the kingdom. But when we receive the child in the name of Christ, the very childhood that we receive to our arms is humanity. We love its humanity in its childhood, for childhood is the deepest heart of humanity—its divine heart; and so in the name of the child we receive all humanity. Therefore, although the lesson is not about humanity, but about childhood, it returns upon our race, and we receive our race with wider arms and deeper heart. There is, then, no other lesson lost by receiving this; no heartlessness shown in insisting that the child was a loveable—a childlike child.

If there is in heaven a picture of that wonderful teaching, doubtless we shall see represented in it a dim childhood shining from the faces of all that group of disciples of which the centre is the Son of God with a child in his arms. The childhood, dim in the faces of the men, must be shining trustfully clear in the face of the child. But in the face of the Lord himself, the childhood will be triumphant—all his wisdom, all his truth upholding that radiant serenity of faith in his Father. Verily, O Lord, this childhood is life! Verily, O Lord, when thy tenderness shall have made the world great, then, children like thee, will all men smile in the face of the great God!

But to advance now to the highest point of this teaching of our Lord: "He that receiveth me receiveth him that sent me." To receive a child in the name of God is to receive God himself. How to receive him? As alone he can be received,—by knowing him as he is. To know him is to have him in us. And that we may know him, let us now receive this revelation of him, in the words of our Lord himself. Here is the argument of highest import founded upon the teaching of our Master in the utterance before us.

God is represented in Jesus, for that God is like Jesus: Jesus is represented in the child, for that Jesus is like the child. Therefore God is represented in the child, for that he is like the child. God is child-like. In the true vision of this fact lies the receiving of God in the child.

Having reached this point, I have nothing more to do with the argument; for if the Lord meant this—that is, if this be a truth, he that is able to receive it will receive it: he that has ears to hear it will hear it. For our Lord's arguments are for the presentation of the truth, and the truth carries its own conviction to him who is able to receive it.

But the word of one who has seen this truth may help

the dawn of a like perception in those who keep their faces turned towards the east and its aurora; for men may have eyes, and, seeing dimly, want to see more. Therefore let us brood a little over the idea itself, and see whether it will not come forth so as to commend itself to that spirit, which, one with the human spirit where it dwells, searches the deep things of God. For, although the true heart may at first be shocked at the truth, as Peter was shocked when he said, "That be far from thee, Lord," yet will it, after a season, receive it and rejoice in it.

Let me then ask, do you believe in the Incarnation? And if you do, let me ask further, Was Jesus ever less divine than God? I answer for you, Never. He was lower, but never less divine. Was he not a child then? You answer, "Yes, but not like other children." I ask, "Did he not look like other children?" If he looked like them and was not like them, the whole was a deception, a masquerade at best. I say he was a child, whatever more he might be. Childhood belongs to the divine nature. Obedience, then, is as divine as Will, Service as divine as Rule. How? Because they are one in their nature; they are both a doing of the truth. The love in them is the same. The Fatherhood and the Sonship are one, save that the Fatherhood looks down lovingly, and the Sonship looks up lovingly. Love is all. And God is all in all. He is ever seeking to get down to us—to be the divine man to us. And we are ever saying, "That be far from thee, Lord!" We are careful, in our unbelief, over the divine dignity, of which he is too grand to think. Better pleasing to God, it needs little daring to say, is the audacity of Job, who, rushing into his presence, and flinging the door of his presence-chamber to the wall, like a troubled, it may be angry, but yet faithful child, calls aloud in the ear of him whose perfect Fatherhood he has yet to learn: "Am I a sea or a whale, that thou settest a watch over me?"

Let us dare, then, to climb the height of divine truth to which this utterance of our Lord would lead us.

Does it not lead us up hither: that the devotion of God to his creatures is perfect? that he does not think about himself but about them? that he wants nothing for himself, but finds his blessedness in the outgoing of blessedness?

Ah! it is a terrible—shall it be a lonely glory this? We will draw near with our human response, our abandonment of self in the faith of Jesus. He gives himself to us—shall not we give ourselves to him? Shall we not give ourselves to each other whom he loves?

For when is the child the ideal child in our eyes and to our hearts? Is it not when with gentle hand he takes his father by the beard, and turns that father's face up to his brothers and sisters to kiss? when even the lovely selfishness of love-seeking has vanished, and the heart is absorbed in loving?

In this, then, is God like the child: that he is simply and altogether our friend, our father—our more than friend, father, and mother—our infinite love-perfect God. Grand and strong beyond all that human imagination can conceive of poet-thinking and kingly action, he is delicate beyond all that human tenderness can conceive of husband or wife, homely beyond all that human heart can conceive of father or mother. He has not two thoughts about us. With him all is simplicity of purpose and meaning and effort and end—namely, that we should be as he is, think the same thoughts, mean the same thing, possess the same blessedness. It is so plain that any one may see it, every one ought

## THE CHILD IN THE MIDST. 111

to see it, every one shall see it. It must be so. He is utterly true and good to us, nor shall anything withstand his will.

The God who is ever uttering himself in the changeful profusions of nature; who takes millions of years to form a soul that shall understand him and be blessed; who never needs to be, and never is, in haste; who welcomes the simplest thought of truth or beauty as the return for seed he has sown upon the old fallows of eternity; who rejoices in the response of a faltering moment to the age-long cry of his wisdom in the streets; the God of music, of painting, of building, the Lord of Hosts, the God of mountains and oceans; whose laws go forth from one unseen point of wisdom, and thither return without an atom of loss; the God of history working in time unto Christianity; this God is the God of little children, and he alone can be perfectly, abandonedly simple and devoted. The deepest, purest love of a woman has its well-spring in him. Our longing desires can no more exhaust the fulness of the treasures of the Godhead, than our imagination can touch their measure. Of him not a thought, not a joy, not a hope of one of his creatures can pass unseen; and while one of them remains unsatisfied, he is not Lord over all.

Therefore, with angels and with archangels, with the spirits of the just made perfect, with the little children of the kingdom, yea, with the Lord himself, and for all them that know him not, we praise and magnify and laud his name in itself, saying, *Our Father*. We do not draw back for that we are unworthy, nor even for that we are hard-hearted and care not for the good. For it is his childlikeness that makes him our God and Father. The perfection of his relation to us swallows up all our imperfections, all our defects, all our evils; for our childhood is born of his fatherhood. That man is perfect in faith who can come to God in the utter dearth of his feelings and his desires, without a glow or an aspiration, with the weight of low thoughts, failures, neglects, and wandering forgetfulness, and say to him, "Thou art my refuge, because thou art my home."

LORD of all power and might, grant us, we beseech thee, a deep and true insight into thy glorious truth, that being justified by grace and renewed in the spirit of our minds by the indwelling of the Holy Ghost, the Comforter, we may be sanctified for thy service both here and hereafter, and at length enter into the joy of our Lord and Saviour Jesus Christ. *Amen.*

## XI.

## FAITH THE PROOF OF THE UNSEEN.

"Now faith is the substance of things hoped for, the evidence of things not seen."—Hebrews 11 : 1.

I read the verse over to you as it is down here; but, as it stands, it never conveyed any idea to my mind at all; and I am very glad it is altered in the New Revision. For, of all things if we are Christians, having the least claim to the name, it is with the spirit and not the letter that we have to do; and this translation has neither letter nor spirit. Happy ought the man to be, who finds the dark things in the dear Book cleared up for him, and who learns that what had been as a pebble under his feet was a nut with a kernel in it, a life in it, a power of growth planted within his spirit. The true heart goes to the blessed Book, not as an idolater, but as a disciple; not to worship the Book, but to learn the will of him who made the Book, and who has made his spirit to understand the Book.

I think the meaning of the phrase is this : faith is the foundation, the root, the underlying substance of hope. If you have any hope, it comes from some faith in you. Hope, you may say, is a bud upon the plant of faith, a bud from the root of faith; the flower is joy and peace. Now the "evidence of things not seen—" I cannot, as I say, find any meaning in that at all; but the true meaning is the most profound fact in human history; it is the *trying* or the *proving* of things not seen. Upon that turns the life of every man, especially, perhaps, in the present day. This thing of faith means the whole recognized relation of man to God and his fellows; it is the right position of the human soul which is made to understand the truth—the right position of that soul toward the truth. Taking it in its simplest original development, it is the highest effort of the whole human intellect, imagination, and will, in the highest direction. Never does our nature put forth itself in such power, with such effort, with such energy, as when it has faith in God.

About faith they used often to say that it was antithetically opposed to works. There never was greater nonsense. They would say that St. Paul taught faith, and St. James taught works; and indeed one would feel something like this sometimes—that St. Paul had gone too far, and that St. James had to write his epistle to set him right. It is not any of us, friends, that will find St. Paul or St. James wrong, nor was there the smallest difference between them. On the contrary, I assert that faith is simply the greatest work that man can do.

In the present stage of history, it seems as if it were more difficult to believe than ever it was before. To some people, and to many people in certain moods, it seems also as if there were less faith in the world than ever there was before. I should like to help you, if I can, friends, about all this. I should like if, on the minds of young men particularly—although there is sad enough ground for including young women too—if I could impress upon them that, let the thing look to them as it may, it is a wrong notion and a false idea of Christianity that has come into their minds, partly because their own doors were opened narrow, partly because their own aspirations were so low, partly because they have been so little in earnest for the truth; it is the notion that they have a Christianity which is about to vanish away and must perish; but the true thing—God's notion of it; what Christ felt and thought while he was here; what he thinks and feels now when he is here still—is that which shall never pass away, but is the real fountain of truth and life to all generations.

But, first of all, let me say a word to the man or woman who is troubled with the difficulty of believing. Nowadays, there is such a talk about science, and such a contempt poured forth on the man, who thinks to walk without that kind of science for the guide of his life, who has a different goal, a different ambition, whose thoughts stretch further than the things of this life—these things he sees and hears and handles! If there be a man among us, friends, such a man who does the work of the world, and does it well, but his head is in heaven, that is the kind of thing we all ought to be and to seek. And there are perhaps a few even now of this kind, and there are more growing.

Let me say to you about your own fears and doubts and difficulties, it is a great thing to believe. Are you fit to believe? Why should you be able to believe? I have just said that I believe it to be the loftiest exercise of the human being and of human nature. How can you expect to believe? Are you like Nathanael—an Israelite indeed, a man without guile? What are your ways? What have you been about? What are your desires in life? How have you been ordering yourself? It may be that, although the power of God upon you makes you feel that you ought to believe, you are such that you cannot believe, and it is your own fault.

Fully do I recognize the difficulty. I question if there is a doubt or a sense of difficulty which prevails now that has not passed through my own mind as a thing to be encountered and understood and settled. It is natural that we should doubt, with such cries especially on all side of us, and the intellect so much more awake than ever it was before, and indeed the conscience not more asleep than before; and with one on this side, and one on that side, crying out: "I have reached, I have seen, and I have found no God." Settle this with yourselves to begin with. Not all the intellect or metaphysics of the world could prove that there is no God, and not all the intellect in the world could prove that there is a God. If you could prove that there is a God, that implies that you could go all around him, and buttress up his being with your human argument that he should exist. As soon might a child on his mother's bosom, looking up into his mother's face, write a treatise on what a woman was, and what a mother was.

But do not think that God is angry with you because you find it hard to believe. It is not so; that is not like God. He knows perfectly well that what the scientific man calls truth is simply an impossibility with regard to God. When you read a proposition of Euclid, there is a kind of proof which commends itself to your mind and understanding; you say, "So it is, and it cannot be otherwise." But there is no such proof with regard to the mighty God: and God knows it. And therefore I say, if you doubt his existence, he is not angry with you for that.

But I am speaking of those who would fain believe if they could. I ask you, have you been trying the things not seen? Have you been proving them? This is what God put in your hands. He says: "I tell you I am:

act you upon that; for I know your conscience moves you to it; act you upon that, and you will find whether I am or not, and what I am." Do you see? Faith in its true sense does not belong to the intellect alone, nor to the intellect first, but to the conscience, to the will; and that man is a faithful man who says, "I cannot prove that there is a God, but, O God, if thou hearest me anywhere, help me to do thy will." There is faith. "Do this," and he does it. It is obedience, friends, that is faith; it is doing that thing which you, let me say, even only suppose to be the will of God; for if you are wrong, and do it because you think it is his will, he will set you right. It is the turning of the eye to the light; it is the sending of the feet into the path that is required, putting the hands to do the things which the conscience says ought to be done.

You will notice that all this chapter from which I have taken the text is a list of people that did things. Some of them were made kings, and some of them were sawn asunder for it; but it was all faith, and nothing but faith. There was a truth; there was a live truth; a truth that had welled through and called up the knowledge of truth in us, nay, called up in us the very possibility of feeling truth. And according to this law these men walked through all the world; and all the worlds together set themselves againt them; and in the name of the original vital law of the universe—namely, the living God—they walked right on and met their fate. Yes: victory and the participation of the divine nature —that was their faith.

Therefore, friends, the practical thing is just this, and it is the one lesson we have to learn, that, whatever our doubts or difficulties may be, we must do the thing we know in order to learn the thing we do not know. But whether we learn it or not, "If ye know these things," saith the Master, "happy are ye if ye do them." It is the doing that is everything, and the doing is faith, and there is no division between them.

Then I would say a word to those who are farther on. They have been trying to serve God for many years now, and they do not seem to themselves to have made much of it. They find that they are troubled in their souls still—not whether they be of God; but does he manage everything now? "Where is he? I have never seen him; if he would but speak to myself! I have been crying for him all these years, and I have never had a sign out of the great blank. Oh, if he would but show himself; if he would but do something—give me the meanest sign that he really is, and that he cares about me!" You say, "I feel as if I could go on forever then." Friends, I believe there is no sign God could give you, but what you would begin to doubt again. I do not believe there is even any miracle he could work before your eyes, that by and by you would not begin to doubt, and be just as lost as before. God will not give us little things to spoil our appetite for great things. He will never be content until we are one with him as he is one with Christ. God will not give us signs and wonders and these inferior things; for be sure God's common and usual way is far better than this miraculous way, as we call it: because, if it were all miracle, then we would make it all common.

You may be sure, then, that God's usual way of doing things is the best way. I say he will not give us signs of anything outside to give us confidence in him. Nothing will serve God's turn but this—that our faith shall be complete, and shall go instantly with our perception of what he his. It is by the vision in

## FAITH THE PROOF OF THE UNSEEN. 119

our souls, the feeling and perception in our souls, of what God is, that we are able to believe in him. Let a man once see God as Christ saw him, and he believes. Any glimmer of the truth in regard to our Lord's nature helps him to believe—enables him to go on, and on, and on. He says: "I know enough to make life a grand and blessed and strong thing to me, and I am going on." We will see. "I cannot convey to you," he may say, "my conviction; that will only come with the conviction itself; you must see, else you do not know; but life to me is enough." So would he say; but then, "What is the way to this?" you ask. Ah, my friends, if you have been at it for twenty or thirty or forty years, surely you have learned by this time what you have just to go on doing—that is, hearkening to Christ and doing his will. Let me try you a bit.

What is your first thought in the morning? Is it, "God is life"? or is it, "How am I to order my day's work?" Is it, "God is very rich and I am his child, and he will see to me"? or is it, "How on earth am I to get through this that lies before me to-day?" Are you afraid? Are the cares of this world troublesome to you? Well, you have not got on much. But if you are not trying to suppress them, I am afraid you have not got on at all; and if you have been thirty or forty years trying to serve Christ, it has been a kind of service that he does not care much about, and it is no wonder you do not get on. You have been very careful in reading your Bible and going to church, and doing this or that thing which you think belongs to religion; but have you been doing the thing Christ told you? If you do that, I do not care whatever else you do; you cannot be wrong then.

The same holds with you as with the beginner who

is troubled as to whether there is a God or not. But you that believe in a God do not trust him; whereas the other is not sure that there is a God; and you think it is very horrible of him to doubt the existence of a God. And yet you, believing that there is a God, are afraid of the trouble, the poverty, the opinion of the world, and are ambitious to get on this way or that! Oh, I had almost sooner say you do not believe in a God, than say that you believe in God, and yet he is nothing to you! And when you feel inclined to say heavy and hard things about your atheistic neighbor, think that there may be a beam in your own eye even worse, if we can bear to call it so, than the mote in his. Indeed, friends, it is because our life does not shine that men have stood up and said, "There is no light." You see a man greedy and grasping, as much taken up with the things of this world as if he were to live, I will not say to the age of Methuselah, but to the age of seventy-five or eighty. He works in the world as if he were to live forever in it; and sometimes, I think, the punishment which would fit him best would be to be condemned to live forever in the world. What a thing that would be! Ah, the man who is most sure that there is no God, and that he can get on pretty well without him, I think the better way would be just to let him live on and on and on, until he got heartily sick of himself and hated himself, and would gladly yield anything to get out of himself.

Ah, friends, there is a worse thing than dying never to wake again; there is a worse thing than dying forever, and going soul and brain to the dust; and that is to wake up and find that there is no God! That is the horror of horrors to me—to tell me that I am to live forever, and there is no God! For anything any man knows, who does not believe in a God, it may be so. He cannot tell with certainty that he is going to die forever because he sees no more of those that have gone before. Why should not they go on to some other sphere as they came into this one? Without any warning or any choice, they do not know until they find themselves here. Why should it not be so in another state of existence? But to find yourselves there without a God! There is no use praying to be killed, because there is no God to hear your prayer. You can no more annihilate yourselves than make yourselves. The whole thing would be utter misery.

But what is to be done with you and me, who cannot finish ourselves? Poor creatures! we feel that, if God is like us, he had better cease. But, if we see he is like us—only he is perfect, absolute in grandeur and loveliness—ah, then we can say "I shall get rid of this bad in me—this poor mean stuff in me—and I shall become glorious, true, and excellent, like him."

This is worth living for, nothing else is; it is for this that Christ tells us to put confidence in him and obey his word, and we will see the Father. "Behold I stand at the door, and knock: if any man hear my voice, and open the door, I will come in to him, and will sup with him, and he with me." When God is seated at the very fireside of our hearts, then there is no more doubt. I say, friends, it is a good thing that you should have doubt until you see that nothing less than that will do. Faith is the trying of the things unseen—the putting of them to the test; and whatever your doubts and fears are, try God by obedience, and then you will get help to carry you on. Less than that will not do. The darkness of life's closing time will come round about you, and find you very doubtful, very sad, looking—looking

—into the darkness, and wondering, "Shall I wake, or shall I sleep?" But if you believe that the man Jesus Christ died and rose again, the whole thing is full of the dawn of an eternal morning, coming up beyond the hills of this life, and full of such hope as the highest imagination of the poet has not a glimer of as yet.

Do you hope for anything, friends? Thank God, that comes from your faith. No man that has not faith can hope. But do not think the world is going all to the devil. There is a better and stronger faith coming. Even those who do not believe are on the whole better in this century than those who did not believe in the last. The world is not worse than it was. What we have to do is to let our light shine. Do you get any light? Let it shine. I do not mean, be an example to other people. You have no business to set yourselves up for an example. You have to be and to do, and that is letting the light shine. It now ought not to be possible to mistake a Christian for a man of the world. His very dealings with every man that comes near him have something to show, something that Christ would have done that a man of the world would not do. Tell me how you would like Christ to come in upon you at any moment in the midst of your business talk. Would you be ready to turn to him and say, "Master, this is how I am saying the thing to my friend; this is how I see it in the light of thy love." Would you be ready for that, or do you think a great part of your being and your life can be conducted upon other laws than Christian? If a man does that, he is altogether wrong —altogether wrong. Christ is God, the All-in-all, or nothing at all. If we were as the bush—if every Christian were as the bush that burned with fire—that would be the shining of our light before men. Atheism would soon vanish, reproved, judged, condemned by the very presence of faith.

I would have you, then, friends, remember that faith is the trying of the things that you do not see, and that you cannot be sure about. A thing that you do not see, and which not seeing you have doubts about, you can yet try—that is faith. And if you are honest, that will be a great opportunity and a great help to you. It will start a fresh faith which you have not thought of before, and give your life a new impulse. Faith is intended to put to the test the unseen world of truth, law, hope, redemption. God grant us all faith enough to carry us on from point to point till the faith shall vanish into light, and we have never to think about faith more, nor to think about Church more, nor the Bible more, nor prayer more, but our whole being shall be a delighted consciousness of the presence of God and his Christ.

O LORD, our heavenly FATHER, almighty and everlasting GOD, who hast safely brought us to the beginning of this day, defend us in the same with thy mighty power, and grant that this day we fall into no sin, neither run into any kind of danger; but that all our doings may be ordered by thy governance, to do always that which is righteous in thy sight, through JESUS CHRIST our LORD. *Amen.*

## XII.

## DIVINE AND HUMAN RELATIONSHIP.

"For whosoever shall do the will of my Father which is in heaven, the same is my brother, and sister, and mother."—Matthew 12 : 50.

A little sad, was it not, that his mother and his brethren were not sitting about him? For, as another evangelist says, "he looked round on those that were about him." His disciples, who were learning of him, were nearest to him naturally, and his mother and his brethren were outside. They did not know him yet.

It takes a long time, and, what is more, a true heart, to know anybody. There are people that belong to the same family through the whole of a long life, and yet do not know each other to the very end. Do you remember they had set out to stop him? That is why they were outside; but for their stopping him they would have been at home. That lovely mother of his was not the first to understand him aright. Of course she understood him a good deal, and when the sword should have gone through her soul, she would understand him well. But there were other women, and they not so lovely as she, far less lovely in some ways, who understood him better, because the sword had passed through their souls, and they knew the evil thing which brought them to his feet. These were outside desiring to speak to him, because they said, "He is beside himself." He was going too far, and they must stop him.

## DIVINE AND HUMAN RELATIONSHIP.

It was the necessity of his relations to see that he did not play the part of a madman. There are tens of thousands of so-called Christian people who are quite capable of doing the same thing at the present day, simply because they have little more of Christ in or about them than the common name that is given freely enough now, and is easy enough to carry. Nay, more, there are tens of thousands of those who are honest towards Christ, but yet know so little of what was in him or what he meant to do, that they would stop him. It is a sad thing, friends, for any of us to be called by his name, and not know him. It is the business of our human being to know Christ, and nothing else is our business. If it is true that we are made in the image of God, the sole, paramount, all-including and absorbing business of existence is to know that image of God in which we are made, to know it in the living Son of God—the one only ideal man. The nearer I come to the change, the more absolutely I am convinced of this, and I have no words strong enough to put the statement in. But, alas, for most of us, we like to pare away the words of Christ, instead of looking at them until they fill heaven and earth.

Let us see what he meant in these lovely, awful, precious words. For the love of Christ is an awful thing. There is nothing in that which goes half way, or which makes exception. The Son of God loves so utterly that he will have his children clean, and if hurt and sorrow, pain and torture, will do to deliver any one of them from the horrible thing, from the death that he cherishes at the very root of his soul, the loving Christ, though it hurts him all the time, and though he feels every sting himself, will do it.

"Who are my mother and my brethren?" So he

asks; and then he answers: "Whosoever does the will of my Father in heaven." You observe he is always talking about his Father in heaven. You would think he knew nothing else. He has but one word, as it seems, over and over again. It has been said that he was possessed with love for humanity, and that is true; but he was possessed before that, and as the beginning of that, with love to his Father in heaven. That was the root, the power, the energy of all that was manifest even in the eternal Son of God himself. It could not be otherwise. He was not to be misled with any outside shows of power and beauty. He knew the heart of them all, and that it was the living will of God, by which all things arose, subsisted, and went on growing and growing. The Father—the Father—the Father was all in all in the heart of the Son, and because the Father, therefore the children of the Father, all the men and women, savage and refined, throughout the universe.

And does it make us at all sorrowful that he said the words to his disciples, that he does not seem to include the rest of the company, and seems to exclude his mother and brethren? Is it a hard word, do you think? Oh, friends, the power of God himself can give you nothing worth having, but this that he would give, which the few about him had already taken, and which some of us have begun to take. Life is the only thing—life, that is the essential of well-being. It is because we are but half-alive now, half-created, you may say, and not nearly that, that we are not blessed. We so often choose death, the thing that separates and kills, for everything that parts us from our fellow, and everything that parts us from God, is a killing of us. Whosoever is wide and free, and will do the will of God—not understand it, not care about it, not theorize about it, but do it—is a son of God. It is in the act that man stands up as a son of God. He may be ever such a philosopher, ever such a theologian, ever such a patriot or benevolent man; but it is only he who, in the act, in the doing of the thing, stands up before God, that is a son of God. That is the divine dignity: "My Father worketh hitherto, and I work." It is he who works that is the son of God.

Do I mean outside works or inside works? I mean whatever a man does, whether it be the giving up all that he has to go and preach the gospel, or whether it be putting down the smallest rising thought of injustice, of anger and wrong, of selfishness in his soul. The act is where the will of man stands up against liking, against temptation, and leads him simply to do that which God would have him to do, easy or difficult; it may be to mount a throne, it may be to be sawn asunder. The man who does what God would have him do, what is he? "My brother," says Christ. The woman who does that? "My sister," says Christ. And as if he would go to the very depth of tenderness, he is not satisfied with saying "brother" or "sister." Woman, that has longed to have children and has none, did you ever think you might have a Son of God for your son? If you would be the "mother" of the Son of God, do the will of his Father, and yours and you will not mourn long.

But was he putting away his mother? Was it an unkind, an unfilial thing to say? Did he, in saying, "Who is my mother, who is my brother?" repudiate the earthly mother and the earthly brother and sister? No, verily. But, friends, it is a profound, absolute fact that our relation to God is infinitely nearer than any relation by nature. Our mother does not make us; we come forth of her, but forth also of the very soul of God. We are nearer, unspeakably nearer, infinitely and unintelligibly (to our very poor intellects) nearer to God than to the best, loveliest, dearest mother on the face of the earth. The Lord, first of all, only spake an absolute fact; but then he goes deeper and deeper still. This cannot be until the thing is known and acknowledged. But look: if a mother has two children, one of whom is as bad as a boy can be, and the other as good; the one is her child and the other is not her child; they are both born of her body, but the one that loves her and obeys her is born of her soul; yea, of her very spirit, and she says "This is my child," and she says to the other, with groans, "You are none of mine." And his being no child is the misery of the thing; she would die for the one who is no child, but for the one who is her child she would live forever. And so when we become the sons and daughters of God indeed by saying, "Oh, my Father, I care for nothing but what thou carest for; I will not lament for this thing; because I see thou dost not care about it, I will not care either;" when you say, "This is sore to bear, but it is thy will, and therefore I thank thee for it, so sure am I of thy will, O my Father in heaven:" when we come to be able to talk like that, then we are in the same mind as Jesus Christ, whose delight, and whose only delight, was to do the will of his Father in heaven. But for God's sake, do not cling to your own poor will. It is not worth having. It is a poor, miserable, degrading thing to fall down and worship the inclination of your own heart, which may have come from any devil, or from any accident of your birth, or from the weather, or from anything. Take the will of God, eternal, pure, strong, living and true, the only good thing; take that, and Christ will be your brother. If we knew the glory of that, I believe we could even delight in going against the poor small things that we should like in ourselves, delight even in thwarting ourselves.

To return to my subject. Was Christ refusing his mother? Was he saying, "I come of another breed, and I have nothing to do with you?" Was that the spirit of it? The Son of God forbid! Never, never! But I must show here a deeper and a better thing. It is of the wisdom and tenderness of God that we come into the world as we do, that we form families, little centres, and groups of spiritual nerves and power in the world. I do not see how in any other way we come to understand God. And, oh! you parents, who make it impossible for your children to understand God, what shall be said of or for you? If we had not fathers and mothers to love, I do not know how our hearts would understand God at all. I know not how I ever should. Then, again, if we had no brothers and sisters to love, how ever should we begin to learn this essential thing, that we should love our neighbor—that is, every man who comes near us to be affected with look or word—as ourselves? It were an impossibility. God begins with us graciously and easily. He brings us near, first, to mother, then to father, then to sister, then to brother—brings us so near to them that we cannot escape them. The months of infancy and the years of childhood are unspeakably precious from this fact, that we cannot escape the holy influences of family. So many are our needs, so quiescent are our needs, that love is, as it were, heaped upon us and forced into us: and we are taught—as we cannot help learning—to love.

But woe to the man or woman who stops there, and can only love because the child, or the sister, or the brother is his or hers! The same human soul, the same hungry human affection, the same aspiring, although blotted and spoiled, human spirit, is within every head, dwelling in every heart, and we are brothers and sisters wherever God has made man or woman; and until we have learned that, we are only going on, it may be a little, to learn Christ, but we have not yet learned him. What! Shall Christ love a man, and I not love him? Shall Christ say to a woman, "My sister," and I not bow before her? It is preposterous. But then my own mother, my own father, my own brothers and sisters—if they be his too, they come first, they come nearer. But I do assert that there is a closer, infinitely closer, relation between any one that loves God and any other that loves God, than there is between any child and any mother where they do not both love him. The one has its root, the other has its leaves and flowers as well. We cannot love anybody too much; but we do not, we can never, love our own child aright until we have learned to love—not the mildness of the child—but the humanity of the child, the goodness, the thing that God meant, that came out of his will. That is the thing we have to love even in our children, or else the love is a poor dying thing, because we ourselves are dying. I am supposing that we do not possess the love of God, which is the only eternal thing. But if we love God, dearer and dearer grow the faces of father and mother, wife and child, until there is no end to it. It goes on, not only eternally in time, but eternally in growth, expanding.

We do not understand it, because we are no farther on.

Every bit we get farther, we understand more, and perceive more, and feel more; and the child of God is infinite, because he is a child of God. The child is like the Father. We have our share in God's infinitude, and therefore the Lord Christ himself called us "gods" when he quoted from the Psalms. Whoever can, let him understand the words, "I say, ye are gods." The children of God must be gods in some sense. Little gods, indeed, but what is their completion and salvation? "Ye shall sit down with me in my throne, even as I am set down with my Father in his throne." And brothers and sisters, I cannot conceive any other sufficing redemption than this, that we should be set down on the throne of the King of kings, with the Lord our Master, as he said. Do you call this presumption? I appeal to Christ, for he has spoken. I believe in nothing but Christ; and so I trust to believe everything that is true, to know it when I see it.

Are you lonely? Has lover or friend forsaken you? Has death taken father or mother, husband or wife, sister or brother from you? If you could see aright, that is a trifle; a profound trifle, though, for God's trifles are precious and great. Dear in the sight of God is the death of his saints. But it is a trifle. I will tell you what would be the terrible thing. Have you been false to them? Have you wronged them? Have you been such that there has been a separation, a tearing of your souls asunder? That is death, and the devil, and damnation. Why is it death that we fear? He hath abolished death. He died and he was not dead; up he rose again radiant with light and victory. So are they all who believe in him; for he said,

"He that liveth and believeth in me shall never die." You may defy death. Only have the "patience of Christ;" there is given us that phrase; wait in his name and you shall have all you want. For when Christ has had his way with you, you would as soon ask for anything that he did not like as you would beg of God to destroy the universe he had created. There would be nothing to you desirable that is not desirable in his eyes.

Think of this: that you can have One who is more than brother or sister, father or mother, husband or wife, or child,—One from whose heart all these flowed out—One from whom came the love that analyzed itself into these forms because of its infinitude. You can have him for your own friend, for brother, sister, mother, son. Whatever relation is possible in humanity, that relation does the heart of Christ feel to every one that can take it.

Do you want, therefore, to forget, and to take Christ as a make-up for the others that are gone? Never! never! That is not his way. For how constantly does he tell you to love one another? That is the glory of Christ's teaching; that is his gospel; there is not an atom of selfishness in God, or in Christ, for he delights to see us loving one another. He cannot be satisfied except by seeing us love each other perfectly—that is his delight. Nay, more than this, I repeat, we cannot love one of our own aright unless Christ is in us making us love that person to the idea of that relationship. Never father loved child, never child loved father, to the idea of fatherhood and childhood, unless Christ was not only born in him but had grown up in him; and in none has he grown to that degree that he understands thoroughly, feels thoroughly, believes thoroughly—or anything like thoroughly—any relation in life, so far as I know.

Do not take from the glory of the words of Christ; do not be afraid to claim from him what he gives you, and would have you take. Claim him, man, woman, boy, girl, claim him as your own; for without him you are as nothing. Claim him, by taking the will of God for your one care, your one object, your one desire; and Christ will be yours altogether. "Behold I stand at the door, and knock: if any man hear my voice, and open the door, I will come in to him, and will sup with him, and he with me." Partaking of the same food together—that food being the very will of God: "it is my meat and drink to do thy will:" that is the very food concerning which our Lord says: "man shall not live by bread alone, but by every word that proceedeth out of the mouth of God." That is the will of God; it is the very food and drink of the true heart; and when Jesus and the man who has opened to him the door sit down together, it is to share together in the understanding of the will of the Father of both—that Father to whom he went when he said: "Go to my brethren, and say unto them, I ascend unto my Father, and your Father; and to my God and your God."

## XIII.

## THE SLEEP OF LAZARUS.

"Our friend Lazarus sleepeth; but I go, that I may awake him out of sleep."—John 11: 11.

When Jesus Christ the Son of God, and therefore our elder brother, was going about on the earth, eating and drinking with his brothers and sisters, there was one family he loved especially—a family of two sisters and a brother; for, although he loves everybody as much as they can be loved, there are some who can be loved more than others. Only God is always trying to make us such that we can be loved more and more. There are several stories—oh, such lovely stories!—about that family and Jesus. And we have to do with one of them now.

They lived near the capital of the country, Jerusalem, in a village they called Bethany; and it must have been a great relief to our Lord, when he was worn out with the obstinacy and pride of the great men of the city, to go out to the quiet little town, and into the refuge of Lazarus's house, where every one was more glad at the sound of his feet than at any news that could come to them.

They had at this time behaved so ill to him in Jerusalem, taking up stones to stone him, even though they dared not quite do it, mad with anger as they were—and all because he told them the truth—that he had

## THE SLEEP OF LAZARUS.

gone away to the other side of the great river that divided the country, and taught the people in that quiet place. While he was there his friend Lazarus was taken ill, and the two sisters, Martha and Mary, sent a messenger to him to say to him, "Lord, your friend is very ill." Only they said it more beautifully than that: "Lord, behold, he whom thou lovest is sick." You know when any one is ill we always want the person whom he loves most to come to him. This is very wonderful. In the worst things that can come to us, the first thought is of love. People like the Scribes and Pharisees might say, "What good can that do him?" And we may not in the least suppose the person we want knows any secret that can cure his pain; yet love is the first thing we think of. And here we are more right than we know; for, at the long last, love will cure everything; which truth, indeed, this story will set forth to us.

No doubt the heart of Lazarus, ill as he was, longed after his friend, and, very likely, even the sight of Jesus might have given him such strength that the life in him could have driven out the death which had already got one foot across the threshold. But the sisters expected more than this. They believed that Jesus, whom they knew to have driven disease and death out of so many hearts, had only to come and touch him—nay, only to speak a word, to look at him, and their brother was saved. Do you think they presumed in thus expecting? The fact was they did not believe enough; they had not yet learned to believe that he could cure him all the same, whether he came to them or not, because he was always with them. We cannot understand this; but our understanding is never a measure of what is true.

Jesus knew that his Father did not want him to go to his friends yet. So he sent them a message to the effect that there was a particular reason for this sickness, that the end of it was not the death of Lazarus, but the glory of God. This I think he told them by the same messenger they sent to him; and then, instead of going to them he remained where he was.

But, oh, my friends, what shall I say about this wonderful message? Think of being sick for the glory of God! of being shipwrecked for the glory of God! of being drowned for the glory of God! How can the sickness, the fear, the broken-heartedness of his creatures be for the glory of God? What kind of a God can that be? Why just a God so perfectly, absolutely good, that the things that look least like it are only the means of clearing our eyes to let us see how good he is. For he is so good that he is not satisfied with *being* good. He loves his children so, that except he can make them good like himself, make them blessed by seeing how good he is, and desiring the same goodness in themselves, he is not satisfied. He is not like a fine, proud benefactor, who is content with doing that which will satisfy his sense of his own glory, but like a mother who puts her arm round her child, and whose heart is sore till she can make her child see the love which is her glory. The glorification of the Son of God is the glorification of the human race, for the glory of God is the glory of man, and that glory is love! Welcome sickness, welcome sorrow, welcome death, revealing that glory!

The next two verses sound very strangely together, and yet they almost seem typical of all the perplexities of God's dealings. The old painters and poets represented Faith as a beautiful woman holding in her hand

## THE SLEEP OF LAZARUS.

a cup of wine and water, with a serpent coiled up within. High hearted Faith! she scruples not to drink of the life-giving wine and water; she is not repelled by the upcoiled serpent. The serpent she takes but for the type of the eternal wisdom that looks repellent because it is not understood. The wine is good, the water is good, and if the hand of the supreme Fate put that cup in her hand, the serpent itself must be good too, harmless at least to hurt the truth of the water and the wine. But let us read the verses.

"Now Jesus loved Martha, and her sister, and Lazarus. When he heard, therefore, that he was sick, he abode two days still in the same place where he was."

Strange! his friend was sick: he abode two days where he was! But remember what we have already heard. The glory of God was infinitely more for the final cure of a dying Lazarus—who, give him all the life he could have, would yet, without that glory, be in death—than the mere presence of the Son of God. I say *mere* presence, for, compared with the glory of God, the very presence of his Son, so dissociated, is nothing. He abode where he was that the glory of God, the final cure of humanity, the love that triumphs over death, might shine out and redeem the hearts of men, so that death could not touch them.

After the two days, the hour had arrived. He said to his disciples, "Let us go back to Judæa." They expostulated, because of the danger, saying, "Master, the Jews of late sought to stone thee; and goest thou thither again?" The answer which he gave them I am not sure whether I can thoroughly understand, but I think, in fact, I know, it must bear on the same region of life—the will of God. I think what he means by walking in the day, is simply doing the will of God.

That was the sole, the all-embracing light in which Jesus ever walked. I think he means that now he saw plainly what the Father wanted him to do. If he did not see that the Father wanted him to go back to Judæa, and yet went, that would be to go stumblingly, to walk in the darkness. There are twelve hours in the day—one time to act—a time of light and a clear call of duty; there is a night when a man not seeing where or hearing how, must be content to rest. Something not inharmonious with this, I think, he must have intended; but I do not see the whole thought clearly enough to be sure that I am right. I do think further that it points at a clearer condition of human vision and conviction than I am good enough to understand; though I hope one day to rise into this upper stratum of light.

Whether his scholars had heard anything of Lazarus yet I do not know. It looks a little as if Jesus had not told them the message he had had from the sisters. But he told them now that he was asleep, and that he was going to wake him. You would think they might have understood this. The idea of going so many miles to wake a man might have surely suggested death. But the disciples were sorely perplexed with many of his words. Sometimes they looked far away for the meaning when the meaning lay in their very hearts; sometimes they looked into their hands for it when it was lost in the grandeur of the ages. But he meant them to see into all that he said by and by, although they could not see into it now. When they understood him better, then they would understand what he said better. And to understand him better they must be more like him, and to make them more like him he must go away and give them his Spirit—awful mystery which no man but himself can understand.

## THE SLEEP OF LAZARUS.

Now he had to tell them plainly that Lazarus was dead. They had not thought of death as a sleep. I suppose this was altogether a new and Christian idea. Do not suppose that it applied more to Lazarus than to other dead people. He was none the less dead that Jesus meant to take a weary two days' journey to his sepulchre and wake him. If death is not a sleep, Jesus did not speak the truth when he said Lazarus slept. You may say it was a figure; but a figure that is not like the thing it figures is simply a lie.

They set out to go back to Judæa. Here we have a glimpse of the faith of Thomas, the doubter. For a doubter is not without faith. The very fact that he doubts, shows that he has some faith. When I find any one hard upon doubters, I always doubt the *quality* of his faith. It is of little use to have a great cable if the hemp is so poor that it breaks like the painter of a boat. I have known people whose power of believing chiefly consisted in their incapacity for seeing difficulties. Of what fine sort a faith must be that is founded in stupidity, or far worse, in indifference to the truth and the mere desire to get out of hell! That is not a grand belief in the Son of God, the radiation of the Father. Thomas's want of faith was shown in the grumbling, self-pitying way in which he said, "Let us also go that we may die with him." His Master had said that he was going to wake him. Thomas said, "that we may die with him." You may say, "he did not understand him." True, it may be, but his unbelief was the cause of his not understanding him. I suppose Thomas meant this as a reproach to Jesus for putting them all in danger by going back to Judæa; if not, it was only a poor piece of sentimentality. So much for Thomas's unbelief. But he had good and true faith, notwithstanding; for *he went with his Master*.

By the time they reached the neighborhood of Bethany, Lazarus had been dead four days. Some one ran to the house and told the sisters that Jesus was coming. Martha, as soon as she heard it, rose and went to meet him. It might be interesting at another time to compare the difference of the behavior of the two sisters upon this occasion with the difference of their behavior upon another occasion likewise recorded; but with the man dead in his sepulchre, and the hope dead in these two hearts, we have no inclination to enter upon fine distinctions of character. Death and grief bring out the great family likenesses in the living as well as in the dead.

When Martha came to Jesus she showed her true, but imperfect, faith by almost attributing her brother's death to Jesus' absence. But even in the moment, looking in the face of the Master, a fresh hope, a new budding of faith began in her soul. She thought— " what if, after all, he were to bring him to life again!" O trusting heart, how thou leavest the dull plodding intellect behind thee! While the conceited intellect is reasoning upon the impossibility of the thing, the expectant faith beholds it accomplished. Jesus, responding instantly to her faith, granting her half-born prayer, says, "Thy brother shall rise again;" not meaning the general truth recognized, or at least assented to by all but the Sadducees, concerning the final resurrection of the dead, but meaning, " Be it unto you as thou wilt; I will raise him again." For there is no steering for a fine effect in the words of Jesus. But these words are too good for Martha to take them as he meant them. Her faith is not equal to the belief that

## THE SLEEP OF LAZARUS.

he actually will do it. The thing she could hope for afar off she could hardly believe when it came to her very door. "Oh, yes," she said, her mood falling again to the level of the commonplace, "of course at the last day." Then the Lord turns away her thoughts from the dogmas of her faith to himself, the Life, saying, "I am the resurrection and the life; he that believeth in me, though he were dead, yet shall he live. And whosoever liveth and believeth in me, shall never die. Believest thou this?" Martha, without understanding what he said more than in a very poor part, answered in words which preserved her honesty entire, and yet included all he asked, and a thousandfold more than she could yet believe: "Yea, Lord, I believe that thou art the Christ, the Son of God, which should come into the world."

I dare not pretend to have more than a grand glimmering of the truth of Jesus' words, "shall never die." But I am pretty sure that when Martha came to die she found that there was indeed no such thing as she had meant when she used the ghastly word, *death*, and said with her first new breath, "Verily, Lord, I am not dead."

But look how the declaration of her confidence in the Christ operated upon herself. She instantly thought of her sister; the hope that the Lord would do something swelled within her, and, leaving Jesus, she went to find Mary. Whoever has had a true word with the elder brother, straightway will look around him to find his brother, his sister. The family feeling blossoms: he wants his friend to share the glory withal. Martha wants Mary to go to Jesus too.

Mary heard her, forgot her visitors, rose, and went. They thought she went to the grave: she went to meet its conqueror. But when she came to him, the woman who had chosen the good part praised of Jesus, had but the same words to embody her hope and her grief that her careful and troubled sister had uttered a few minutes before. How often during those four days had not the self-same words passed between them: "Ah, if he had been here, our brother had not died!" She said so to himself, now, and wept, and her friends who had followed her wept likewise. A moment more, and the Master groaned; yet a moment, and he too wept. "Sorrow is catching," but this was not the mere infection of sorrow. It went deeper than mere sympathy; for he groaned in his spirit, and was troubled. What made him weep? It was when he saw them weeping that he wept. But why should he weep, when he knew how soon their weeping would be turned into rejoicing? It was not for their weeping, so soon to be over, that he wept, but for the human heart everywhere swollen with tears, yea, with grief that can find no such relief as tears; for these, and for all his brothers and sisters tormented with pain for lack of faith in his Father in heaven, Jesus wept. He saw the blessed well-being of Lazarus on the one side, and on the other the streaming eyes from whose sight he had vanished. The vail between was so thin! yet the sight of those eyes could not pierce it: their hearts must go on weeping—without cause, for his Father was so good. I think it was the helplessness he felt in the impossibility of at once sweeping away the phantasm death from their imagination that drew the tears from the eyes of Jesus. Certainly it was not for Lazarus; it could hardly be for these, his friends—save as they represented the humanity which he would help, but could not help even as he was about to help them.

## THE SLEEP OF LAZARUS.

The Jews saw herein proof that he loved Lazarus; but they little thought it was for them and their people, and for the Gentiles, whom they despised, that his tears were now flowing—that the love which pressed the fountains of his weeping was love for every human heart, from Adam on through the ages.

Some of them went a little further, nearly as far as the sisters, saying, "Could he not have kept the man from dying?" But it was such a poor thing, after all, that they thought he might have done. They regarded merely this unexpected illness, this early death; for I dare say Lazarus was not much older than Jesus. They did not think that, after all, Lazarus must die some time; that the beloved could be saved, at best, only for a little while. Jesus seems to have heard the remark, for he again groaned in himself.

Meantime they were drawing near the place where he was buried. It was a hollow in the face of a rock, with a stone laid against it. I suppose the bodies were laid on something like shelves inside the rock, as they are in many sepulchres. They were not put into coffins, but wound round and round with linen.

When they came before the door of death, Jesus said to them, "Take away the stone." The nature of Martha's reply, the realism of it, as they would say nowadays, would seem to indicate that her dawning faith had sunk again below the horizon; that in the presence of the insignia of death, her faith yielded, even as the faith of Peter failed him when he saw around him the grandeur of the high priest, and his Master bound and helpless. Jesus answered—oh, what an answer! To meet the corruption which filled her poor human fancy, "the glory of God" came from his lips: human fear; horror speaking from the lips of a woman in the very jaws of a devouring death; and then "said I not unto thee?" from the mouth of him who was so soon to pass worn and bloodless through such a door!

Before the open throat of the sepulchre Jesus began to speak to his Father aloud. He had prayed to him before in his heart—most likely while he groaned in his spirit. Now he thanked him that he had comforted him, and given him Lazarus as a first-fruit from the dead. But he will be true to the listening people, as well as to his ever-hearing Father, therefore he tells why he said the word of thanks aloud—a thing not usual with him, for his Father was always hearing him. Having spoken it for the people, he would say that it was for the people. The end of it all was that they might believe that God had sent him—a far grander gift than having the dearest brought back from the grave—for he is the Life of men.

"Lazarus, come forth!" And Lazarus came forth, creeping helplessly, with inch-long steps of his linen-bound limbs. "Ha! ha! brother! sister!" cries the human heart. The Lord of Life hath taken the prey from the spoiler! he hath emptied the grave! Here comes the dead man, welcome as never was child from the womb—new-born—and in him all the human race new-born from the grave! "Loose him and let him go!" and the work is done. The sorrow is over, and the joy is come. Home, home, Martha, Mary, with your Lazarus! He too will go with you, the Lord of the living. Home, and get the feast ready, Martha! Prepare the food for him who comes hungry from the grave, for him who has called him hence. Home, Mary, to help Martha! What a household yours will be! What wondrous speech will pass between the dead come to life, and the living come to die!

## THE SLEEP OF LAZARUS.

But what pang is this that makes Lazarus draw hurried breath, and turns Martha's cheeks so white? Ah! at the little window of the heart, the pale eyes of the defeated Horror look in. What, is he there still? Ah, yes, he will come for Martha, come for Mary, come yet again for Lazarus—yea, come for the Lord of Life himself, and carry all away. But look at the Lord. He knows all about it, and he smiles. Does Martha think of the words he spoke, "He that liveth and believeth in me shall never die!" Perhaps she does, and like the moon before the sun, her face returns the smile of her Lord.

This, my friends, is a fancy in form, but it embodies a dear truth. What is it to you and me that he raised Lazarus? We are not called upon to believe that he will raise from the tomb that joy of our hearts which lies buried there beyond our sight. Stop! Are we not? We *are* called upon to believe this. Else the whole story were for us a poor mockery. What is it to us that the Lord raised Lazarus? Is it nothing to know that our Brother is Lord over the grave? Will the harvest be behind the first-fruits? If he tells us he cannot, for good reasons, raise up our vanished love to-day, or to-morrow, or for all the years of our life to come, shall we not mingle the smile of faithful thanks with the sorrow of present loss, and walk diligently, waiting? That he called forth Lazarus showed that he was in his keeping, that he is Lord of the living, and that all live to him—that he has a hold of them, and can draw them forth when he will. If this is not true, then the raising of Lazarus is false—I do not mean merely false in fact, but false in meaning. If we believe in him, then in his name, both for ourselves and for our friends, we must deny death and believe in life. Lord Christ, fill our hearts with thy life!

## XIV.

## THE NEW NAME.

"To him that overcometh, I will give a white stone, and in the stone a new name written, which no man knoweth saving he that receiveth it."—Revelation 2: 17.

Whether the Book of the Revelation be written by the same man who wrote the Gospel according to St. John or not, there is, at least, one element common to the two—the mysticism.

I use the word *mysticism* as representing a certain mode of embodying truth, common, in various degrees, to almost all, if not all, the writers of the New Testament. The attempt to define it thoroughly would require an essay. I will hazard but one suggestion towards it: A mystical mind is one which, (having perceived that the highest expression, of which the truth admits, lies in the symbolism of nature and the human customs that result from human necessities), prosecutes thought about truth so embodied by dealing with the symbols themselves after logical forms. This is the highest mode of conveying the deepest truth; and the Lord himself often employed it, as, for instance, in the whole passage ending with the words, "If therefore the light that is in thee be darkness, how great is the darkness!"

The mysticism in the Gospel of St. John is of the

simplest, and, therefore, noblest nature. No dweller on this planet can imagine a method of embodying truth that shall be purer, loftier, truer to the truth embodied. There may be higher modes in other worlds, or there may not—I cannot tell; but of all our modes these forms are best illustrations of the highest. Apparently the mysticism of St. John's own nature enabled him to remember and report with sufficient accuracy the words of our Lord, always, it seems to me, of a recognizably different kind from those of any of the writers of the New Testament—chiefly, perhaps, in the simplicity of their poetical mysticism.

But the mysticism in the Book of Revelation is more complicated, more gorgeous, less poetic, and occasionally, I think, perhaps arbitrary, or approaching the arbitrary; *reminding* one, in a word, of the mysticism of Swedenborg. Putting aside both historical and literary criticism, in neither of which with regard to the authorship of these two books have I a right even to an opinion, I would venture to suggest that possibly their difference in tone is just what one might expect when the historian of a mystical teacher, and the recorder of his mystical sayings, proceeds to embody his own thoughts, feelings, and inspirations; that is when the revelation flows no longer from the lips of the Master, but through the disciple's own heart, soul, and brain. For surely no one will venture to assert that the Spirit of God could speak as freely by the lips of the wind-swayed, reed-like, rebukable Peter, or of the Thomas who could believe his own eyes, but neither the word of his brethren, nor the nature of his Master, as by the lips of him who was blind and deaf to everything but the will of him that sent him.

Truth is truth, whether from the lips of Jesus or Balaam. But, in its deepest sense, *the truth* is a condition of heart, soul, mind, and strength towards God and towards our fellow—not an utterance, not even a *right* form of words; and therefore such truth coming forth in words is, in a sense, the person that speaks. And many of the utterances of truth in the Revelation, commonly called of St. John, are not merely lofty in form, but carry with them the conviction that the writer was no mere "trumpet of a prophecy," but spoke that he did know, and testified that he had seen.

In this passage about the gift of the white stone, I think we find the essence of religion.

What the notion in the mind of the writer with regard to the white stone was, is, I think, of comparatively little moment. I take the stone to belong more to the arbitrary and fanciful than to the true mystical imagery, although for the bringing out of the mystical thought in which it is concerned, it is of high and honorable dignity. For fancy itself will subserve the true imagination of the mystic, and so be glorified. I doubt if the writer himself associated any essential meaning with it. Certainly I will not allow that he had such a poor notion in it as that of a voting pebble —white, because the man who receives it is accepted or chosen. The word is used likewise for a precious stone set as a jewel. And the writer thought of it mystically, a mode far more likely to involve a reference to nature than to a political custom. What his mystic meaning may be, must be taken differently by different minds. I think he sees in its whiteness purity, and in its substance indestructibility. But I care chiefly to regard the stone as the vehicle of the name,—as the form whereby the name is represented

# THE NEW NAME. 149

as passing from God to the man, and what is involved in this communication is what I wish to show. If my reader will not acknowledge my representation as St. John's meaning, I yet hope so to set it forth that he shall see the representation to be true in itself, and then I shall willingly leave the interpretation to its fate.

I say, in brief, the giving of the white stone with the new name is the communication of what God thinks about the man to the man. It is the divine judgment, the solemn holy doom of the righteous man, the "Come, thou blessed," spoken to the individual.

In order to see this, we must first understand what is the idea of a name,—that is, what is the perfect notion of a name. For, seeing that the mystical energy of a holy mind here speaks of God as giving something, we must understand that the essential thing, and not any of its accidents or imitations, is intended.

A name of the ordinary kind in this world, has nothing essential in it. It is but a label by which one man and a scrap of his external history may be known from another man and a scrap of his history. The only names which have significance are those which the popular judgment or prejudice or humor bestows, either for ridicule or honor, upon a few out of the many. Each of these is founded upon some external characteristic of the man, upon some predominant peculiarity of temper, some excellence or the reverse of character, or something which he does or has done well or ill enough, or at least, singularly enough, to render him, in the eyes of the people, worthy of such distinction from other men. As far as they go, these are real names, for, in some poor measure, they express individuality.

The true name is one which expresses the character, the nature, the being, the *meaning* of the person who bears it. It is the man's own symbol,—his soul's picture, in a word,—the sign which belongs to him and to no one else. Who can give a man this, his own name? God alone. For no one but God sees what the man is, or even, seeing what he is, could express in a name-word the sum and harmony of what he sees. To whom is this name given? To him that overcometh. When is it given? When he has overcome. Does God then not know what a man is going to become? As surely as he sees the oak which he put there lying in the heart of the acorn. Why then does he wait till the man has become by overcoming ere he settles what his name shall be? He does not wait; he knows his name from the first. But as—although repentance comes because God pardons—yet the man becomes aware of the pardon only in the repentance; so it is only when the man has become his name that God gives him the stone with the name upon it, for then first can he understand what his name signifies. It is the blossom, the perfection, the completion, that determines the name; and God foresees that from the first, because he made it so; but the tree of the soul, before its blossom comes, cannot understand what blossom it is to bear, and could not know what the word meant, which, in representing its own unarrived completeness, named itself. Such a name cannot be given until the man *is* the name.

God's name for a man must then be the expression in a mystical word—a word of that language which all who have overcome understand—of his own idea of the man, that being whom he had in his thought when he began to make the child, and whom he kept in

## THE NEW NAME. 151

his thought through the long process of creation that went to realize the idea. To tell the name is to seal the success—to say, "In thee also I am well pleased."

But we are still in the region of symbol. For supposing that such a form were actually observed between God and him that overcometh, it would be no less a symbol—only an acted one. We must therefore look deeper still for the fulness of its meaning. Up to this point little has been said to justify our expectations of discovery in the text. Let us, I say, look deeper. We shall not look long before we find that the mystic symbol has for its centre of significance the fact of the personal individual relation of every man to his God. That every man has affairs, and those his first affairs, with God, stands to the reason of every man who associates any meaning or feeling with the words, Maker, Father, God. Were we but children of a day, with the understanding that some one had given us that one holiday, there would be something to be thought, to be felt, to be done, because we knew it. For then our nature would be according to our fate, and we could worship and die. But it would be only the praise of the dead, not the praise of the living, for death would be the deepest, the lasting, the overcoming. We should have come out of nothingness, not out of God. He could only be our Maker, not our Father, our Origin. But now we know that God cannot be the God of the dead—must be the God of the living; inasmuch as to know that we died, would freeze the heart of worship, and we could not say Our God, or feel him worthy of such worship as we could render. To him who offers unto this God of the living his own self of sacrifice, to him that overcometh, him who has brought his individual life back to its source, who knows that he is *one* of God's children, *this* one of the Father's making, he giveth the white stone. To him who climbs on the stair of all his God-born efforts and God-given victories up to the height of his being—that of looking face to face upon his ideal self in the bosom of the Father—God's *him*, realized in him through the Father's love in the Elder Brother's devotion—to him God gives the new name written.

But I leave this, because that which follows embraces and intensifies this individuality of relation in a fuller development of the truth. For the name is one "which no man knoweth saving he that receiveth it." Not only then has each man his individual relation to God, but each man has his peculiar relation to God. He is to God a peculiar being, made after his own fashion, and that of no one else; for when he is perfected he shall receive the new name which no one else can understand. Hence, he can worship God as no man else can worship him—can understand God as no man else can understand him. This or that man may understand God more, may understand God better than he, but no other man can understand God *as* he understands him. God give me grace to be humble before thee, my brother, that I drag not my simulacrum of thee before the judgment-seat of the unjust judge, but look up to thyself for what revelation of God thou and no one else canst give! As the fir-tree lifts up itself with a far different need from the need of the palm-tree, so does each man stand before God, and lift up a different humanity to the common Father. And, for each, God has a different response. With every man he has a secret—the secret of the new name. In every man there is a loneliness, an inner chamber of peculiar life into which God only can enter. I say not it is *the innermost chamber*—but a

## THE NEW NAME.

chamber into which no brother, nay, no sister, can come.

From this it follows that there is a chamber also—(O God, humble and accept my speech)—a chamber in God himself, into which none can enter but the one, the individual, the peculiar man,—out of which chamber that man has to bring revelation and strength for his brethren. This is that for which he was made—to reveal the secret things of the Father.

By his creation, then, each man is isolated with God; each, in respect of his peculiar making, can say, "*my* God;" each can come to him alone, and speak with him face to face, as a man speaketh with his friend. There is no *massing* of men with God. When he speaks of gathered men, it is as a spiritual *body*, not a *mass*. For in a body every smallest portion is individual, and, therefore, capable of forming a part of the body.

See, now, what a significance the symbolism of our text assumes. Each of us is a distinct flower or tree in the spiritual garden of God,—precious, each for his own sake, in the eyes of him who is even now making us,—each of us watered and shone upon and filled with life, for the sake of his flower, his completed being, which will blossom out of him at last to the glory and pleasure of the great gardener. For each has within him a secret of the Divinity; each is growing towards the revelation of that secret to himself, and so to the full reception, according to his measure, of the divine. Every moment that he is true to his true self, some new shine of the white stone breaks on his inward eye, some fresh channel is opened upward for the coming glory of the flower, the conscious offering of his whole being in beauty to the Maker. Each man, then, is in

God's sight worth. Life and action, thought and intent, are sacred. And what an end lies before us! To have a consciousness of our own ideal being flashed into us from the thought of God! Surely for this may well give way all our paltry self-consciousnesses, our self-admirations and self-worships! Surely to know what he thinks about us will pale out of our souls all our thoughts about ourselves! and we may well hold them loosely now, and be ready to let them go. Towards this result St. Paul had already drawn near, when he, who had begun the race with a bitter cry for deliverance from the body of his death, was able to say that he judged his own self no longer.

"But is there not the worst of all dangers involved in such teaching—the danger of spiritual pride?" If there be, are we to refuse the Spirit for fear of the pride? Or is there any other deliverance from pride except the Spirit? Pride springs from supposed success in the high aim: with attainment itself comes humility. But here there is no room for ambition. Ambition is the desire to be above one's neighbor; and here there is no possibility of comparison with one's neighbor: no one knows what the white stone contains except the man who receives it. Here is room for endless aspiration towards the unseen ideal; none for ambition. Ambition would only be higher than others; aspiration would be high. Relative worth is not only unknown—to the children of the kingdom, it is unknowable. Each esteems the other better than himself. How shall the rose, the glowing heart of the summer heats, rejoice against the snowdrop risen with hanging head from the white bosom of the snow? Both are God's thoughts; both are dear to him; both are needful to the completeness of his earth and the

## THE NEW NAME.

revelation of himself. "God has cared to make me for himself," says the victor with the white stone, "and has called me that which I like best; for my own name must be what I would have it, seeing it is myself. What matter whether I be called a grass of the field, or an eagle of the air? a stone to build into his temple, or a Boanerges to wield his thunder? I am his; his idea, his making; perfect in my kind, yea, perfect in his sight; full of him, revealing him, alone with him. Let him call me what he will. The name shall be precious as my life. I seek no more."

Gone then will be all anxiety as to what his neighbor may think about him. It is enough that God thinks about him. To be something to God—is not that praise enough? To be a thing that God cares for and would have complete for himself, because it is worth caring for—is not that life enough?

Neither will he thus be isolated from his fellows. For that we say of one, we say of all. It is as *one* that the man has claims amongst his fellows. Each will feel the sacredness and awe of his neighbor's dark and silent speech with his God. Each will regard the other as a prophet, and look to him for what the Lord hath spoken. Each, as a high priest returning from his Holy of Holies, will bring from his communion some glad tidings, some gospel of truth, which, when spoken, his neighbors shall receive and understand. Each will behold in the other a marvel of revelation, a present son or daughter of the Most High, come forth from him to reveal him afresh. In God, each will draw nigh to each.

Yes, there will be danger—danger as everywhere; but he giveth more grace. And if the man who has striven up the heights should yet fall from them into the deeps, is there not that fire of God, the consuming fire, which burneth and destroyeth not?

To no one who has not already had some speech with God, or who has not at least felt some aspiration towards the fount of his being, can all this appear other than foolishness. So be it.

But, Lord, help them and us, and make our being grow into thy likeness. If through ages of strife and ages of growth, yet let us at last see thy face, and receive the white stone from thy hand.


O GOD, thou King eternal, immortal, invisible, may we, who cannot see thee with the eye of flesh, behold the steadfastly with the eye of faith, that we faint not under the many temptations and afflictions of this mortal life, but endure as seeing thee who art invisible; that when we shall have done and suffered thy will upon the earth, we may behold the vision of God in heaven, and be made partakers of those unspeakable joys which thou hast promised to them that love thee, through Jesus Christ, our Lord. *Amen.*

## XV.

## THE GOD OF THE LIVING.

"He is not a God of the dead, but of the living: for all live unto him."
—Luke 20: 38.

It is a recurring cause of perplexity in our Lord's teaching that he is too simple for us; that while we are questioning with ourselves about the design of Solomon's carving upon some gold-plated door of the temple, he is speaking about the foundations of Mount Zion, yea, of the earth itself, upon which it stands. If the reader of the Gospel supposes that our Lord was here using a verbal argument with the Sadducees, namely, "I *am* the God of Abraham, Isaac, and Jacob; therefore they *are*," he will be astonished that no Sadducee was found with courage enough to reply: "All that God meant was to introduce himself to Moses as the same God who had aided and protected his fathers while they were alive, saying, I am he that was the God of thy fathers. They found me faithful. Thou, therefore, listen to me, and thou too shalt find me faithful *unto* the death."

But no such reply suggested itself even to the Sadducees of that day, for their eastern nature could see argument beyond logic. Shall God call himself the God of the dead, of those who were alive once, but whom he either could not or would not keep alive?

Is that the Godhood, and its relation to those who worship it? The changeless God of an ever-born and ever-perishing torrent of life; of which each atom cries with burning heart, *My God!* and straightway passes into the Godless cold! "Trust in me, for I took care of your fathers once upon a time, though they are gone now. Worship and obey me, for I will be good to you for threescore years and ten, or thereabouts; and after that, when you are not, and the world goes on all the same without you, I will call myself your God still." God changes not. Once God he is always God. If he has once said to a man, "I am thy God, and that man has died the death of the Sadducee's creed," then we have a right to say that God is the God of the dead.

"And wherefore should he not be so far the God of the dead, if during the time allotted to them here, he was the faithful God of the living?" What God-like relation can the ever-living, life-giving, changeless God hold to creatures who partake not of his life, who have death at the very core of their being, are not worth their Maker's keeping alive? To let his creatures die would be to change, to abjure his Godhood, to cease to be that which he had made himself. If they are not worth keeping alive, then his creating is a poor thing, and he is not so great, nor so divine as even the poor thoughts of those his dying creatures have been able to imagine him.

But our Lord says, "All live unto him." With him death is not. Thy life sees our life, O Lord. All of whom *all* can be said, are present to thee. Thou thinkest about us, eternally more than we think about thee. The little life that burns within the body of this death, glows unquenchable in thy true-seeing eyes. If thou didst forget us for a moment, then indeed death would

## THE GOD OF THE LIVING.

be. But unto thee we live. The beloved pass from our sight, but they pass not from thine. This that we call death, is but a form in the eyes of men. It looks something final, an awful cessation, an utter change. It seems not probable that there is anything beyond. But if God could see us before we were, and make us after his ideal, that we shall have passed from the eyes of our friends can be no argument that he beholds us no longer.

"All live unto him." Let the change be ever so great, ever so imposing; let the unseen life be ever so vague to our conception, it is not against reason to hope that God could see Abraham after his Isaac had ceased to see him; saw Isaac after Jacob ceased to see him; saw Jacob after some of the Sadducees had begun to doubt whether there ever had been a Jacob at all. He remembers them; that is, he carries them in his mind: he of whom God thinks, lives. He takes to himself the name of *Their God*. The Living One cannot name himself after the dead; when the very Godhood lies in the giving of life. Therefore they must be alive. If he speaks of them, remembers his own loving thoughts of them, would he not have kept them alive if he could; and if he could not, how could he create them? Can it be an easier thing to call into life than to keep alive?

"But if they live to God, they are aware of God. And if they are aware of God, they are conscious of their own being: whence then the necessity of a resurrection?"

For their relation to others of God's children in mutual revelation; and for fresh revelation of God to all.—But let us inquire what is meant by the resurrection of the body. "With what body do they come?"

Surely we are not required to believe that the same body is raised again. That is against science, common sense, Scripture. St. Paul represents the matter quite otherwise. One feels ashamed of arguing such a puerile point. Who could wish his material body, which has indeed died over and over again since he was born, never remaining for one hour composed of the same matter, its endless activity depending upon its endless change, to be fixed as his changeless possession, such as it may then be, at the moment of death, and secured to him in worthless identity for the ages to come? A man's material body will be to his consciousness at death no more than the old garment he throws aside at night, intending to put on a new and a better in the morning. To desire to keep the old body seems to me to argue a degree of sensual materialism excusable only in those pagans who in their Elysian fields could hope to possess only such a thin, fleeting, dreamy, and altogether funebrial existence, that they might well long for the thicker, more tangible bodily being in which they had experienced the pleasures of a tumultuous life on the upper world. As well might a Christian desire that the hair which has been shorn from him through all his past life should be restored to his risen and glorified head.

Yet not the less is the doctrine of the Resurrection gladdening as the sound of the silver trumpet of its visions, needful as the very breath of life to our longing souls. Let us know what it means, and we shall see that it is thus precious.

Let us first ask what is the use of this body of ours. It is the means of Revelation to us, the *camera* in which God's eternal shows are set forth. It is by the body that we come into contact with Nature, with our

## THE GOD OF THE LIVING.

fellow-men, with all their revelations of God to us. It is through the body that we receive all the lessons of passion, of suffering, of love, of beauty, of science. It is through the body that we are both trained outwards from ourselves, and driven inwards into our deepest selves to find God. There is glory and might in this vital evanescence, this slow glacier-like flow of clothing and revealing matter, this ever uptossed rainbow of tangible humanity. It is no less of God's making than the spirit that is clothed therein.

We cannot yet have learned all that we are meant to learn through the body. How much of the teaching even of this world can the most diligent and most favored man have exhausted before he is called to leave it! Is all that remains to be lost? Who that has loved this earth can but believe that the spiritual body of which St. Paul speaks will be a yet higher channel of such revelation? The meek who have found that their Lord spake true, and have indeed inherited the earth, who have seen that all matter is radiant of spiritual meaning, who would not cast a sigh after the loss of mere animal pleasure, would, I think, be the least willing to be without a body, to be unclothed without being again clothed upon. Who, after centuries of glory in heaven, would not rejoice to behold once more that patient-headed child of winter and spring, the meek snowdrop? In whom, amidst the golden choirs, would not the vision of an old sunset wake such a song as the ancient dwellers of the earth would with gently flattened palm hush their throbbing harps to hear?

All this revelation, however, would render only *a* body necessary, not this body. The fulness of the word *Resurrection* would be ill met if this were all. We need not only a body to convey revelation to us, but a body to reveal us to others. The thoughts, feelings, imaginations which arise in us, must have their garments of revelation, whereby shall be made manifest the unseen world within us to our brothers and sisters around us; else is each left in human loneliness. Now, if this be one of the uses my body served on earth before, the new body must be like the old. Nay, it must be the same body, glorified as we are glorified, with all that was distinctive of each from his fellows more visible than ever before. The accidental, the non-essential, the unrevealing, the incomplete, will have vanished. That which made the body what it was in the eyes of those who loved us will be tenfold there. Will not this be the resurrection of the body? of the same body though not of the same dead matter? Every eye shall see the beloved, every heart will cry, "My own again!—more mine because more himself than ever I beheld him!" For do we not say on earth, "He is not himself to-day," or "She looks her own self;" "She is more like herself than I have seen her for long"? And is not this when the heart is glad and the face is radiant? For we carry a better likeness of our friends in our hearts than their countenances, save at precious seasons, manifest to us.

Who will dare to call anything less than this a resurrection? Oh, how the letter killeth! There are some who can believe that the dirt of their bodies will rise the same as it went down to the friendly grave, who yet doubt if they will know their friends when they rise again. And they call *that* believing in the resurrection!

What! shall a man love his neighbor as himself, and must he be content not to know him in heaven? Better be content to lose our consciousness, and know

## THE GOD OF THE LIVING. 163

ourselves no longer. What! shall God be the God of the families of the earth, and shall the love that he has thus created towards father and mother, brother and sister, wife and child, go moaning and longing to all eternity; or worse, far worse, die out of our bosoms? Shall God be God, and shall this be the end?

Ah, my friends! what will resurrection or life be to me, how shall I continue to love God as I have learned to love him through you, if I find he cares so little for this human heart of mine, as to take from me the gracious visitings of your faces and forms? True, I might have a gaze at Jesus, now and then; but he would not be so good as I had thought him. And how should I see him if I could not see you? God will not take you, has not taken you from me to bury you out of my sight in the abyss of his own unfathomable being, where I cannot follow and find you, myself lost in the same awful gulf. No, our God is an unvailing, a revealing God. He will raise you from the dead, that I may behold you; that that which vanished from the earth may again stand forth, looking out of the same eyes of eternal love and truth, holding out the same mighty hand of brotherhood, the same delicate and gentle, yet strong hand of sisterhood, to me, this me that knew you and loved you in the days gone by. I shall not care that the matter of the forms I loved a thousand years ago has returned to mingle with the sacred goings on of God's science upon that far-off world wheeling its nursery of growing loves and wisdoms through space; I shall not care that the muscle which now sends the ichor through your veins is not formed of the very particles which once sent the blood to the pondering brain, the flashing eye, or the nervous right arm; I shall not care, I say, so long as it is yourselves that are before me, beloved; so long as through these forms I know that I look on my own, on my loving souls of the ancient time; so long as my spirits have got garments of revealing after their own old lovely fashion, garments to reveal themselves to me. The new shall then be dear as the old, and for the same reason, that it reveals the old love. And in the changes which, thank God, must take place when the mortal puts on immortality, shall we not feel that the nobler our friends are, the more they are themselves; that the more the idea of each is carried out in the perfection of beauty, the more like they are to what we thought them in our most exalted moods, to that which we saw in them in the rarest moments of profoundest communion, to that which we beheld through the vail of all their imperfections when we loved them the truest?

Lord, evermore give us this Resurrection, like thine own in the body of thy Transfiguration! Let us see and hear, and know, and be seen, and heard, and known, as thou seest, hearest, and knowest. Give us glorified bodies through which to reveal the glorified thoughts which shall then inhabit us, when not only shalt thou reveal God, but each of us shall reveal thee.

And for this, Lord Jesus, come thou, the child, the obedient God, that we may be one with thee, and with every man and woman whom thou hast made, in the Father.

## XVI.

## THE TEMPTATION IN THE WILDERNESS.

"But he answered and said, It is written, Man shall not live by bread alone, but by every word that proceedeth out of the mouth of God."—Matthew 4 : 4.

"Then was Jesus led up of the Spirit into the wilderness, to be tempted of the devil. And when he had fasted forty days and forty nights, he was afterward an hungred. And when the tempter came to him, he said, If thou be the Son of God, command that these stones be made bread. But he answered and said, It is written, Man shall not live by bread alone, but by every word that proceedeth out of the mouth of God. Then the devil taketh him up into the holy city, and setteth him on a pinnacle of the temple, and saith unto him, If thou be the Son of God, cast thyself down; for it is written, He shall give his angels charge concerning thee, and in their hands they shall bear thee up, lest at any time thou dash thy foot against a stone. Jesus said unto him, It is written again, Thou shalt not tempt the Lord thy God. Again, the devil taketh him up into an exceeding high mountain, and showeth him all the kingdoms of the world, and the glory of them; and saith unto him, All these things will I give thee, if thou wilt fall down and worship me. Then saith Jesus unto him, Get thee hence, Satan; for it is written, Thou shalt worship the Lord thy God, and him only shalt thou serve. Then the devil leaveth him; and, behold, angels came and ministered unto him."

This narrative must have one of two origins. Either it is an invention, such as many tales told of our Lord in the earlier periods of Christianity ; or it came from our Lord himself, for, according to the story, except the wild beasts, of earthly presence there was none at his Temptation.

As to the former of the two origins : The story bears upon it no sign of human invention. The man who could see such things as are here embodied, dared not invent such an embodiment for them. To one in doubt about the matter it will be helpful, I think, to compare this story with the best of those for which one or other of the apocryphal gospels is our only authority—say the grand account of the Descent into Hell in the Gospel according to Nicodemus.

If it have not this origin, there is but the other that it can have—Our Lord himself. To this I will return presently.

And now, let us approach the subject from another side. With this in view, I ask you to think how much God must know of which we know nothing. Think what an abyss of truth was our Lord, out of whose divine darkness, through that revealing countenance, that uplifting voice, those hands whose tenderness has made us great, broke all holy radiations of human significance. Think of his understanding, imagination, heart, in which lay the treasures of wisdom and knowledge. Must he not have known, felt, imagined, rejoiced in things that would not be told in human words, could not be understood by human hearts ? Was he not always bringing forth out of the light inaccessible?

Was not his very human form a vail hung over the face of the truth that, even in part by dimming the effulgence of the glory, it might reveal? What could be conveyed must be thus conveyed: an infinite More must lie behind. And even of those things that might be partially revealed to men, could he talk to his Father and talk to his disciples in altogether the same forms, in altogether the same words? Would what he said to God on the mountain-tops, in the dim twilight or the gray dawn, never be such that his disciples could have understood it no more than the people, when the voice of God spoke to him from heaven, could distinguish that voice from the inarticulate thundering of the element?

There is no attempt made to convey to us even the substance of the battle of those forty days. Such a conflict of spirit as for forty days absorbed all the human necessities of *The Man* in the cares of the Godhead could not be rendered into forms intelligible to us, or rather, could not be in itself intelligible to us, and therefore could not take any form of which we could lay hold. It is not till the end of those forty days that the divine event begins to dawn out from the sacred depths of the eternal thought, becomes human enough to be made to appear, admits of utterance, becomes capable of being spoken in human forms to the ears of men, though yet only in a dark saying, which he that hath ears to hear may hear, and he that hath a heart to understand may understand. For the mystery is not left behind, nor can the speech be yet clear unto men.

At the same moment, when the approaching event comes within human ken, may from afar be dimly descried by the God-upheld intelligence, the same humanity seizes on the Master, and he is "an hungred." The first sign that he has come back to us, that the strife is approaching its human result, is his hunger. On what a sea of endless life do we float, are our poor necessities sustained—not the poorest of them dissociated from the divine! Emerging from the storms of the ocean of divine thought and feeling into the shallower waters that lave the human shore, bearing with him the treasures won in the strife, our Lord is straightway an hungred; and from this moment the temptation is human, and can be in some measure understood by us.

But could it even then have been conveyed to the human mind in merely intellectual forms? Or, granting that it might, could it be so conveyed to those who were only beginning to have the vaguest, most error-mingled and confused notions about our Lord and what he came to do? No. The inward experiences of our Lord, such as could be conveyed to them at all, could be conveyed to them only in a parable. For far plainer things than these, our Lord chose this form. The form of the parable is the first in which truth will admit of being embodied. Nor is this all: it is likewise the fullest; and to the parable will the teacher of the truth ever return. Is he, who asserts that the passage contains a simple narrative of actual events, prepared to believe, as the story, so interpreted, indubitably gives us to understand, that a visible demon came to our Lord and, himself the prince of wordly wisdom, thought, by quoting Scripture after the manner of the priests to persuade a good man to tempt God; thought, by the promise of power, to prevail upon him to cast aside every claim he had upon the human race, in falling down and worshiping one whom he knew to be the adversary of Truth, of Humanity, of God? How could Satan be so foolish? or, if Satan might be so foolish, wherein could such temptation so presented have tempted our Lord? and wherein would a victory over such be a victory for the race?

Told as a parable, it is all full of meaning as it would be bare if received as a narrative. Our Lord spake then this parable unto them, and so conveyed more of the truth with regard to his temptation in the wilderness, than could have been conveyed by any other form in which the truth he wanted to give them might have been embodied.

And now arises the question upon the right answer to which depends the whole elucidation of the story. *How could the Son of God be tempted?*

If any one say that he was not moved by those temptations, he must be told that then they were no temptations to him, and he was not tempted; nor was his victory of more significance than that of the man who, tempted to bear false witness against his neighbor, abstains from robbing him of his goods. For human need, struggle, and hope, it bears no meaning; and we must reject the whole as a fantastic folly of crude invention; a mere stage-show; a lie for the poor sake of the fancied truth; a doing of evil that good might come; and, with how many fragments soever of truth its mud may be filled, not in any way to be received as a divine message.

But asserting that these were real temptations if the story is to be received at all, am I not involving myself in a greater difficulty still? For how could the Son of God be tempted with evil—with that which must to him appear in its true colors of discord, its true shapes of deformity? Or how could he then be the Son of his Father who cannot be tempted with evil?

In the answer to this lies the centre, the essential germ of the whole interpretation: He was not tempted with Evil but with Good; with inferior forms of good, that is, pressing in upon him, while the higher forms of good held themselves aloof, biding their time, that is, God's time. I do not believe that the Son of God could be tempted with evil, but I do believe that he could be tempted with good—to yield to which temptation would have been evil in him—ruin to the universe.

"But does not all evil come from good?" Yes; but it has come *from* it. It is no longer good. A good corrupted is no longer a good. Such could not tempt our Lord. Revenge may originate in a sense of justice, but it is revenge not justice; an evil thing, for it would be fearfully unjust. Evil is evil whatever it may have come from. The Lord could not have felt tempted to take vengeance upon his enemies, but he might have felt tempted to destroy the wicked from the face of the earth—to destroy them from the face of the earth, I say, not to destroy them for ever. To that I do not think he could have felt tempted.

But we shall find illustration enough of what I mean in the matter itself. Let us look at the individual temptations represented in the parable.

The informing idea which led to St. Mathew's arrangement seems to me superior to that showing itself in St. Luke's. In the two accounts, the closes, while each is profoundly significant, are remarkably different. Now let us follow St. Matthew's record. And we shall see how the devil tempted him *to* evil, but not *with* evil.

First, He was hungry, and the devil said, *Make bread of this stone.*

The Lord had been fasting for forty days—a fast

impossible except during intense mental absorption. Let no one think to glorify this fast by calling it miraculous. Wonderful such fasts are on record on the part of holy men; and inasmuch as the Lord was more of a man than his brethren, insomuch might he be farther withdrawn in the depths of his spiritual humanity from the outer region of his physical nature. So much the slower would be the goings on of that nature; and fasting in his case might thus be extended beyond the utmost limits of similar fasts in others. This, I believe, was all—and this *all* infinite in its relations. This is the grandest, simplest, and most significant, and, therefore, the divinest way of regarding his fast. Hence, at the end of the forty days, it was not hunger alone that made food tempting to him, but that exhaustion of the whole system, wasting itself all the time it was forgotten, which, reacting on the mind when the mind was already worn out with its own tension, must have deadened it so, that (speaking after the experience of his brethren, which alone will explain his,) it could for the time see or feel nothing of the spiritual, and could only *believe in* the unfelt, the unseen.

What a temptation was here! There is no sin in wishing to eat; no sin in procuring food honestly that one may eat. But it rises even into an awful duty, when a man knows that to eat will restore the lost vision of the eternal; will, operating on the brain, and thence on the mind, render the man capable of hope as well as of faith, of gladness as well as of confidence, of praise as well as of patience. Why then should he not eat? Why should he not put forth the power that was in him that he might eat? Because such power was his, not to take care of himself, but to work the work of him that sent him. Such power was his not even to honor his Father save as his Father chose to be honored, who is far more honored in the ordinary way of common wonders, than in the extraordinary way of miracles. Because it was God's business to take care of him, his to do what the Father told him to do. To make that stone bread would be to take the care out of the Father's hands, and turn the divinest thing in the universe into the merest commonplace of self-preservation.

And in nothing was he to be beyond his brethren, save in faith. No refuge for him, any more than for them, save in the love and care of the Father. Other refuge, let it be miraculous power or what you will, would be but hell to him. God is refuge. God is life.

"Was he not to eat when it came in his way? And did not the bread come in his way, when his power met that which could be changed into it?"

Regard that word *changed*. The whole matter lies in that. Changed from what? From what God had made it. Changed into what? Into what he did not make it. Why changed? Because the Son was hungry, and the Father would not feed him with food convenient for him! The Father did not give him a stone when he asked for bread. It was Satan that brought the stone and told him to provide for himself. The Father said, That is a stone. The Son would not say, That is a loaf. No one creative *fiat* shall contradict another. The Father and the Son are of one mind. The Lord could hunger, could starve, but would not change into another thing what his Father had made one thing.

There was no such change in the feeding of the multitudes. The fish and the bread were fish and bread before. I think this is significant as regards the true nature of a miracle, and its relation to the ordinary ways of God. There was in these miracles, and I think in all, only a hastening of appearances; the doing of that in a day, which may ordinarily take a thousand years, for with God time is not what it is with us. He makes it. And the hastening of a process does not interfere in the least with cause and effect in the process, nor does it render the process one whit more miraculous. Indeed, the wonder of the growing corn is to me greater than the wonder of feeding the thousands. It is easier to understand the creative power going forth at once—immediately—than through the countless, the lovely, the seemingly forsaken wonders of the corn-field. To the merely scientific man all this is pure nonsense, or at best belongs to the region of the fancy. The time will come, I think, when he will see that there is more in it, namely, a higher reason, a loftier science, how incorrectly soever herein indicated.

If we regard the answer Jesus gave the devil, we shall see the root of the matter at once; "Man shall not live by bread alone, but by every word that proceedeth out of the mouth of God." Yea, even by the word which made that stone that stone. Everything is all right. It is life indeed for him to leave that stone, which the Father had made a stone. It would be death to him to alter one word that God had spoken.

"Man shall not live by bread alone." There are other ways of living besides that which comes by bread. A man will live by the word of God, by what God says to him, by what God means between God and him, by the truths of being which the Father alone can reveal to his child, by the communion of love between them. Without the bread he will die, as men say; but he will not find that he dies. He will only find that the tent which hid the stars from him is gone, and that he can see the heavens; or rather, the earthly house will melt away from around him, and he will find that he has a palace-home about him, another and loftier word of God clothing upon him. So the man lives by the word of God even in refusing the bread which God does not give him, for, instead of dying because he does not eat, he rises into a higher life even of the same kind.

For I have been speaking of the consciousness of existence, and not of that higher spiritual life on which all other life depends. That of course can for no one moment exist save from the heart of God. When a man tries to live by bread and not by the word that comes out of that heart of God, he may think he lives, but he begins to die or is dead. Our Lord says, "I can do without the life that comes of bread: without the life that comes of the word of my Father, I die indeed." Therefore he does not think twice about the matter. That God's will be done is all his care. That done, all will be right, and all right with him, whether he thinks about himself or not. For the Father does not forget the child who is so busy trusting in him, that he cares not even to pray for himself.

In the higher aspect of this first temptation, arising from the fact that a man cannot feel the things he believes except under certain conditions of physical well-being dependent upon food, the answer is the same: A man does not live by his feelings any more than by bread, but by the Truth, that is, the Word, the Will, the uttered Being of God.

I am even ashamed to yield here to the necessity of writing what is but as milk for babes, when I would gladly utter, if I might, only that which would be as bread for men and women. What I must say is this: that, by *the Word of God*, I do not understand *The*

*Bible*. The Bible is *a* Word of God, the chief of his written words, because it tells us of The Word, the Christ; but everything God has done and given man to know is a word of his, a will of his; and inasmuch as it is a will of his, it is a necessity to man, without which he cannot live: the reception of it is man's life. For inasmuch as God's utterances are a whole, every smallest is essential: he speaks no foolishness—there are with him no vain repetitions. But by *the word* of the God and not Maker only, who is God just because he *speaks* to men, I must understand, in the deepest sense, every revelation of himself in the heart and consciousness of man, so that the man knows that God is there, nay, rather, that he is here. Even Christ himself is not the Word of God in the deepest sense *to a man*, until he is this Revelation of God to the man,—until the Spirit that is the meaning in the Word has come to him,—until the speech is not a sound as of thunder, but the voice of words; for a word is more than an utterance—it is a sound to be understood. No word, I say, is fully a Word *of* God until it is a Word *to* man, until the man therein recognizes God.

This is that for which the word is spoken. The words of God are as the sands and the stars,—they cannot be numbered; but the end of all and each is this—to reveal God. Nor, moreover, can the man know that any one of them is the word of God, save as it comes thus to him, is a revelation of God in him. It is *to* him that it may be *in* him; but till it is *in* him he cannot *know* that it was *to* him. God must be God *in* man before man can know that he is God, or that he has received aright, and for that for which it was spoken, any one of his words.

No doubt the humble spirit will receive the testimony of every one whom he reveres, and look in the direction indicated for a word from the Father; but till he thus receives it in his heart, he cannot know what the word spoken of is.

If, by any will of God—that is, any truth in him—we live, we live by it tenfold when that will has become a word to us. When we receive it, his will becomes our will, and so we live by God. But the word of God once understood, a man must live by the faith of what God is, and not by his own feelings even in regard to God. It is the Truth itself, that which God is, known by what goeth out of his mouth, that man lives by. And when he can no longer *feel* the truth, he shall not therefore die. He lives because God is true; and he is able to know that he lives because he knows, having once understood the word, that God is truth. He believes in the God of former vision, lives by that word therefore, when all is dark and there is no vision.

O GOD, everlasting and almighty, whose grace hath appeared, bringing salvation to all men, teach us to deny ungodliness and worldly lusts, and to live soberly, righteously and godly in this present world, looking for the blessed hope, even the glorious appearing of the great God and our Saviour Jesus Christ, who gave himself for us that he might redeem us from all iniquity. *Amen.*

## XVII.

## THE SECOND AND THIRD TEMPTATIONS.

"Then saith Jesus unto him, Get thee hence, Satan: for it is written, Thou shalt worship the Lord thy God, and him only shalt thou serve."—Matthew 4: 10.

We now come to the second attempt of the Enemy. "Then if God is to be so trusted, try him. Fain would I see the result. Show thyself his darling. Here is the word itself for it: He shall give his angels charge concerning thee; not a stone shall hurt thee. Take him at his word. Throw thyself down, and strike the conviction into me that thou art the Son of God. For thou knowest thou dost not look like what thou sayest thou art."

Again, with a written word, in return, the Lord meets him. And he does not quote the Scripture for logical purposes—to confute Satan intellectually, but as giving even Satan the reason of his conduct. Satan quotes Scripture as a verbal authority: our Lord meets him with a Scripture, by the truth in which he regulates his conduct.

If we examine it, we shall find that this answer contains the same principle as the former, namely this, that to the Son of God the will of God is Life. It was a temptation to show the powers of the world that he was the Son of God; that to him the elements were subject; that he was above the laws of Nature, because he was the Eternal Son; and thus stop the raging of the heathen, and the vain imaginations of the people. It would be but to show them the truth. But he was the *Son* of God: what was his *Father's* will? Such was not the divine way of convincing the world of sin, of righteousness, of judgment. If the Father told him to cast himself down, that moment the pinnacle pointed naked to the sky. If the devil threw him down, let God send his angels; or, if better, allow him to be dashed to pieces in the valley below. But never will he forestall the divine will. The Father shall order what comes next. The Son will obey. In the path of his work he will turn aside for no stone. There let the angels bear him in their hands if need be. But he will not choose the path because there is a stone in it. He will not choose at all. He will go where the Spirit leads him.

I think this will throw some light upon the words of our Lord, "If ye have faith and doubt not, if ye shall say unto this mountain, Be thou removed, and be thou cast into the sea; it shall be done." Good people, amongst them John Bunyan, have been tempted to tempt the Lord their God upon the strength of this saying, just as Satan sought to tempt our Lord on the strength of the passage he quoted from the Psalms. Happily for such, the assurance to which they would give the name of faith generally fails them in time. Faith is that which, knowing the Lord's will, goes and does it; or, not knowing it, stands and waits, content in ignorance as in knowledge, because God wills; neither pressing into the hidden future, nor careless of the knowledge which opens the path of action. It is its noblest exercise to act with uncertainty of the result when the duty itself is certain, or even when a course,

## THE SECOND AND THIRD TEMPTATIONS. 179

seems with strong probability to be the duty. In the latter case a man may be mistaken, and his work will be burned, but by that very fire he will be saved. Nothing saves a man more than the burning of his work, except the doing of work that can stand the fire.

But to put God to the question in any other way than by saying, What wilt thou have me to do? is an attempt to compel God to declare himself, or to hasten his work. This probably was the sin of Judas. It is presumption of a kind similar to the making of a stone into bread. It is, as it were, either a forcing of God to act where he has created no need for action, or the making of a case wherein he shall seem to have forfeited his word if he does not act. The man is therein dissociating himself from God so far that, instead of acting by the divine will from within, he acts in God's face, as it were, to see what he will do. Man's first business is, "What does God want me to do?" not "What will God do if I do so and so?" To tempt a parent after the flesh in such a manner would be impertinence: to tempt God so is the same vice in its highest form—a natural result of that condition of mind which is worse than all the so-called cardinal sins, namely, spiritual pride, which attributes the tenderness and love of God not to man's being and man's need, but to some distinguishing excellence in the individual himself, which causes the Father to love him better than his fellows, and so pass by his faults with a smile. Not thus did the Son of God regard his relation to his Father. The faith which will remove mountains is that confidence in God which comes from seeking nothing but his will. A man who was thus faithful would die of hunger sooner than say to the stone, *Be bread;* would meet the scoffs of the unbelieving without reply and with apparent defeat, sooner than say to the mountain, *Be thou cast into the sea*, even if he knew that it would be torn from its foundations at the word, except he knew first that God would have it so.

And thus I am naturally brought to consider more fully how this should be a real temptation to the Son of Man. It would be good to confound his adversaries; to force conviction upon them that he was the God-supported messenger he declared himself. Why should he have adversaries a moment longer to interfere between him and the willing hearts which would believe if they could? The answer to all this was plain to our Lord, and is plain to us now: It was not the way of the Father's will. It would not fall in with that gradual development of life and history by which the Father works, and which must be the way to breed free, God-loving wills. It would be violent, theatrical, therefore poor in nature and in result,—not God-like in any way. Everything in God's doing comes harmoniously with and from all the rest. Son of Man, his history shall be a man's history, shall be The Man's history. Shall that begin with an exception? Yet it might well be a temptation to him who longed to do all he could for men. He was the Son of God: why should not the sons of God know it?

But as this temptation in the wilderness was an epitome and type of the temptations to come, against which for forty days he had been making himself strong, revolving truth beyond our reach, in whose light every commonest duty was awful and divine, a vision fit almost to oppress a God in his humiliation, so we shall understand the whole better if we look at his life in relation to it. As he refused to make stones bread, so throughout that life he never wrought a miracle to help himself; as he refused to cast himself from the temple to convince Satan or glory visibly in his Sonship, so he steadily refused to give the sign which the human Satans demanded, notwithstanding the offer of conviction which they held forth to bribe him to the grant. How easy it seems to have confounded them, and strengthened his followers! But such conviction would stand in the way of a better conviction in his disciples, and would do his adversaries only harm. For neither could in any true sense be convinced by such a show : it could but prove his power. It might prove so far the presence of a God; but would it prove that God? Would it bring him nearer to them, who could not see him in the face of his Son? To say *Thou art God*, without knowing what the *Thou* means—of what use is it? God is a name only, except we know *God*. Our Lord did not care to be so acknowledged.

On the same principle, the very miracles which from their character did partially reveal his character to those who already had faith in him, he would not do where unbelief predominated. He often avoided cities and crowds, and declined mighty works because of unbelief. Except for the loving help they gave the distressed, revealing him to their hearts as the Redeemer from evil, I doubt if he would have wrought a single miracle. I do not think he cared much about them. Certainly, as regarded the onlookers, he did not expect much to result from those mighty deeds. A mere marvel is practically soon forgotten, and long before it is forgotten, many minds have begun to doubt the senses, their own even, which communicated it. Inward sight alone can convince of truth; signs and wonders never. No number of signs can do more than convey a probability that he who shows them knows that of which he speaks. They cannot convey the truth. But the vision of the truth itself, in the knowledge of itself, a something altogether beyond the region of signs and wonders, is the power of God, is salvation. This vision was in the Lord's face and form to the pure in heart who were able to see God; but not in his signs and wonders to those who sought after such.

Yet it is easy to see how the temptation might for a moment work upon a mind that longed to enter upon its labors with the credentials of its truth. How the true heart longs to be received by its brethren—to be known in its truth! But no. The truth must show itself in God's time, in and by the labor. The kingdom must come in God's holy human way. Not by a stroke of grandeur, but by years of love, yea, by centuries of seeming bafflement, by æons of labor, must he grow into the hearts of the sons and daughters of his Father in heaven. The Lord himself *will* be bound by the changeless laws which are the harmony of the Father's being and utterance. He will *be*, not seem. He will be, and thereby, not therefore, seem. Yet, once more, even on him, the idea of asserting the truth in holy power such as he could have put forth, must have dawned in grandeur. The thought was good: to have yielded to it would have been the loss of the world; nay, far worse—ill inconceivable to the human mind— the God of obedience had fallen from his throne, and— all is blackness.

But let us not forget that the whole is a faint parable —faint I mean in relation to the grandeur of the reality, as the ring and the shoes are poor types (yet how dear!) of the absolute love of the Father to his prodigal children.

We shall now look at the third temptation. The first

## THE SECOND AND THIRD TEMPTATIONS. 183

was to help himself in his need; the second, perhaps, to assert the Father; the third to deliver his brethren.

To deliver them, that is, after the fashion of men—from the outside still. Indeed, the whole Temptation may be regarded as the contest of the seen and the unseen, of the outer and inner, of the likely and the true, of the show and the reality. And as in the others, the evil in this last lay in that it was a temptation to save his brethren, instead of doing the will of his Father.

Could it be other than a temptation to think that he might, if he would, lay a righteous grasp upon the reins of government, leap into the chariot of power, and ride forth conquering and to conquer? Glad visions arose before him of the prisoner breaking jubilant from the cell of injustice; of the widow lifting up the bowed head before the devouring Pharisee; of weeping children bursting into shouts at the sound of the wheels of the chariot before which oppression and wrong shrunk and withered, behind which sprung the fir-tree instead of the thorn, and the myrtle instead of the brier. What glowing visions of holy vengeance, what rosy dreams of human blessedness—and all from his hand—would crowd such a brain as his!—not like the castles-in-the-air of the aspiring youth, for he builds at random, because he knows that he cannot realize; but consistent and harmonious as well as grand, because he knew them within his reach. Could he not mould the people at his will? Could he not, transfigured in his snowy garments, call aloud in the streets of Jerusalem, "Behold your King"? And the fierce warriors of his nation would start at the sound; the ploughshare would be beaten into the sword, and the pruning-hook into the spear; and the nation, rushing to his call, learn war yet again indeed,—a grand, holy war—a crusade—no;

we should not have had *that* word; but a war against the tyrants of the race—the best, as they called themselves—who trod upon their brethren, and would not suffer them even to look to the heavens.—Ah! but when were his garments white as snow? When, through them, glorifiying them as it passed, did the light stream from his glorified body? Not when he looked to such a conquest; but when, on a mount like this, he "spake of the decease that he should *accomplish* at Jerusalem"! Why should this be "the sad end of the war"? "Thou shalt worship the Lord thy God, and him only shalt thou serve." Not even thine own visions of love and truth, O Saviour of the world, shall be thy guides to thy goal, but the will of thy Father in heaven.

But how would he, thus conquering, be a servant of Satan? Wherein would this be a falling-down and a worshiping of him (that is, an acknowledging of the worth of him) who was the lord of misrule and its pain?

I will not inquire whether such an enterprise could be accomplished without the worship of Satan—whether men could be managed for such an end without more or less of the trickery practised by every ambitious leader, every self-serving conqueror—without double-dealing, tact, flattery, finesse. I will not inquire into this, because, on the most distant supposition of our Lord being the leader of his country's armies, these things drop out of sight as impossibilities. If these were necessary, such a career for him refuses to be for a moment imagined. But I will ask whether to know better and do not so well, is not a serving of Satan;—whether to lead men on in the name of God as towards the best when the end is not the best, is not a serving of Satan;—whether to flatter their pride by making them conquerors of the enemies of their nation instead of their own evils, is not a serving of Satan;—in a word, whether, to desert the mission of God, who knew that men could not be set free in that way, and sent him to be a man, a true man, the one man, among them, that his life might become their life, and that so they might be as free in prison or on the cross, as upon a hill-side or on a throne,—whether, so deserting the truth, to give men over to the lie of believing other than spirit and truth to be the worship of the Father, other than love the fulfilling of the law, other than the offering of their best selves the service of God, other than obedient harmony with the primal love and truth and law, freedom,—whether, to desert God thus, and give men over thus, would not have been to fall down and worship the devil.

Not all the sovereignty of God, as the theologians call it, delegated to the Son, and administered by the wisdom of the Spirit that was given to him without measure, could have wrought the kingdom of heaven in one corner of our hearth. Nothing but the obedience of the Son, the obedience unto the death, the absolute *doing* of the will of God because it was the truth, could redeem the prisoner, the widow, the orphan. But it would redeem them by redeeming the conquest-ridden conqueror too, the stripe-giving jailor, the unjust judge, the devouring Pharisee himself with the insatiable moth-eaten heart. The earth should be free because Love was stronger than Death. Therefore should fierceness and wrong and hypocrisy and God-service play out their weary play. He would not pluck the spreading branches of the tree; he would lay the axe to its root. It would take time; but the tree would be dead at last—dead, and cast into the lake of fire. It would take time ; but his Father had time enough and to spare. It would take courage and strength and self-denial and endurance ; but his Father could give him all. It would cost pain of body and mind, yea, agony and torture ; but those he was ready to take on himself. It would cost him the vision of many sad and, to all but him, hopeless sights ; he must see tears without wiping them, hear sighs without changing them into laughter, see the dead lie, and let them lie ; see Rachel weeping for her children and refusing to be comforted ; he must look on his brothers and sisters crying as children over their broken toys, and must not mend them ; he must go on to the grave, and they not know that thus he was setting all things right for them. His work must be one with and completing God's Creation and God's History. The disappointment and sorrow and fear he could, he would bear. The will of God should be done. Man should be free—not merely man as he thinks of himself, but man as God thinks of him. The divine idea shall be set free in the divine bosom ; the man on earth shall see his angel face to face. He shall grow into the likeness of the divine thought, free not in his own fancy, but in absolute divine fact of being, as in God's idea. The great and beautiful and perfect will of God *must* be done.

"Get thee hence, Satan : for it is written, Thou shalt worship the Lord thy God, and him only shalt thou serve." It was when Peter would have withstood him as he set his face steadfastly to meet this death at Jerusalem, that he gave him the same kind of answer that he now gave to Satan, calling him Satan too. "Then the devil leaveth him, and behold angels came and ministered unto him." So saith St. Matthew. They brought him the food he had waited for, walking in the strength of the word. He would have died if it had not come now. "And when the devil had ended all the temptation, he departed from him for a season." So saith St. Luke. Then Satan ventured once more. When?

Was it then, when at the last moment, in the agony of the last faint, the Lord cried out, "Why hast thou forsaken me?" when, having done the great work, having laid it aside clean and pure as the linen cloth that was ready now to infold him, another cloud than that on the mount overshadowed his soul, and out of it came a voiceless persuasion that, after all was done, God did not care for his work or for him?

Even in those words the adversary was foiled—and for ever. For when he seemed to be forsaken, his cry was still, "*My God! my God!*"

ALMIGHTY and eternal God, who hast graciously bestowed on us the clear light of thy truth, whereby we, notwithstanding our sins, can attain through Christ a childlike trust in thee; we humbly pray thee give us thy Holy Spirit, that we may trust thee with our whole hearts, and may deny ourselves, and bear the cross after thy dear Son in steadfast patience, through Jesus Christ, our Lord.
*Amen.*

## XVIII.

## THE CRY, "ELOI, ELOI."

"My God, my God, why hast thou forsaken me?"—Matthew 27 : 46.

I do not know that I should dare to approach this of all utterances into which human breath has ever been moulded, most awful in import, did I not feel that, containing both germ and blossom of the final devotion, it contains therefore the deepest practical lesson the human heart has to learn. The Lord, the Revealer, hides nothing that can be revealed, and will not warn away the foot that treads in naked humility even upon the ground of that terrible conflict between him and Evil, when the smoke of the battle, that was fought not only with garments rolled in blood but with burning and fuel of fire, rose up between him and his Father, and, for the one terrible moment ere he broke the bonds of life, and walked weary and triumphant into his arms, hid God from the eyes of his Son. He will give us even to meditate the one thought that slew him at last, when he could bear no more, and fled to the Father to know that he loved him, and was well pleased with him.

For Satan had come at length yet again, to urge him with his last temptation; to tell him that although he had done his part, God had forgotten his; that although he had lived by the word of his mouth, that mouth

## THE CRY, "ELOI, ELOI."

had no word more to speak to him; that although he had refused to tempt him, God had left him to be tempted more than he could bear; that although he had worshiped none other, for that worship God did not care. The Lord hides not his sacred sufferings, for truth is light, and would be light in the minds of men. The Holy Child, the Son of the Father, has nothing to conceal, but all the Godhead to reveal. Let us then put off our shoes, and draw near, and bow the head, and kiss those feet that bear forever the scars of our victory. In those feet we clasp the safety of our suffering, our sinning brotherhood.

It is with the holiest fear that we should approach the terrible fact of the sufferings of our Lord. Let no one think that those were less because he was more. The more delicate the nature, the more alive to all that is lovely and true, lawful and right, the more does it feel the antagonism of pain, the inroad of death upon life; the more dreadful is that breach of the harmony of things whose sound is torture. He felt more than man could feel, because he had a larger feeling. He was even therefore worn out sooner than another man would have been. These sufferings were awful indeed when they began to invade the region about the will; when the struggle to keep consciously trusting in God began to sink in darkness; when the Will of The Man put forth its last determined effort in that cry after the vanishing vision of the Father: *My God, my God, why hast thou forsaken me?* Never had it been so with him before. Never before had he been unable to see God beside him. Yet never was God nearer him than now. For never was Jesus more divine. He could not see, could not feel him near; and yet it is "*My* God" that he cries.

Thus the Will of Jesus, in the very moment when his faith seems about to yield, is finally triumphant. It has no *feeling* now to support it, no beatific vision to absorb it. It stands naked in his soul and tortured, as he stood naked and scourged before Pilate. Pure and simple and surrounded by fire, it declares for God. The sacrifice ascends in the cry, *My God*. The cry comes not out of happiness, out of peace, out of hope. Not even out of suffering comes that cry. It was a cry *in* desolation, but it came out of Faith. It is the last voice of Truth, speaking when it can but cry. The divine horror of that moment is unfathomable by human soul. It was blackness of darkness. And yet he would believe. Yet he would hold fast. God was his God yet. *My God*—and in the cry came forth the Victory, and all was over soon. Of the peace that followed that cry, the peace of a perfect soul, large as the universe, pure as light, ardent as life, victorious for God and his brethren, he himself alone can ever know the breadth and length, and depth and height.

Without this last trial of all, the temptations of our Master had not been so full as the human cup could hold; there would have been one region through which we had to pass wherein we might call aloud upon our Captain-Brother, and there would be no voice or hearing: he had avoided the fatal spot! The temptations of the desert came to the young, strong man with his road before him, and the presence of his God around him; nay, gathered their very force from the exuberance of his conscious faith. "Dare and do, for God is with thee," said the devil. "I know it, and therefore I will wait," returned the king of his brothers. And now, after three years of divine action, when his course is run, when the old age of finished work is come, when the whole frame is tortured until the regnant brain falls whirling down the blue gulf of fainting, and the giving up of the ghost is at hand, when the friends have forsaken him and fled, comes the voice of the enemy again at his ear: "Despair and die, for God is not with thee. All is in vain. Death, not Life, is thy refuge. Make haste to Hades, where thy torture will be over. Thou hast deceived thyself. He never was with thee. He was the God of Abraham. Abraham is dead. Whom makest thou thyself?" "My God, my God, why hast thou forsaken me?" the Master cries. For God was his God still, although he had forsaken him—forsaken *his vision* that his faith might glow out triumphant; forsaken *himself?* no; come nearer to him than ever: come nearer, even as—but with a yet deeper, more awful pregnancy of import—even as the Lord himself withdrew from the bodily eyes of his friends, that he might dwell in their profoundest being.

I do not think it was our Lord's deepest trial when in the garden he prayed that the cup might pass from him, and prayed yet again that the will of the Father might be done. For that will was then present with him. He was living and acting in that will. But now the foreseen horror has come. He is drinking the dread cup, and the Will has vanished from his eyes. Were that Will visible in his suffering, his will could bow with tearful gladness under the shelter of its grandeur. But now his will is left alone to drink the cup of The Will in torture. In the sickness of this agony, the Will of Jesus arises perfect at last; and of itself, unsupported now, declares—a naked consciousness of misery hung in the waste darkness of the universe—declares for God, in defiance of pain, of death, of apathy, of self, of negation, of the blackness within and around it; calls aloud upon the vanished God.

This is the Faith of the Son of God. God withdrew, as it were, that the perfect Will of the Son might arise and go forth to find the Will of the Father.

Is it possible that even then he thought of the lost sheep who could not believe that God was their Father; and for them, too, in all their loss and blindness and unlove, cried, saying the word they might say, knowing for them that *God* means *Father* and more, and knowing now, as he had never known till now, what a fearful thing it is to be without God and without hope? I dare not answer the question I put.

But wherein or what can this Alpine apex of faith have to do with the creatures who call themselves Christians, creeping about in the valleys, hardly knowing that there are mountains above them, save that they take offence at, and stumble over, the pebbles washed across their path by the glacier streams? I will tell you. We are and remain such creeping Christians, because we look at ourselves and not at Christ; because we gaze at the marks of our own soiled feet, and the trail of our own defiled garments, instead of up at the snows of purity, whither the soul of Christ clomb. Each, putting his foot in the footprint of the Master, and so defacing it, turns to examine how far his neighbor's footprint corresponds with that which he still calls the Master's, although it is but his own. Or, having committed a petty fault, I mean a fault such as only a petty creature could commit, we mourn over the defilement to ourselves, and the shame of it before our friends, children, or servants, instead of hastening to make the due confession and amends to our fellow, and then, forgetting our paltry self, with its well-earned disgrace, lift up our eyes to the glory which alone will quicken the true man in us, and kill the peddling creature we so wrongly call our *self*. The true self is that which can look Jesus in the face, and say, *My Lord*.

When the inward sun is shining, and the wind of thought, blowing where it lists amid the flowers and leaves of fancy and imagination, rouses glad forms and feelings, it is easy to look upwards, and say, *My God*. It is easy when the frosts of external failure have braced the mental nerves to healthy endurance and fresh effort after labor, it is easy then to turn to God and trust in him, in whom all honest exertion gives an ability as well as a right to trust. It is easy in pain, so long as it does not pass certain undefinable bounds, to hope in God for deliverance, or pray for strength to endure. But what is to be done when all feeling is gone? when a man does not know whether he believes or not, whether he loves or not? when art, poetry, religion are nothing to him, so swallowed up is he in pain, or mental depression, or disappointment, or temptation, or he knows not what? It seems to him then that God does not care for him, and certainly he does not care for God. If he is still humble, he thinks that he is so bad that God cannot care for him. And he then believes for the time that God loves us only because and when and while we love him; instead of believing that God loves us always because he is our God, and that we live only by his love. Or he does not believe in a God at all, which is better.

So long as we have nothing to say to God, nothing to do with him, save in the sunshine of the mind when we feel him near us, we are poor creatures, willed upon, not willing; reeds, flowering reeds, it may be, and pleasant to behold, but only reeds blown about of the wind; not bad, but poor creatures.

And how, in such a condition, do we generally act? Do we not sit mourning over the loss of our feelings? or worse, make frantic efforts to rouse them? or ten times worse, relapse into a state of temporary atheism, and yield to the pressing temptation? or, being heartless, consent to remain careless, conscious of evil thoughts and low feelings alone, but too lazy, too content to rouse ourselves against them? We know we must get rid of them some day, but meantime—never mind; we do not *feel* them bad, we do not feel anything else good; we are asleep and we know it, and we cannot be troubled to wake. No impulse comes to arouse us, and so we remain as we are.

God does not, by the instant gift of his Spirit, make us always feel right, desire good, love purity, aspire after him and his will. Therefore either he will not, or he cannot. If he will not, it must be because it would not be well to do so. If he cannot, then he would not if he could; else a better condition than God is conceivable to the mind of God—a condition in which he could save the creatures whom he has made, better than he can save them. The truth is this: He wants to make us in his own image, *choosing* the good, *refusing* the evil. How should he effect this if he were *always* moving us from within, as he does at divine intervals, towards the beauty of holiness? God gives us room *to be;* does not oppress us with his will; "stands away from us," that we may act from ourselves, that we may exercise the pure will for good. Do not, therefore, imagine me to mean that we can do anything of ourselves without God. If we choose the right at last, it is all God's doing, and only the more his that it is ours, only in a far more marvelous way his than if he had kept us filled with all holy impulses precluding the need of choice. For up to this very point, for this very point, he has been educating us, leading us, pushing us, driving us, enticing us, that we may choose him and his will, and so be tenfold more his children, of his own best making, in the freedom of the will found our own first in its loving sacrifice to him, for which in his grand fatherhood he has been thus working from the foundations of the earth, than we could be in the most ecstatic worship flowing from the divinest impulse, without this *willing* sacrifice. For God made our individuality as well as, and a greater marvel than, our dependence; made our *apartness* from himself, that freedom should bind us divinely dearer to himself, with a new and inscrutable marvel of love; for the Godhead is still at the root, is the making root of our individuality, and the freer the man, the stronger the bond that binds him to him who made his freedom. He made our wills, and is striving to make them free; for only in the perfection of our individuality and the freedom of our wills can we be altogether his children. This is full of mystery, but can we not see enough in it to make us very glad and very peaceful?

Not in any other act than one which, in spite of impulse or of weakness, declares for the Truth, for God, does the will spring into absolute freedom, into true life.

See, then, what lies within our reach every time that we are thus lapped in the folds of night. The highest condition of the human will is in sight, is attainable. I say not the highest condition of the Human Being; that surely lies in the Beatific Vision, in the sight of God. But the highest condition of the Human Will, as distinct, not as separated from God, is when, not seeing God, not seeming to itself to grasp him at all, it yet holds him fast. It cannot continue in this condition, for, not finding, not seeing God, the man would die; but the will thus asserting itself, the man has passed from death into life, and the vision is nigh at hand. Then first, thus free, in thus asserting its freedom, is the individual will one with the Will of God; the child is finally restored to the father; the childhood and the fatherhood meet in one; the brotherhood of the race arises from the dust; and the prayer of our Lord is answered, "I in them and thou in me, that they may be made perfect in one." Let us then arise in God-born strength every time that we feel the darkness closing, or become aware that it has closed around us, and say, "I am of the Light and not of the Darkness."

Troubled soul, thou art not bound to feel, but thou art bound to arise. God loves thee whether thou feelest or not. Thou canst not love when thou wilt, but thou art bound to fight the hatred in thee to the last. Try not to feel good when thou art not good, but cry to him who is good. He changes not because thou changest. Nay, he has an especial tenderness of love towards thee for that thou art in the dark, and hast no light, and his heart is glad when thou dost arise and say, "I will go to my Father." For he sees thee through all the gloom through which thou canst not see him. Will thou his will. Say unto him: "My God, I am very dull and low and hard; but thou art wise and high and tender, and thou art my God. I am thy child. Forsake me not." Then fold the arms of thy faith, and wait in quietness until light goes up in thy darkness. Fold the arms of thy Faith I say, but not of thy Action: bethink thee of something that

## THE CRY, "ELOI, ELOI." 197

thou oughtest to do, and go and do it, if it be but the sweeping of a room, or the preparing of a meal, or a visit to a friend. Heed not thy feelings: Do thy work.

As God lives by his own will, and we live in him, so has he given to us power to will in ourselves. How much better should we not fare if, finding that we are standing with our heads bowed away from the good, finding that we have no feeble inclination to seek the source of our life, we should yet *will* upwards toward God, rousing that essence of life in us, which he has given us from his own heart, to call again upon him who is our Life, who can fill the emptiest heart, rouse the deadest conscience, quicken the dullest feeling, and strengthen the feeblest will!

Then, if ever the time should come, as perhaps it must come to each of us, when all consciousness of well-being shall have vanished, when the earth shall be but a sterile promontory, and the heavens a dull and pestilent congregation of vapors, when man nor woman shall delight us more, nay, when God himself shall be but a name, and Jesus an old story, then, even then, when a Death far worse than "that phantom of grisly bone" is griping at our hearts, and having slain love, hope, faith, forces existence upon us only in agony, then, even then, we shall be able to cry out with our Lord, "My God, my God, why hast thou forsaken me?" Nor shall we die then, I think, without being able to take up his last words as well, and say, "*Father, into thy hands I commend my spirit.*"

## XIX.

## THE WAY.

"If thou wouldest be perfect."—Matthew 19 ; 21.

For reasons many and profound, amongst the least because of the fragmentary nature of the records, he who would read them without the candle of the Lord —that is, the light of truth in his inward parts—must not merely fall into a thousand errors—a thing for such a one of less moment—but must fail utterly of perceiving and understanding the life therein struggling to reveal itself—the life, that is, of the Son of Man, the thought, the feeling, the intent of the Lord himself, that by which he lived, that which is himself, that which he poured out for us. Yet the one thing he has to do with is this life of Jesus, his inner nature and being, manifested through his outer life, according to the power of sight in the spiritual eye that looks thereupon.

In contemplating the incident revealing that life of which I would now endeavor to unfold the truth, those who do not study the Greek Testament must use the revised version. Had I not known and rejoiced in it long before the revision appeared, I should have owed the revisers endless gratitude, if for nothing more than the genuine reading of St. Mathew's report of the story of the youth who came to our Lord. Whoever does not welcome the change must fail to see its preciousness.

## THE WAY. 199

Reading, then, from the revised version, we find in St. Matthew the commencement of the conversation between Jesus and the young man very different from that given in the Gospels of St. Mark and St. Luke. There is not for that the smallest necessity for rejecting either account; they blend perfectly, and it is to me a joy unspeakable to have both. Put together, they give a completed conversation. Here it is as I read it; let my fellow-students look to the differing—far from opposing—reports, and see how naturally they combine.

"Good Master," said the kneeling youth, and is interrupted by the Master. "Why callest thou me good?" he returns: "None is good save one, even God." Daring no reply to this, the youth leaves it, and betakes himself to his object in addressing the Lord. "What good thing shall I do," he says, "that I may have eternal life?" But again the Lord takes hold of the word *good*. "Why askest thou me concerning that which is good," he rejoins: "One there is who is good. But if thou wouldest enter into life, keep the commandments."—"Which?"—"Thou shalt not kill, Thou shalt not commit adultery, Thou shalt not steal, Thou shalt not bear false witness, Honor thy father and thy mother; and, Thou shalt love thy neighbor as thyself."—"All these things have I observed: what lack I yet?"—"If thou wouldest be perfect, go, sell that thou hast, and give to the poor, and thou shalt have treasure in heaven; and come, follow me."

Let us regard the story.—As Jesus went out of a house (see St. Mark 10: 10, 17), the young man came running to him, and, kneeling down in the way, addressed him as "Good Master."

The words with which the Lord interrupts his address

reveal the whole attitude of the Lord's being. At that moment, at every and each moment, just as much as when in the garden of Gethsemane, or encountering any of those hours which men call crises of life, his whole thought, his whole delight, was in the thought, in the will, in the being of his Father. The joy of the Lord's life, that which made it life to him, was the Father; of him he was always thinking, to him he was always turning. I suppose most men have some thought of pleasure or satisfaction, or strength to which they turn when action pauses, life becomes for a moment still, and the wheel sleeps on its own swiftness: with Jesus it needed no pause of action, no rush of renewed consciousness, to send him home; his thought was ever and always his Father. To its home in the heart of the Father his heart ever turned. That was his treasure-house, the jewel of his mind, the mystery of his gladness, claiming all degrees and shades of delight, from peace and calmest content to ecstasy. His life was hid in God. No vain show could enter at his eyes; every truth and grandeur of life passed before him as it was; neither ambition nor disappointment could distort them to his eternal childlike gaze; he beheld and loved them from the bosom of the Father. It was not for himself he came to the world—not to establish his own power over the doings, his own influence over the hearts of men: he came that they might know the Father who was his joy, his life. The sons of men were his Father's children like himself: that the Father should have them all in his bosom was the one thought of his heart: that should be his doing for his Father, cost him what it might! He came to do his will, and on the earth was the same he had been from the beginning, the eternal first. He was not interested in himself, but in his

Father, and in his Father's children. He did not care to be himself called *good*. It was not of consequence to him. He was there to let men see the goodness of the Father in whom he gloried. For that he entered the weary dream of the world, in which the glory was so dulled and clouded. You call me good! you should know my Father!

For the Lord's greatness consisted in his Father's being greater than he: he who calls into being is greater than one who is called. The Father was always the Father, the Son was always the Son; yet the Son is not of himself, but by the Father; he does not live by his own power, like the Father. If there were no Father, there would be no Son. All that is the Lord's is the Father's, and all that is the Father's he has given to the Son. The Lord's goodness is of the Father's goodness; because the Father is good, the Son is good. When the word *good* enters the ears of the Son, his heart lifts it at once to his Father, the Father of all. His words contain no denial of goodness to himself: in his grand self-regard he was not the original of his goodness, neither did he care for his own goodness, except to be good: it was to him a matter of course. But for his Father's goodness, he would spend life, suffering, labor, death, to make that known! His other children must learn to give him his due, and love him as did the primal Son! The Father was all in all to the Son; and the Son no more thought of his own goodness than an honest man thinks of his honesty. When the good man sees goodness, he thinks of his own evil: Jesus had no evil to think of, but neither does he thinks of his goodness; he delights in his Father's. "Why callest thou me good? None is good save one, even God."

Checked thus, the youth turns to the question which,

working in his heart, had brought him running, and made him kneel: what good thing shall he do that he may have eternal life? It is unnecessary to inquire precisely what he meant by *eternal life*. Whatever shape the thing took to him, that shape represented a something he needed and had not got—a something which, it was clear to him, could be gained only in some path of good. But he thought to gain a thing by a *doing*, when the very thing desired was a *being*: he would have that as a possession which must possess him. The Lord cared neither for isolated truth nor for orphaned deed. It was truth in the inward parts, it was the good heart, the mother of good deeds, he cherished. It was the live, active, knowing, breathing good he came to further. He cared for no speculation in morals or religion. It was good men he cared about, not notions of good things or even good actions, save as the outcome of life, save as the bodies in which the primary actions of love and will in the soul took shape and came forth. Could he by one word have set at rest all the questionings of philosophy as to the supreme good and the absolute truth, I venture to say that word he would not have uttered. But he would die to make men good and true. His whole heart would respond to the cry of sad publican or despairing Pharisee, "How am I to be good?"

When the Lord says, "Why askest thou me concerning that which is good?" we must not put emphasis on the *me*, as if the Lord refused the question, as he had declined the epithet: he was the proper person to ask, only the question was not the right one: the good thing was a small matter; the good Being was all in all. "Why ask me about the good thing? There is one living good, in whom the good thing, and all good, is alive and ever operant. Ask me not about the good thing, but the good Person, the good Being, the origin of all good"—who, because he is, can make good. He is the one live good, ready with his life to communicate living good, the power of being—and so doing—good, for he makes good itself to exist. It is not with this good thing and that good thing we have to do, but with that Power whence comes our power even to speak the word *good*. We have to do with him to whom no one can look without the need of being good waking up in his heart; to think about him is to begin to be good. To do a good thing is to do a good thing; to know God is to be good. It is not to make us do all things right he cares, but to makes us hunger and thirst after a righteousness possessing which we shall never need to think of what is or is not good, but shall refuse the evil and choose the good by motion of the will which is at once necessity and choice. You see again he refers him immediately as before to his Father.

But I am anxious that no one should mistake. Observe the question in the young man's mind is not about the doing or not doing of something he knows to be right. Had such been the case, the Lord would have permitted no question at all; the one thing he insists upon is the *doing* of the thing we know we ought to do. In the instance present, the youth looking out for some unknown good thing to do, he sends him back to the doing of what he knows, and that in answer to his question concerning the way to eternal life.

A man must have something to do in the matter, and may well ask such a question of any teacher! The Lord does not for a moment turn away from it, and only declines the form of it to help the youth to what he really needs. He has, in truth, already more than hinted where the answer lies, namely, in God himself; but that the young man is not capable of receiving: he must begin with him farther back: "If thou wouldest enter into life, keep the commandments:" for verily, if the commandments have nothing to do with entering into life, why were they ever given to men? This is his task—he must keep the commandments.

Then the road to eternal life is the keeping of the commandments? Had the Lord not said so, what man of common moral sense would ever dare say otherwise? What else can be the way into life but the doing of what the Lord of life tells the creatures he has made, and whom he would have live forever, that they must do? It is the beginning of the way. If a man had kept all those commandments, yet would he not therefore have in him life eternal; nevertheless, without keeping of the commandments, there is no entering into life; the keeping of them is the path to the gate of life; it is not life, but it is the way—so much of the way to it. Nay, the keeping of the commandments, consciously or unconciously, has closest and essential relation to eternal life.

The Lord says nothing about the first table of the law: why does he not tell this youth, as he did the lawyer, that to love God is everything? He had given him a glimpse of the essence of his own life, had pointed the youth to the heart of all—for him to think of afterwards: he was not ready for it yet. He wanted eternal life: to love God with all our heart, and soul, and strength, and mind, is to know God, and to know him is life eternal; that is the end of the whole saving matter; it is no human beginning, it is the grand end and eternal beginning of all things; but the youth was not capable of it. To begin with that would be as sensible as to say to one asking how to reach the top of some mountain, "Just set your foot on that shining snow-clad peak, high there in the blue, and you will at once be where you wish to go!" Love God with all your heart, and eternal life is yours : it would have been to mock him. Why? he could not yet see or believe that that was eternal life! He was not yet capable of looking upon life even from afar! How many *Christians* are? How many know that they are not? The Lord answers his question directly, tells him what to do—a thing he can do—to enter into life; he must keep the commandments!—and when he asks, "Which?" specifies only those that have to do with his neighbor, ending with the highest and most difficult of them.

"But no man can perfectly keep a single commandment of the second table any more than of the first."

Surely not—else why should they have been given? But is there no meaning in the word *keep*, or *observe*, except it be qualified by *perfectly?* Is there no keeping but a perfect keeping?—"None that God cares for."— There I think you utterly wrong. That no keeping but a perfect one will *satisfy* God, I hold with all my heart and strength ; but that there is none else he cares for, is one of the lies of the enemy. What father is not pleased with the first tottering attempt of his little one to walk? What father would be satisfied with anything but the manly step of the full-grown son?

When the Lord has definitely mentioned the commandments he means, the young man returns at once that he has observed those from his youth up ; are we to take his word for it? The Lord at least takes his word for it : he looked on him and loved him. Was the Lord deceived in him? Did he tell an untruth? or did the Master believe he had kept the commandments perfectly? There must be a keeping of the commandments, which, although anything but perfect, is yet acceptable to the heart of him from whom nothing is hid. In that way the youth had kept the commandments. He had for years been putting forth something of his life-energy to keep them. Nor, however he had failed of perfection, had he missed the end for which they were given him to keep. For the immediate end of the commandments never was that men should succeed in obeying them, but that finding they could not do that which yet must be done, finding the more they tried the more was required of them, they should be driven to the source of life and law—of their life and his law—to seek from him such reinforcement of life as should make the fulfilment of the law as possible, yea, as natural, as necessary. This result had been wrought in the youth. His observance had given him no satisfaction; he was not at rest; but he desired eternal life —of which there was no word in the law: the keeping of the law had served to develop a hunger which no law or its keeping could fill. Must not the imperfection of his keeping of the commandments, even in the lower sense in which he read them, have helped to reveal how far they were beyond any keeping of his, how their implicit demands rose into the infinitude of God's perfection?

Having kept the commandments, the youth needed and was ready for a further lesson: the Lord would not leave him where he was; he had come to seek and to save. He saw him in sore need of perfection—the thing the commonplace Christian thinks he can best do without—the thing the elect hungers after with an eternal hunger. Perfection, the perfection of the

Father, is eternal life. "If thou wouldst be perfect," said the Lord. What an honor for the youth to be by him supposed desirous of perfection! And what an enormous demand does he, upon the supposition, make of him! To gain the perfection he desired, the one thing lacking was, that he should sell all that he had, give it to the poor, and follow the Lord! Could this be all that lay between him and entering into life? God only knows what the victory of such an obedience might at once have wrought in him! Much, much more would be necessary before perfection was reached, but certainly the next step, to sell and follow, would have been the step into life: had he taken it, in the very act would have been born in him that whose essence and vitality is eternal life, needing but process to develop it into the glorious consciousness of oneness with The Life.

There was nothing like this in the law: was it not hard? —hard to let earth go, and take heaven instead? for eternal life, to let dead things drop? to turn his back on Mammon, and follow Jesus? lose his rich friends, and be of the Master's household? Let him say it was hard who does not know the Lord, who has never thirsted after righteousness, never longed for the life eternal!

The youth had got on so far, was so pleasing in the eyes of the Master, that he would show him the highest favor he could; he would take him to be with him—to walk with him, and rest with him, and go from him only to do for him what he did for his Father in heaven —to plead with men, be a mediator between God and men. He would set him free at once, a child of the kingdom, and heir of the life eternal.

I do not suppose that the youth was one whom ordinary people would call a lover of money; I do not believe he was covetous, or desired even the large increase of his possessions; I imagine he was just like most good men of property: he valued his possessions —looked on them as a good. I suspect that in the case of another, he would have regarded such possession almost a merit, a desert; would value a man more who had means, value a man less who had none—like most of my friends here. They have not a notion how entirely they will one day have to alter their judgment, or have it altered for them, in this respect: well for them if they alter it for themselves!

From this false way of thinking, and all the folly and unreality that accompany it, the Lord would deliver the young man. As the thing was, he was a slave; for a man is in bondage to whatever he cannot part with that is less than himself. He could have taken his possessions from him by an exercise of his own will, but there would have been little good in that; he wished to do it by the exercise of the young man's will: that would be a victory indeed for both! So would he enter into freedom and life, delivered from the bondage of Mammon by the lovely will of the Lord in him, one with his own. By the putting forth of the divine energy in him, he would escape the corruption that is in the world through lust—that is, the desire or pleasure of *having*.

The young man would not. Was the Lord then premature in his demand upon him? Was the youth not ready for it? Was it meant for a test, and not as an actual word of deliverance? Did he show the child a next step on the stair too high for him to set his foot upon? I do not believe it. He gave him the very next lesson in the divine education for which he was ready. It was possible for him to respond; to give birth by obedience, to the redeemed and redeeming will, and so be free. It was time the demand should be made upon him. Do you say, "But he would not respond, he would not obey"? Then it was time, I answer, that he should refuse, that he should know what manner of spirit he was of, and meet the confusions of soul, and the sad searchings of heart, that must follow. A time comes to every man when he must obey, or make such refusal—*and know it.*

Shall I then be supposed to mean that the refusal of the young man was of necessity final? that he was therefore lost? that, because he declined to enter into life, the door of life was closed against him? Verily, I have not so learned Christ. And that the lesson was not lost, I see in this, that "he went away sorrowful." Was such sorrow, in the mind of an earnest youth, likely to grow less or to grow more? Was all he had gone through in the way of obedience to be of no good to him? Could the nature of one who had kept the commandments be so slight that, after having sought and talked with Jesus, held communion with him who is the Life, he would care less about eternal life than before? Many, alas! have looked upon his face, yet have never seen him, and have turned back; some have kept company with him for years, and denied him; but their weakness is not the measure of the patience or the resources of God. Perhaps this youth was never one of the Lord's so long as the Lord was on the earth; but perhaps, when he saw that the Master himself cared nothing for the wealth he had told him to cast away, that, instead of ascending the throne of his fathers, he let the people do with him what they would, and left the world the poor man he lived in it, by its meanest door, perhaps then the young ruler became one of those who sold all they had, and came and laid the money at the apostles' feet.

In the meantime, he had that in his soul which made it heavy: by the gravity of his riches the world held him, and would not let him rise. He counted his weight his strength, and it was his weakness. Moneyless in God's upper air, he would have had power indeed. Money is the power of this world—a power for defeat and failure to him who holds it—a weakness to be overcome ere a man can be strong; yet many decent people fancy it a power of the world to come! It is indeed a little power, as food and drink, as bodily strength, as the winds and the waves are powers; but it is no mighty thing for the redemption of men; yea, to the redemption of those who have it, it is the saddest obstruction. To make this youth capable of eternal life, clearly—and the more clearly that he went away sorrowful—the first thing was to make a poor man of him! He would doubtless have gladly devoted his wealth to the service of the Master, yea, and gone with him, *as a rich man*, to spend it for him, but part with it to free him for his service—that he could not *yet*!

And how now would he go on with his keeping of the commandments? Would he not begin to see more plainly his shortcomings, the larger scope of their requirements? Might he not feel the keeping of them more imperative than ever, yet impossible without something he had not? The commandments can never be kept while there is a strife to keep them; the man is overwhelmed in the weight of their broken pieces. It needs a clean heart to have pure hands, all the power of a live soul to keep the law—a power of life, not of struggle; the strength of love, not the effort of duty.

## THE WAY. 211

One day the truth of his conduct must dawn upon that young man with absolute clearness. Bitter must be the discovery. He had refused the life eternal! had turned his back upon The Life! In deepest humility and shame, yet with the profound consolation of repentance, he would return to the Master, and bemoan his unteachableness. There are those who, like St. Paul, can say, "I did wrong, but I did it in ignorance; my heart was not right, and I did not know it." The remorse of such must be very different from that of one who, brought to the point of being capable of embracing the truth, turned from it and refused to be set free. To him the time will come, God only knows its hour, when he will see the nature of his deed, *with the knowledge that he was dimly seeing it so even when he did it:* the alternative had been put before him. And all those months, or days, or hours, or moments, he might have been following the Master, hearing the words he spoke, through the windows of his eyes looking into the very gulfs of Godhead!

The sum of the matter in regard to the youth is this: he had begun early to climb the eternal stair: he had kept the commandments, and by every keeping had climbed: but, because he was *well to do*—a phrase of unconscious irony—he felt well to be—quite, but for that lack of eternal life! His possessions gave him a standing in the world—a position of consequence—of value in his eyes. He knew himself looked up to; he liked to be looked up to; he looked up to himself because of his *means,* forgetting that *means* are but tools, and poor tools, too. To part with his wealth would be to sink to the level of his inferiors! Why should he not keep it? why not use it in the service of the Master? What wisdom could there be in throwing away such a grand advantage? He could devote it, but he could not cast it from him! He could devote it, but he could not devote himself! He could not make himself naked as a little child, and let his Father take him! To him it was not the word of wisdom the "Good Master" spoke. How could precious money be a hindrance to entering into life? How could a rich man believe he would be of more value without his money? that the casting of it away would make him one of God's Anakim? that the battle of God could be better fought without its impediment? that his work refused, as an obstruction, the aid of wealth? But the Master had repudiated money that he might do the will of his Father; and the disciple must be as his Master. Had he done as the Master told him, he would soon have come to understand. Obedience is the opener of eyes.

There is this danger to every good youth in keeping the commandments, that he will probably think of himself more highly than he ought to think. He may be correct enough as to facts, and in his deductions and consequent self-regard, be anything but fair. He may think himself a fine fellow, when he is but an ordinarily reasonable youth, trying to do but the first thing necessary to the name or honor of a man. Doubtless such a youth is exceptional among youths; but the number of fools not yet acknowledging the first condition of manhood nowise alters the fact that he who has begun to recognize duty, and acknowledge the facts of his being, is but a tottering child on the path of life. He is on the path; he is as wise as at the time he can be; the Father's arms are stretched out to receive him; but he is not therefore a wonderful being; not therefore a model of wisdom; not at all the admirable creature his largely remaining folly would, in his worst

## THE WAY

moments (that is, when he feels best), persuade him to think himself; he is just one of God's poor creatures. What share this besetting sin of *the good young man* may have had in the miserable failure of this one, we need not inquire; but it may well be that he thought the Master undervalued his work as well as his wealth, and was less than fair to him.

To return to the summing up of the matter—the youth, climbing the stair of eternal life, had come to a landing-place where not a step more was visible. On the cloud-swathed platform he stands looking in vain for further ascent. What he thought with himself he wanted, I cannot tell; his idea of eternal life I do not know; I can hardly think it was but the poor idea of living forever, all that commonplace minds grasp at for eternal life—its mere concomitant shadow, in itself not worth thinking about, not for a moment to be disputed, and taken for granted by all devout Jews: when a man has eternal life, that is, when he is one with God, what should he do but live forever? without oneness with God, the continuance of existence would be to me the all but unsurpassable curse—the unsurpassable itself being, a God other than the God I see in Jesus; but whatever his idea, it must have held in it, though perhaps only in solution, all such notions as he had concerning God and man and a common righteousness. While thus he stands, then, alone and helpless, behold the form of the Son of Man! It is God himself come to meet the climbing youth, to take him by the hand, and lead him up his own stair, the only stair by which ascent can be made. He shows him the first step of it through the mist. His feet are heavy; they have golden shoes. To go up that stair, he must throw aside his shoes. He must walk bare-footed into life eternal. Rather than so, rather than stride free-limbed up the everlasting stair to the bosom of the Father, he will keep his precious shoes! It is better to drag them about on the earth, than part with them for a world where they are useless!

But how miserable his precious things, his golden vessels, his embroidered garments, his stately house, must have seemed when he went back to them from the face of the Lord! Surely, it cannot have been long before, in shame and misery, he cast all from him, even as Judas cast from him the thirty pieces of silver, in the agony of every one who wakes to the fact that he has preferred money to the Master! For, although never can man be saved without being freed from his possessions, it is yet only *hard*, not *impossible*, for a rich man to enter into the kingdom of God.

O GOD, who desirest not sacrifice, and hast no delight in burnt-offering, but has showed us what is good; and who requirest of us to do justly, to love mercy, and to walk humbly with thee, grant us, we pray thee, true repentance; and so direct and govern our hearts and lives that we may render a constant and unfeigned obedience to thy holy laws; that, offering to thee the sacrifices of righteousness, we may be accepted in thy sight, and may obtain our petitions, through Jesus Christ, our Lord. *Amen.*

## XX.

## THE HARDNESS OF THE WAY.

"CHILDREN, HOW HARD IS IT!"—Mark 10: 24.

I suspect there is scarcely a young man, rich and thoughtful, who is not ready to feel our Lord's treatment of this young man hard. He is apt to ask, "Why should it be difficult for a rich man to enter into the kingdom of heaven?" He is ready to look upon the natural fact as an arbitrary decree, arising, shall I say, from some prejudice in the divine mind, or, at least, from some objection to the joys of well-being, as regarded from the creature's side. Why should the rich fare differently from other people in respect of the world to come?

They do not perceive that the law is that they *shall* fare like other people, whereas they want to fare as rich people. A condition of things, in which it would be easy for a rich man to enter into the kingdom of heaven, is to me inconceivable. There is no kingdom of this world into which a rich man may not easily enter—in which, if he be but rich enough, he may not be the first. A kingdom into which it would be easy for a rich man to enter could be no kingdom of heaven. The rich man does not by any necessity of things belong to the kingdom of Satan, but into that kingdom he is especially welcome; whereas into the kingdom of heaven he will be just as welcome as another man.

I suspect also that many a rich man turns from the

record of this incident with the resentful feeling that there lies in it a claim upon his whole having; while there are many, and those by no means only of the rich, who cannot believe the Lord really meant to take the poor fellow's money from him. To the man born to riches they seem not merely a natural, but an essential, condition of well-being; and the man who has *made* his money, feels it his by the labor of his soul, the travail of the day, and the care of the night. Each feels a right to have and to hold the things he possesses; and if there is a necessity for his entering into the kingdom of heaven, it is hard indeed that right and that necessity should confront each other and constitute all but a bare impossibility! Why should he not "make the best of both worlds?" He would compromise if he might; he would serve Mammon a little, and God much. He would not have such a "best of both worlds" as comes of putting the lower in utter subservience to the higher—of casting away the treasure of this world, and taking the treasure of heaven instead. He would gain as little as may be of heaven —but something, with the loss of as little as possible of the world. That which he desires of heaven is not its best; that which he would not yield of the world is its most worthless.

I can well imagine an honest youth, educated in Christian forms, thus reasoning with himself: "Is the story of general relation? Is this demand made upon me? If I make up my mind to be a Christian, shall I be required to part with all I possess? It must have been comparatively easy in those times to give up the kind of things they had! If I had been he, I am sure I should have done it—at the demand of the Saviour in person. Things are very different now!

Wealth did not then imply the same social relations as now! I should be giving up so much more! Neither do I love money as he was in danger of doing: in all times the Jews have been Mammon-worshipers! I try to do good with my money! Besides, am I not a Christian already? Why should the same thing be required of me as of a young Jew? If every one who, like me, has a conscience about money, and cares to use it well, had to give up all, the power would be at once in the hands of the irreligious; they would have no opposition, and the world would go to the devil! We read often in the Bible of rich men, but never of any other who was desired to part with all that he had. When Ananias was struck dead, it was not because he did not give up all his money, but because he pretended to have done so. St. Peter expressly says: 'While it remained, was it not thine own? and after it was sold, was it not in thine own power?' How would the Lord have been buried but for the rich Joseph? Besides, the Lord said here, 'If thou wouldst be perfect, go, sell that thou hast.' I cannot be perfect; it is hopeless; and he does not expect it."

It would be more honest if he said, "I do not want to be perfect, I am content to be saved." Such as he do not care for being perfect as their Father in heaven is perfect, but for being what they call *saved*. They little think that without perfection there is no salvation—perfection is salvation: they are one. "And again," he adds, in conclusion triumphant, "the text says, 'How hard is it for them that trust in riches to enter into the kingdom of God!' I do not trust in my riches; I know that they can do nothing to save me!"

I will suppose myself in immediate communication with such a youth. I should care little to set forth anything called truth, except in siege for surrender to the law of liberty. If I cannot persuade, I would be silent. Nor would I labor to instruct the keenest intellect; I would rather learn for myself. To persuade the heart, the will, the action, is alone worth the full energy of a man. His strength is first for his own, then for his neighbor's manhood. He must first pluck out the beam out of his own eye, then the mote out of his brother's—if, indeed, the mote in his brother's be more than the projection of the beam in his own. To make a man happy as a lark, *might be* to do him grievous wrong: to make a man wake, rise, look up, turn, is worth the life and death of the Son of the Eternal.

I say then to the youth : Have you kept—have you been keeping the commandments? "I will not dare say that," I suppose him to answer: "I ought to know better than that young ruler how much is implied in the keeping of the commandments!" But, I ask, insisting—does your answer imply that, counting the Lord a hard master, you have taken the less pains to do as he would have you? or that, bending your energies to the absolute perfection he requires, you have the more perceived the impossibility of fulfilling the law? Can you have failed to note that it is the youth, who has been for years observing the commandments, on whom the further, and to you startling, command is laid, to part with all he has? Surely not! Are you then one on whom, because of correspondent condition, the same command could be laid? Have you, in any sense, like that in which the youth answered the question, kept the commandments? Have you, unsatisfied with the result of what keeping you have given them, and filled with desire to be perfect, gone kneeling to the Master to learn more of the way to eternal life? or

## THE HARDNESS OF THE WAY. 219

are you so well satisfied with what you are, that you have never sought eternal life, never hungered and thirsted after the righteousness of God, the perfection of your being? If this latter be your condition, then be comforted; the Master does not require of you to sell what you have and give to the poor. *You* follow him! *You* go with him to preach good tidings!—you who care not for righteousness! You are not one whose company is desirable to the Master. Be comforted, I say; he does not want you; he will not ask you to open your purse for him; you may give or withhold, it is nothing to him What! is he to be obliged to come to one outside his kingdom— to the untrue, the ignoble—for money? Bring him a true heart, an obedient hand: he has given his life-blood for that; but your money—he neither needs it nor cares for it.

"Pray, do not deal harshly with me. I confess I have not been what I ought; but I want to repent, and would fain enter into life. Do not think, because I am not prepared, without the certainty that it is required of me, to cast from me all I have, that I have no regard for higher things."

Once more, then—*go and keep the commandments.* It is not come to your money yet: the commandments are enough for you. You are not yet a child of the kingdom. You do not care for the arms of your Father; you value only the shelter of his roof. As to your money, let the commandments direct you how to use it. It is in you but pitiable presumption to wonder whether it is required of you to sell all that you have. When in keeping the commandments you have found the great reward of loving righteousness—the further reward of discovering that, with all the energy you can put forth, you are but an unprofitable servant; when you have come to know that the law can be kept only by such as need no law; when you have come to feel that you would rather pass out of being than live on such a poor, miserable, selfish life as alone you can call yours; when you are aware of a something beyond all that your mind can think, yet not beyond what your heart can desire—a something that is not yours, seems as if it never could be yours, which yet your life is worthless without; when you have come, therefore, to the Master with the cry, "What shall I do that I may inherit eternal life?"—it may be then that he will say to you, "Sell all that you have, and give to the poor, and come, follow me." If he do, then will you be of men most honorable, if you obey—of men most pitiable, if you refuse. Till then, you would be of no comfort to him, no pleasure to his friends. For the young ruler to have sold all and followed him would have been to accept God's patent of peerage: to you it is not offered. Were one of the disobedient, in the hope of the honor, to part with every straw he possessed, he would but be sent back to keep the commandments in the new and easier circumstances of his poverty.

Does this comfort you? Then alas for you! A thousand times alas! Your relief is to know that the Lord has no need of you—does not require you to part with your money, does not offer you himself instead! You do not indeed sell him for thirty pieces of silver, but you are glad not to buy him with all that you have! Wherein do you differ from the youth of the story? In this: that he was invited to do more, to do everything, to partake of the divine nature; you have not had it in your power to refuse; you are not fit to be invited. Such as you can never enter the kingdom.

You would not even know you were in heaven, if you were in it; you would not see it around you, if you sat on the very footstool of the throne.

"But I do not trust in my riches; I trust in the merits of my Lord and Saviour. I trust in his finished work. I trust in the sacrifice he has offered."

Yes; yes! you will trust in anything but the Man himself who tells you it is hard to be saved! Not all the merits of God and his Christ can give you eternal life; only God and his Christ can; and they cannot, would not if they could, without your keeping the commandments. The knowledge of the living God *is* eternal life. What have you to do with his merits? You have to know his being—himself. And as to trusting in your riches, who ever imagined he could have eternal life by his riches? No man, with half a conscience, half a head, and no heart at all, could suppose that any man, trusting in his riches to get him in, could enter the kingdom. That would be too absurd. The money-confident Jew might hope that, as his riches were a sign of the favor of God, that favor would not fail him at the last; or their possession might so enlarge his self-satisfaction that he could not entertain the idea of being lost; but *trust in his riches !* no! It is the last refuge of the riches-lover, the riches-worshiper, the man to whom their possession is essential for his peace, to say he does not trust in them to take him into life. Doubtless the man, who thinks of nothing so much, trusts in them in a very fearful sense; but hundreds who do so will yet say, "I do not trust in my riches; I trust in "—this or that stock-phrase.

"You forget yourself; you are criticising the Lord's own words: he said, 'How hard is it *for them that trust in riches* to enter into the kingdom of heaven!'"

I do not forget myself; to this I have been leading you. Our Lord, I believe, never said those words. The reading of both the Sinaitic and the Vatican manuscripts, the oldest two we have—that preferred by both Westcott and Tischendorf, though not by Tregelles or the Revisers—is, "Children, how hard is it to enter into the kingdom of God!" These words I take to be those of the Lord. Some copyist, with the mind at least of a rich man, dissatisfied with the Lord's way of regarding money, and like yourself anxious to compromise, must forsooth affix his marginal gloss, to the effect that it is not the possessing of riches, but the trusting in them that makes it difficult to enter into the kingdom. *Difficult!* Why, it is eternally impossible for the man who trusts in his riches to enter into the kingdom! it is for the man who has riches that it is difficult. Is the Lord supposed to teach that, for a man who trusts in his riches, it is *possible* to enter the kingdom? that, though impossible with men, this is possible with God? God himself take the Mammon-worshiper into his glory! No; the Lord never said it.

Take then the Lord's words thus: "Children, how hard is it to enter into the kingdom of God!" It is quite like his way of putting this. Calling his hearers first to reflect on the original difficulty for every man of entering into the kingdom of God, he reasserts in yet stronger phrase the difficulty of the rich man: "It is easier for a camel to go through a needle's eye, than for a rich man to enter into the kingdom of God." It always was, always will be, hard to enter into the kingdom of heaven. It is hard even to believe that one must be born from above—must pass into a new and unknown consciousness. The law-faithful Jew, the ceremonial Christian, shrinks from the self-annihilation, the life of grace and truth, the upper air of heavenly delight, the all-embracing love that fills the law full and sets it aside. They cannot accept a condition of being as in itself eternal life. And hard to believe in. this life, this kingdom of God, this simplicity of absolute existence, is hard to enter. How hard? As hard as the Master of salvation could find words to express the hardness: "If any man cometh unto me, and hateth not.... his own life also, he cannot be my disciple." And the rich man must find it harder than another to hate his own life. There is so much associated with it to swell out the self of his consciousness, that the difficulty of casting it from him as the mere ugly shadow of the self God made, is vastly increased.

None can know how difficult it is to enter into the kingdom of heaven, but those who have tried—tried hard, and have not ceased to try. I care not to be told that one may pass at once into all possible sweetness of assurance; it is not assurance I desire, but the thing itself; not the certainty of eternal life, but eternal life. I care not what other preachers may say, while I know that in St. Paul the spirit and the flesh were in frequent strife. They only, I repeat, know how hard it is to enter into life, who are in conflict every day, are growing to have this conflict every hour—nay, begin to see that no moment is life, without the presence that maketh strong. Let any tell me of peace and content, yea, joy unspeakable, as the instant result of the new birth; I deny no such statement, refuse no such testimony; all I care to say is, that, if by salvation they mean less than absolute oneness with God, I count it no salvation, neither would be content with it if it included every joy in the heaven of their best imagining.

If they are not righteous even as he is righteous, they are not saved, whatever be their gladness or their content; they are but on the way to be saved. If they do not love their neighbor—not as themselves: that is a phrase ill to understand, and not of Christ: but as Christ loves him—I cannot count them entered into life, though life may have begun to enter into them. Those whose idea of life is simply an eternal one, best know how hard it is to enter into life. The Lord said: "Children, how hard is it to enter into the kingdom!" the disciples little knew what was required of them.

Demands, unknown before, are continually being made upon the Christian: it is the ever fresh rousing and calling, asking and sending of the Spirit that worketh in the children of obedience. When he thinks he has attained, then he is in danger; when he finds the mountain he has so long been climbing show suddenly a distant peak, radiant in eternal whiteness, and all but lost in heavenly places, a peak whose glory-crowned apex it seems as if no human foot could ever reach— then is there hope for him; proof there is then that he has been climbing, for he beholds the yet unclimbed; he sees what he could not see before; if he knows little of what he is, he knows something of what he is not. He learns ever afresh that he is not in the world as Jesus was in the world; but the very wind that breathes courage as he climbs is the hope that one day he shall be like him, seeing him as he is.

Possessions are *things*, and *things* in general, save as affording matter of conquest and means of spiritual annexation, are very ready to prove inimical to the better life. The man, who for consciousness of well-being depends upon anything but life, the life essential, is a slave; he hangs on what is less than himself. He is not perfect, who, deprived of everything, would not sit down calmly content, aware of a well-being untouched; for none the less would he be possessor of all things, the child of the Eternal. Things are given us, this body first of things, that through them we may be trained both to independence and true possession of them. We must possess them; they must not possess us. Their use is to mediate—as shapes and manifestations in lower kind of the things that are unseen, that is, in themselves unseeable, the things that belong, not to the world of speech, but the world of silence, not to the world of showing, but the world of being, the world that cannot be shaken, and must remain.

These things unseen take form in the things of time and space—not that they may exist, for they exist in and from eternal Godhead, but that their being may be known to those in training for the eternal; these things unseen the sons and daughters of God must possess. But instead of reaching out after them, they grasp at their forms, regard the things seen as the things to be possessed, fall in love with the bodies instead of the souls of them. There are good people who can hardly believe that, if the young man had consented to give up his wealth, the Lord would not then have told him to keep it; they too seem to think the treasure in heaven insufficient as a substitute. They cannot believe he would have been better off without his wealth. "Is not wealth power?" they ask. It is indeed power, and so is a wolf hid in the robe; it is power, but as of a brute machine, of which the owner ill knows the handles and cranks, valves and governor. The multitude of those who read the tale are of the same mind as the youth himself—in his worst moment, as he turned and went—with one vast difference, that they are not sorrowful.

*Things* can never be really possessed by the man who cannot do without them—who would not be absolutely, divinely content in the consciousness that the cause of his being is within it—and *with him*. I would not be misunderstood: no man can have the consciousness of God with him, and not be content: I mean that no man, who has not the Father so as to be eternally content in him alone, can possess a sunset or a field of grass or a mine of gold or the love of a fellow creature, according to its nature—as God would have him possess it—in the eternal way of inheriting, having, and holding. He who has God, has all things, after the fashion in which he who made them has them. To man, woman, and child, I say—if you are not content, it is because God is not with you as you need him, not with you as he would be with you, as you *must* have him : for you need him as your body never needed food or air, need him as your soul never hungered after joy, or peace, or pleasure.

It is imperative on us to get rid of the tyranny of *things*. See how imperative : let the young man cling with every fibre to his wealth, what God can do he will do : his child shall not be left in the hell of possession! Comes the angel of death—and where are the things that haunted the poor soul with such manifold hindrance and obstruction? The world, and all that is in the world, drops and slips from his feet, from his hands, carrying with it his body, his eyes, his ears, every pouch, every coffer, that could delude him with the fancy of possession.

When the fetters of gold are gone, on which the man delighted to gaze, though they held him fast to his dungeon-wall, buried from air and sunshine, then first will he feel them in the soreness of their lack, in the weary indifference with which he looks on earth and sea, on space and stars. When the truth begins to dawn upon him that those fetters were a horror and a disgrace, then will the good of saving death appear, and the man begin to understand that *having* never was, never could be, well-being: that it is not by possessing we live, but by life we possess. Thus death may give a new opportunity—with some hope for the multitude counting themselves Christians, who are possessed by *things* as by a legion of devils: who stand well in their church: whose lives are regarded as stainless; who are kind, friendly, give largely, believe in the redemption of Jesus, talk of the world and the church, yet whose care all the time is to heap up, to make much into more, to add house to house and field to field, burying themselves deeper and deeper in the ash-heap of *Things*.

## XXI.

## THE BEGINNING OF MIRACLES.

"This beginning of miracles did Jesus in Cana of Galilee, and manifested forth his glory; and his disciples beleived on him."—John 2 : 11.

Already Jesus had his disciples, although as yet he had done no mighty works. They followed him for himself and for his mighty words. With his mother they accompanied him to a merry-making at a wedding. With no retiring regard, with no introverted look of se'f-consciousness or self-withdrawal, but more human than any of the company, he regarded their rejoicings with perfect sympathy, for, whatever suffering might follow, none knew so well as he that—

> "There is one
> Who makes the joy the last in every song."

The assertion in the old legendary description of his person and habits, that he was never known to smile, I regard as an utter falsehood, for to me it is incredible —almost as a geometrical absurdity. In that glad company the eyes of a divine artist, following the spiritual lines of the group, would have soon settled on his face as the centre whence radiated all the gladness, where, as I seem to see him, he sat in the background beside his mother. Even the sunny face of the bridegroom would appear less full of light than his. But something is at hand which will change his mood. For no true man had he been, if his mood had never changed.

## THE BEGINNING OF MIRACLES. 229

His high, holy, obedient will, his tender, pure, strong heart never changed, but his mood, his feeling did change. For the mood must often, and in many cases ought to be, the human reflex of changing circumstance. The change comes from his mother. She whispers to him that they have no more wine. The bridegroom's liberality had reached the limit of his means, for, like his guests, he was most probably of a humble calling, a craftsman, say, or a fisherman. It must have been a painful little trial to him if he knew the fact; but I doubt if he heard of the want before it was supplied.

There was nothing in this, however, to cause the change in our Lord's mood of which I have spoken. It was no serious catastrophe, at least to him, that the wine should fail. His mother had but told him the fact; only there is more than words in every commonest speech that passes. It was not his mother's words but the tone and the look with which they were interwoven, that wrought the change. She knew that her son was no common man, and she believed in him with an unripe, unfeatured faith. This faith, working with her ignorance and her fancy, led her to expect the great things of the world from him. This was a faith which must fail that it might grow. Imperfection must fail that strength may come in its place. It is well for the weak that their faith should fail them, for it may at the moment be resting its wings upon the twig of some brittle fancy, instead of on a branch of the tree of life.

But, again, what was it in his mother's look and tone that should work the change in our Lord's mood? The request implied in her words could give him no offence, or he granted that request; and he never would have done a thing he did not approve, should his very mother ask him. The *thoughts* of the mother lay not in her words, but in the expression that accompanied them, and it was to those thoughts that our Lord replied. Hence his answer, which has little to do with her spoken request, is the key both to her thoughts and to his. If we do not understand his reply, we *may* misunderstand the miracle—certainly we are in danger of grievously misunderstanding him—a far worse evil. How many children are troubled in heart that Jesus should have spoken to his mother as our translation compels them to suppose he did speak! "Woman, what have I to do with thee? Mine hour is not yet come." His hour for working the miracle *had* come, for he wrought it; and if he had to do with one human soul at all, that soul must be his mother. The "woman," too, sounds strange in our ears. This last, however, is our fault: we allow words to sink from their high rank, and then put them to degraded uses. What word so full of grace and tender imagings to any true man as that one word! The Saviour did use it to his mother; and when he called her *woman*, the good custom of the country and the time was glorified in the word as it came from his lips *fulfilled* of humanity; for those lips were the open gates of a heart full of infinite meanings. Hence whatever word he used had more of the human in it than that word had ever held before.

What he did say was this—"Woman, what is there common to thee and me? My hour is not yet come." What! was not their humanity common to them? Had she not been fit, therefore chosen, to bear him? Was she not his mother? But his words had no reference to the relation between them; they only referred to the present condition of her mind, or rather the nature of the thought and expectation which now occupied it.

## THE BEGINNING OF MIRACLES.

Her hope and his intent were at variance; there was no harmony between his thought and hers; and it was to that thought and that hope of hers that his words were now addressed. To paraphrase the words—and if I do so with reverence and for the sake of the spirit which is higher than the word, I think I am allowed to do so—"Woman, what is there in your thoughts now that is in sympathy with mine? Also the hour that you are expecting is not come yet."

What, then, was in our Lord's thoughts? and what was in his mother's thoughts to call forth his words? She was thinking the time had come for making a show of his power—for revealing what a great man he was —for beginning to let that glory shine, which was, in her notion, to culminate in the grandeur of a righteous monarch—a second Solomon, forsooth, who should set down the mighty in the dust, and exalt them of low degree. Here was the opportunity for working like a prophet of old, and revealing of what a mighty son she was the favored mother.

And of what did the glow of her face, the light in her eyes, and the tone with which she uttered the words, "They have no wine," make Jesus think? Perhaps of the decease which he must accomplish at Jerusalem; perhaps of a throne of glory betwixt the two thieves; certainly of a kingdom of heaven not such as filled her imagination, even although her heaven-descended Son was the king thereof. A kingdom of exulting obedience, not of acquiescence, still less of compulsion, lay germed in his bosom, and he must be laid in the grave ere that germ could send up its first green lobes into the air of the human world. No throne, therefore, of earthly grandeur for him! no triumph for his blessed mother such as she dreamed! There was nothing common in their visioned ends. Hence came the change of mood to Jesus, and hence the words that sound at first so strange, seeming to have so little to do with the words of his mother.

But no change of mood could change a feeling towards mother or friends. The former, although she could ill understand what he meant, never fancied in his words any unkindness to her. She, too, had the face of the speaker to read; and from that face came such answer to her prayer for her friends, that she awaited no confirming words, but in the confidence of a mother who knew her child, said at once to the servants, "Whatsoever he saith unto you, do it."

If any one object that I have here imagined too much, I would remark, first, that the records in the Gospel are very brief and condensed; second, that the germs of a true intelligence must lie in this small seed, and our hearts are the soil in which it must unfold itself; third, that we are bound to understand the story, and that the foregoing are the suppositions on which I am able to understand it in a manner worthy of what I have learned concerning him. I am bound to refuse every interpretation that seems to me unworthy of him, for to accept such would be to sin against the Holy Ghost. If I am wrong in my idea either of that which I receive or of that which I reject, as soon as the fact is revealed to me I must cast the one away and do justice to the other. Meantime this interpretation seems to me to account for our Lord's words in a manner he will not be displeased with even if it fail to reach the mark of the fact. That St. John saw, and might expect such an interpretation to be found in the story, barely as he has told it, will be rendered the more probable if we remember his own similar condition and experience when he and his brother James prayed the Lord for the highest rank in his kingdom, and received an answer which evidently flowed from the same feeling to which I have attributed that given on this occasion to his mother.

"'Fill the water-pots with water.' And they filled them up to the brim. 'Draw out now, and bear unto the governor of the feast.' And they bare it. Thou hast kept the good wine until now.'" It is such a thing of course, that when our Lord gave them wine, it would be of the best, that it seems almost absurd to remark upon it. What the Father would make and will make, and that towards which he is ever working, is *the Best;* and when our Lord turns the water into wine it must be very good.

It is like his Father, too, not to withhold good wine because men abuse it. Enforced virtue is unworthy of the name. That men may rise above temptation, it is needful that they should have temptation. It is the will of him who makes the grapes and the wine. Men will even call Jesus himself a wine-bibber. What matters it, so long as he works as the Father works, and lives as the Father wills?

I dare not here be misunderstood. God chooses that men should be tried, but let a man beware of tempting his neighbor. God knows how and how much, and where and when: man is his brother's keeper, and must keep him according to his knowledge. A man may work the will of God for others, and be condemned therein because he sought his own will and not God's. That our Lord gave this company wine, does not prove that he would have given *any* company wine. To some he refused even the bread they requested at his hands. Because he gave wine to the wedding guests, shall man dig a pit at the corner of every street, that the poor may fall therein, spending their money for that which is not bread, and their labor for that which satisfieth not? Let the poor man be tempted as God wills, for the end of God is victory; let not man tempt him, for his end is his neighbor's fall, or at best he heeds it not for the sake of gain, and he shall receive according to his works.

To him who can thank God with free heart for his good wine, there is a glad significance in the fact that our Lord's first miracle was this turning of water into wine. It is a true symbol of what he has done for the world in glorifying all things. With his divine alchemy he turns not only water into wine, but common things into radiant mysteries, yea, every meal into a eucharist, and the sepulchre into an outgoing gate. I do not mean that he makes any change in the things or ways of God, but a mighty change in the hearts and eyes of men, so that God's facts and God's meanings become their faiths and their hopes. The destroying spirit, who works in the commonplace, is ever covering the deep and clouding the high. For those who listen to that spirit great things cannot be. Such are there, but they cannot see them, for in themselves they do not aspire. They believe, perhaps, in the truth and grace of their first child; when they have spoiled him, they laugh at the praises of childhood. From all that is thus low and wretched, incapable and fearful, he who made the water into wine delivers men, revealing heaven around them, God in all things, truth in every instinct, evil withering and hope springing even in the path of the destroyer.

That the wine should be his first miracle, and that the feeding of the multitudes should be the only other creative miracle, will also suggest many thoughts in

## THE BEGINNING OF MIRACLES.

connection with the symbol he has left us of his relation to his brethren. In the wine and the bread of the eucharist, he reminds us how utterly he has given, is giving himself for the gladness and the strength of his Father's children. Yea, more; for in that he is the radiation of the Father's glory, this bread and wine is the symbol of how utterly the Father gives himself to his children, how earnestly he would have them partakers of his own being. If Jesus was the Son of the Father, is it hard to believe that he should give men bread and wine?

It was not his power, however, but his glory, that Jesus showed forth in the miracle. His power could not be hidden, but it was a poor thing beside his glory. Yea, power in itself is a poor thing. If it could stand alone, which it cannot, it would be a horror. No amount of lonely power could create. It is the love that is at the root of power, the power of power, which alone can create. What then was this his glory? What was it that made him glorious? It was that, like his Father, he ministered to the wants of men. Had they not needed the wine, not for the sake of whatever show of his power would he have made it. The concurrence of man's need and his love made it possible for that glory to shine forth. It is for this glory most that we worship him. But power is no object of adoration, and they who try to worship it are slaves. Their worship is no real worship. Those who trembled at the thunder from the mountain went and worshiped a golden calf; but Moses went into the thick darkness to find his God. How far the expectation of the mother Mary that her son would, by majesty of might, appeal to the wedding guests, and arouse their enthusiasm for himself, was from our Lord's thoughts, may be well seen in the fact that the miracle was not beheld even by the ruler of the feast; while the report of it would probably receive little credit from at least many of those who partook of the good wine. So quietly was it done, so entirely without pre-intimation of his intent, so stolenly, as it were, in the two simple ordered acts, the filling of the water-pots with water, and the drawing of it out again, as to make it manifest that it was done for the ministration. He did not do it even for the show of his goodness, but *to be good*. This alone could show his Father's goodness. It was done because here was an opportunity in which all circumstances combined with the bodily presence of the powerful and the prayer of his mother, to render it fit that the love of his heart should go forth in giving his merry-making brothers and sisters more and better wine to drink.

And herein we find another point in which this miracle of Jesus resembles the working of his Father. For God ministers to us so gently, so stolenly, as it were, with such a quiet, tender loving absence of display, that men often drink of his wine, as these wedding guests drank, without knowing whence it comes— without thinking that the giver is beside them, yea, in their very hearts. For God will not compel the adoration of men: it would be but a pagan worship that would bring to his altars. He will rouse in men a sense of need, which shall grow at length into a longing; he will make them feel after him, until by their search becoming able to behold him, he may at length reveal to them the glory of their Father. He works silently— keeps quiet behind his works, as it were, that he may truly reveal himself in the right time. With this intent also, when men find his wine good and yet do not rise and search for the giver, he will plague them with

## THE BEGINNING OF MIRACLES. 237

sore plagues that the good wine of life may not be to them, and therefore to him and the universe, an evil thing. It would seem that the correlative of creation is search; that as God has *made* us, we must *find* him; that thus our action must reflect his; that thus he glorifies us with a share in the end of all things, which is that the Father and his children may be one in thought, judgment, feeling, and intent, in a word, that they may mean the same thing.

St. John says that Jesus thus "manifested forth his glory, and his disciples believed on him." I doubt if any but his disciples knew of the miracle, or of those others who might see or hear of it, if any believed on him because of it. It is possible to see a miracle, and not believe in it; while many of those who saw a miracle of our Lord believed in the miracle, and yet did not believe in him.

I wonder how many Christians there are who so thoroughly believe God made them that they can laugh in God's name; who understand that God invented laughter and gave it to his children. Such belief would add a keenness to the zest in their enjoyment, and slay that sneering laughter of which a man grimaces to the fiends, as well as that feeble laughter in which neither heart nor intellect has a share. It would help them, also, to understand the depth of this miracle. The Lord of gladness delights in the laughter of a merry heart. These wedding guests could have done without wine, surely without more wine and better wine. But the Father looks with no esteem upon a bare existence, and is ever working, even by suffering, to render life more rich and plentiful. His gifts are to the overflowing of the cup; but when the cup would overflow, he deepens its hollow, and widens its brim. Our Lord is profuse, like his Father, yea, will, at his own sternest cost, be lavish to his brethren. He will give them wine indeed.

But even they who know whence the good wine comes, and joyously thank the giver, shall one day cry out, like the praiseful ruler of the feast to him who gave it not, "Thou hast kept the good wine until now."

O THOU who art more ready to hear than we are to pray, and are wont to give more than either we desire or deserve, pour down upon us the abundance of thy mercy; forgiving us those things of which our conscience is afraid, and giving us those things which we are not worthy to ask, but for thy mercy's sake, through Christ our Lord. *Amen.*

## XXII.

## THE MIRACLES OF HEALING UNSOLICITED.

"Believest thou not that I am in the Father, and the Father in me? the words that I speak unto you, I speak not of myself: but the Father, that dwelleth in me, he doeth the works."—John 14: 10.

On a former occasion I took the healing of Simon's wife's mother as a type of all such miracles viewed from the consciousness of the person healed. In the multitude of cases—for it must not be forgotten that there was a multitude of which we have no individual record—the experience must have been very similar. The evil thing, the antagonist of their life, departed; they knew in themselves that they were healed; they beheld before them the face and form whence the healing power had gone forth, and they believed in the man. What they believed *about* him, farther than that he had healed them and was good, I cannot pretend to say. Some said he was one thing, some another, but they believed in the man himself. They felt henceforth the strongest of ties binding his life to their life. He was now the central thought of their being. Their minds lay open to all his influences, operating in time and by holy gradations. The well of life was henceforth to them an unsealed fountain, and endless currents of essential life began to flow from it through their existence. High love urging gratitude awoke the conscience to intenser life, and the healed began to recoil from evil deeds and vile thoughts as jarring with the new friendship. Mere acquaintance with a good man is a powerful antidote to evil, but the knowledge of *such* a man as those healed by him knew him was the mightiest of divine influences.

In these miracles of healing our Lord must have laid one of the largest of the foundation-stones of his church. The healed knew him henceforth, not by comprehension, but with their whole being. Their very life acknowledged him. They returned to their homes to recall and love afresh. I wonder what their talk about him was like. What an insight it would give into our common nature to know how these men and women thought and spoke concerning him! But the time soon arrived when they had to be public martyrs—that is, witnesses to what they knew, come of it what might. After our Lord's departure came the necessity for those who loved him to gather together, thus bearing their testimony at once. Next to his immediate disciples, those whom he had cured must have been the very heart of the young church. Imagine the living strength of such a heart—personal love to the personal helper he very core of it. The church had begun with the first gush of affection in the heart of the mother Mary, and now "great was the company of those that published" the good news to the world. The works of the Father had drawn the hearts of the children, and they spake of the Elder Brother who had brought those works to their doors. The thoughtful remembrances of those who had heard him speak; the grateful convictions of those whom he had healed; the tender memories of those whom he had taken in his arms and blessed—these were the fine fibrous multitudinous roots which were to the church existence, growth, and continuance, for these were they which sucked in the

## THE MIRACLES OF HEALING UNSOLICITED.

dews and rains of that descending Spirit which was the life of the tree. Individual life is the life of the church.

But one may say: Why then did he not cure all the sick in Judæa? Simply because all were not ready to be cured. Many would not have believed in him if he had cured them. Their illness had not yet wrought its work, had not yet ripened them to the possibility of faith; his cure would have left them deeper in evil than before. "He did not many mighty works there because of their unbelief." God will cure a man, will give him a fresh start of health and hope, and the man will be the better for it, even without having *yet* learned to thank him; but to behold the healer and acknowledge the outstretched hand of help, yet not to believe in the healer, is a terrible thing for the man; and I think the Lord kept his personal healing for such as it would bring at once into some relation of heart and will with himself; whence arose his frequent demand of faith—a demand apparently always responded to: at the word, the flickering belief, the smoking flax burst into a flame. Evil, that is, physical evil, is a moral good—a mighty means to a lofty end. Pain is an evil; but a good as well, which it would be a great injury to take from the man before it had wrought its end. Then it becomes all evil, and must pass.

I now proceed to a group of individual cases in which, as far as we can judge from the narratives, our Lord gave the gift of restoration unsolicited. There are other instances of the same, but they fall into other groups, gathered because of other features.

The first is that, recorded by St. Luke alone, of the "woman which had a spirit of infirmity eighteen years, and was bowed together, and could in no wise lift up herself." It may be that this belongs to the class of demoniacal possession as well, but I prefer to take it here; for I am very doubtful whether the expression in the narrative, "a spirit of infirmity," even coupled with that of our Lord in defending her and himself from the hypocritical attack of the ruler of the synagogue, "this woman—whom Satan hath bound," renders it necessary to regard it as one of the latter kind. This is, however, a matter of small importance—at least from our present point of view.

Bowed earthwards, the necessary blank of her eye the ground and not the horizon, the form divine deformed towards that of the four-footed animals, this woman had been in bondage eighteen years. Necessary as it is to one's faith to believe every trouble fitted for the being who has to bear it, every physical evil not merely the result of moral evil, but antidotal thereto, no one ought to dare judge of the relation between moral condition and physical suffering in individual cases. Our Lord has warned us from that. But in proportion as love and truth prevail in the hearts of men, physical evil will vanish from the earth. The righteousness of his descendants will destroy the disease which the unrighteousness of their ancestor has transmitted to them. But, I repeat, to destroy this physical evil save by the destruction of its cause, by the redemption of the human nature from moral evil, would be to ruin the world. What in this woman it was that made it right she should bear these bonds for eighteen years, who can tell? Certainly it was not that God had forgotten her. What it may have preserved her from, one may perhaps conjecture, but can hardly have a right to utter. Neither can we tell how she had borne the sad affliction; whether in the lovely patience

## THE MIRACLES OF HEALING UNSOLICITED. 243

common amongst the daughters of affliction, or with the natural repining of one made to behold the sun, and doomed ever to regard the ground upon which she trod. While patience would have its glorious reward in the cure, it is possible that even the repinings of prideful pain might be destroyed by the grand deliverance, that gratitude might beget sorrow for vanished impatience. Anyhow the right hour had come when the darkness must fly away.

Supported, I presume, by the staff which yet more assimilated her to the lower animals, she had crept to the synagogue—a good sign surely, for the synagogue was not its ruler. There is no appearance from the story, that she had come there to seek Jesus, or even that when in his presence she saw him before the word of her deliverance had gone forth. Most likely, being bowed together, she heard him before she saw him.

But he saw her. Our translation says he called her to him. I do not think this is correct. I think the word, although it might mean that, does mean simply that he *addressed her*. Going to her, I think, and saying, "Woman, thou art loosed from thy infirmity," "he laid his hands on her, and immediately she was made straight, and glorified God." What an uplifting!—a type of all that God works in his human beings. The head, downbent with sin, care, sorrow, pain, is uplifted; the groveling will sends its gaze heavenward; the earth is no more the one object of the aspiring spirit; we lift our eyes to God; we bend no longer even to his will, but raise ourselves up towards his will, for his will has become our will, and that will is our sanctification.

Although the woman did not beg the Son to cure

her, she may have prayed the Father much. Anyhow proof that she was ready for the miracle is not wanting. She glorified God. It is enough. She not merely thanked the man who had wrought the cure, for of this we cannot doubt; but she glorified the known Saviour, God, from whom cometh down every good gift and every perfect gift.

She had her share in the miracle I think too, as, in his perfect bounty, God gives a share to every one in what work he does for him. I men, that, with the given power, *she* had to *lift herself* up. Such active faith is the needful response in order that a man may be a child of God, and not the mere instrument upon which his power plays a soulless tune.

In this preventing of prayer, in this answering before the call, in this bringing of the blessing to the door, according to which I have grouped this with the following miracles, Jesus did as his Father is doing every day. He was doing the works of his Father. If men had no help, no deliverance from the ills which come upon them, even those which they bring upon themselves, except such as came at their cry; if no salvation descended from God, except such as they prayed for, where would the world be? in what case would the generations of men find themselves? But the help of God is ever coming, ever setting them free whom Satan hath bound; ever giving them a fresh occasion and a fresh impulse to glorify the God of their salvation. For with every such recovery the child in the man is new-born—for some precious moments at least; a gentleness of spirit, a wonder at the world, a sense of the blessedness of being, an opening to calm yet rousing influences appear in the man. These are the descending angels of God. The passion that had blotted out the child will revive; the strife of the world will renew wrath and hate; ambition and greed will blot out the beauty of the earth; envy of others will blind the man to his own blessedness; and self-conceit will revive in him all those prejudices whose very strength lies in his weakness; but the man has had a glimpse of the peace to gain which he must fight with himself; he has for one moment felt what he might be if he trusted in God; and the memory of it may return in the hour of temptation. As the commonest things in nature are the most lovely, so the commonest agencies in humanity are the most powerful. Sickness and recovery therefrom have a larger share in the divine order of things for the deliverance of men than can show itself to the keenest eyes. Isolated in individuals, the facts are unknown; or, slow and obscure in their operation, are forgotten by the time their effects appear. Many things combine to render an enlarged view of the moral influences of sickness and recovery impossible. The kingdom cometh not with observation, and the working of the leaven of its approach must be chiefly unseen. Like the creative energy itself, it works "in secret shadow, far from all men's sight."

The teaching of our Lord which immediately follows concerning the small beginnings of his kingdom, symbolized in the grain of mustard seed and the leaven, may, I think, have immediate reference to the cure of this woman, and show that he regarded her glorifying of God for her recovery as one of those beginnings of a mighty growth. We do find the same similes in a different connection in St. Matthew and St. Mark; but even if we had no instances of fact, it would be rational to suppose that the Lord, in the varieties of place, audience, and occasion, in the dulness likewise of his disciples, and the perfection of the similes he chose, would again and again make use of the same.

I now come to the second miracle of the group, namely that, recorded by all the Evangelists except St. John, of the cure of the man with the withered hand. This, like the preceding, was done in the synagogue. And I may remark, in passing, that all of this group, with the exception of the last—one of very peculiar circumstance—were performed upon the Sabbath, and each gave rise to discussion concerning the lawfulness of the deed. St. Mark says they watched Jesus to see whether he would heal the man on the Sabbath-day; St. Luke adds that he knew their thoughts, and therefore met them with the question of its lawfulness; St. Matthew says they challenged him to the deed by asking him if it was lawful. The mere watching could hardly have taken place without the man's perceiving something in motion which had to do with him. But there is no indication of a request.

There cannot surely be many who have reached half the average life of man without, at some time, having felt the body a burden in some way, and regarded a possible deliverance from it as an enfranchisement. If the spirit of man were fulfilled of the Spirit of God, the body would simply be a living house, an obedient servant—yes, a humble mediator, by the senses, between his thoughts and God's thoughts; but when every breath has, as it were, to be sent for and brought hither with much labor and small consolation—when pain turns faith into a mere shadow of hope—when the withered limb hangs irresponsive, lost and cumbersome, an inert simulacrum of power, swinging lifeless to and fro; —then even the physical man understands his share in the groaning of the creation after a sonship. When, at a word issuing from such a mouth as that of Jesus of Nazareth, the poor, withered, distorted, contemptible hand obeyed and, responsive to the spirit within, spread forth its fingers, filled with its old human might, became capable once more of the grasp of friendship, of the caress of love, of the labor for the bread that sustains the life, little would the man care that other men—even rulers of synagogues, even Scribes and Pharisees, should question the rectitude of him who had healed him. The power which restored the gift of God and completed humanity, must be of God. Argument upon argument might follow from old books and old customs and learned interpretations, wherein man set forth the will of God as different from the laws of his world, but the man whose hand was restored whole as the other, knew it fitting that his hands should match. They might talk; he would thank God for the crooked made straight. Bewilder his judgment they might with their glosses upon commandment and observance, but they could not keep his heart from gladness; and, being glad, whom should he praise but God? If there was another giver of good things he knew nothing of him. The hand was now as God had meant it to be. Nor could he behold the face of Jesus, and doubt that such a man would do only that which was right. It was not Satan, but God that had set him free.

Here, plainly by the record, our Lord gave the man his share, not of mere acquiescence, but of active will, in the miracle. If man is the child of God, he must have a share in the works of the Father. Without such share in the work as faith gives, cure will be of little avail. "Stretch forth thine hand," said the

Healer; and the man made the effort; and the withered hand obeyed, and was no more withered. *In* the act came the cure, without which the act had been confined to the will, and had never taken form in the outstretching. It is the same in all spiritual redemption.

Think for a moment with what delight the man would employ his new hand. This right hand would henceforth be God's hand. But was not the other hand God's too?—God's as much as this? Had not the power of God been always present in that left hand, whose unwithered life had ministered to him all these years? Was it not the life of God that inspired his whole frame? By the loss and restoration in one part, he would understand possession in the whole.

But as the withered and restored limb to the man, so is the maimed and healed man to his brethren. In every man the power by which he does the commonest things is the power of God. The power is not *of* us. Our power does it; but we do not make the power. This, plain as it is, remains, however, the hardest lesson for a man to learn with conviction and thanksgiving. For God has, as it were, put us just so far away from him that we can exercise the divine thing in us, our own will, in returning towards our source. Then we shall learn the fact that we are infinitely more great and blessed in being the outcome of a perfect self-constituting will, than we could be by the conversion of any imagined independence of origin into fact for us— a truth no man *can* understand, feel, or truly acknowledge, save in proportion as he has become one with his perfect origin, the will of God. While opposition exists between the thing made and the maker, there can be but discord and confusion in the judgment of the creature. No true felicitous vision of the facts of the

## THE MIRACLES OF HEALING UNSOLICITED. 249

relation between his God and him; no perception of the mighty liberty constituted by the holy dependence wherein the will of God is the absolutely free choice of the man; no perception of a unity such as cannot exist between independent wills, but only in unspeakable love and tenderness between the causing Will and the caused will, can yet have place. Those who cannot see how the human will should be free in dependence upon the will of God, have not realized that the will of God made the will of man; that, when most it pants for freedom, the will of man is the child of the will of God, and therefore that there can be no natural opposition or strife between them. Nay, more, the whole labor of God is that the will of man should be free as his will is free—in the same way that his will is free—by the perfect love of the man for that which is true, harmonious, lawful, creative. If a man say, "But might not the will of God make my will with the intent of over-riding and enslaving it?" I answer, such a Will could not create, could not be God, for it involves the false and contrarious. That would be to make a will in order that it might be no will. To create in order to uncreate is something else than divine. But a free will is not the liberty to do whatever one likes, but the power of doing whatever one sees ought to be done, even in the very face of otherwise overwhelming impulse. There lies freedom indeed.

I come now to the case of the man who had been paralysed for eight-and-thirty years. There is great pathos in the story. For many, at least, of these years, the man had haunted the borders of legendary magic, for I regard the statement about the angel troubling the pool as only the expression of a current superstition. Oh, how different from the healing of our Lord!

What he had to bestow was free to all. The cure of no man by his hand weakened that hand for the cure of the rest. None were poorer that one was made rich. But this legend of the troubling of the pool fostered the evil passion of emulation, and that in a most selfish kind. Nowhere in the divine arrangement is my gain another's loss. If it be said that this was the mode in which God determined which was to be healed, I answer that the effort necessary was contrary to all we admire most in humanity. According to this rule, Sir Philip Sidney ought to have drunk the water which he handed to the soldier instead. Does the doctrine of Christ, and by that I insist we must interpret the ways of God, countenance a man's hurrying to be before the rest, and gain the boon in virtue of having the least need of it, inasmuch as he was the ablest to run and plunge first into the eddies left by the fantastic angel? Or, if the triumph were to be gained by the help of friends, surely he was in most need of the cure who, like this man—a man such as we hope there are few— had no friends either to plunge him in the waters of fabled hope, or to comfort him in the seasons of disappointment which alone divided the weary months of a life passed in empty expectation.

But the Master comes near. In him the power of life rests as in "its own calm home, its crystal shrine," and he that believeth in him shall not need to make haste. He knew it was time this man should be healed, and did not wait to be asked. Indeed, the man did not know him; did not even know his name. "Wilt thou be made whole?" "Sir, I have no man, when the water is troubled, to put me into the pool: but while I am coming, another steppeth down before me." "Rise, take up thy bed, and walk."

## THE MIRACLES OF HEALING UNSOLICITED.

Our Lord delays the cure in this case with no further speech. The man knows nothing about him, and he makes no demand upon his faith, except that of obedience. He gives him something to do at once. He will find him again by and by. The man obeys, takes up his bed, and walks.

He sets an open path before us; *we* must walk in it. More, we must be willing to believe that the path is open, that we have strength to walk in it. God's gift glides into man's choice. It is needful that we should follow with our effort in the track of his foregoing power. To refuse is to destroy the gift. His cure is not for such as choose to be invalids. They must be willing to be made whole, even if it should involve the carrying of their beds and walking. Some keep in bed who have strength enough to get up and walk. There is a self-care and a self-pity, a laziness and conceit of incapacity, which are as unhealing for the body as they are unhealthy in the mind, corrupting all dignity and destroying all sympathy. Who but invalids need like miracles wrought in them? Yet some invalids are not cured because they will not be healed. They will not stretch out the hand; they will not rise; they will not walk; above all things, they will not work. Yet for their illness it may be that the work so detested is the only cure, or if no cure yet the best amelioration. Labor is not in itself an evil like the sickness, but often a divine, a blissful remedy. Nor is the duty or the advantage confined to those who ought to labor for their own support. No amount of wealth sets one free from the obligation to work—in a world the God of which is ever working. He who works not has not yet discovered what God made him for, and is a false note in the orchestra of the universe. The possession of wealth is as it were pre-payment, and involves an obligation of honor to the doing of correspondent work. He who does not know what to do has never seriously asked himself what he ought to do.

But there is a class of persons, the very opposite of these, who, as extremes meet, fall into a similar fault. They will not be healed either. They will not take the repose in which God giveth to his beloved. Some sicknesses are to be cured with rest, others with labor. The right way is all—to meet the sickness as God would have it met, to submit or to resist according to the conditions of cure. Whatsoever is not of faith is sin; and she who will not go to her couch and rest in the Lord, is to blame even as she who will not rise and go to her work.

There is reason to suppose that this man had brought his infirmity upon himself—I do not mean by the mere neglect of physical laws, but by the doing of what he knew to be wrong. For the Lord, although he allowed the gladness of the deliverance full sway at first, when he found him afterwards did not leave him without the lesson that all health and well-being depend upon purity of life: "Behold, thou art made whole: sin no more lest a worse thing come unto thee." It is the only case of recorded cure in which Jesus gives a warning of the kind. Therefore I think the probability is as I have stated it. Hence, the fact that we may be ourselves to blame for our sufferings is no reason why we should not go to God to deliver us from them. David the king knew this, and set it forth in that grand poem, the 107th Psalm.

In the very next case, we find that Jesus will not admit the cause of the man's condition, blindness from his birth, to be the sin either of the man himself, or of

## THE MIRACLES OF HEALING UNSOLICITED.

his parents. The probability seems, to judge from their behavior in the persecution that followed, that both the man and his parents were people of character, thought, and honorable prudence. He was born blind Jesus said, "that the works of God should be made manifest in him." What works, then? The work of creation for one, rather than the work of healing. The man had suffered nothing in being born blind. God had made him only not so blessed as his fellows, with the intent of giving him equal faculty and even greater enjoyment afterwards, with the honor of being employed for the revelation of his works to men. In him Jesus created sight before men's eyes. For, as at the first God said, "Let there be light," so the work of God is still to give light to the world, and Jesus must work his work, and *be* the light of the world—light in all its degrees and kinds, reaching into every corner where work may be done, arousing sleepy hearts, and opening blind eyes.

Jesus saw the man, the disciples asked their question, and he had no sooner answered it, than "he spat on the ground, made clay of the spittle, and anointed the eyes of the blind man with the clay."—Why this mediating clay? Why the spittle and the touch?—Because the man who could not see him must yet be brought into sensible contact with him—must know that the healing came from the man who touched him. Our Lord took pains about it because the man was blind. And for the man's share in the miracle, having blinded him a second time as it were with the clay, he sends him to the pool to wash it away: clay and blindness should depart together by the act of the man's faith. It was as if the Lord said, "I blinded thee: now, go and see." Here, then, are the links of the chain by which the Lord bound the man to himself. The voice, if heard by the man, which defended him and his parents from the judgment of his disciples; the assertion that he was the light of the world—a something which others had and the blind man only knew as not possessed by him; the sound of the spitting on the ground; the touch of the speaker's fingers; the clay on his eyes; the command to wash; the journey to the pool; the laving water; the astonished sight. "He went his way, therefore, and washed, and came seeing."

But who can imagine, save in a conception only less dim than the man's blindness, the glory which burst upon him when, as the restoring clay left his eyes, the light of the world invaded his astonished soul? The very idea may well make one tremble. Blackness of darkness—not an invading stranger, but the home-companion always there—the negation never understood because the assertion was unknown—creation not erased and treasured in the memory, but to his eyes uncreated!—Blackness of darkness! . . . The glory of the celestial blue! The towers of the great Jerusalem dwelling in the awful space! The room! The life! The tenfold-glorified being! Any wonder might follow on such a wonder. And the whole vision was as fresh as if he had that moment been created, the first of men.

But the best remained behind. A man had said, "I am the light of the world," and lo! here was the light of the world. The words had been vague as a dark form in darkness, but now the thing itself had invaded his innermost soul. But the face of the man who was this light of the world he had not seen. The creator of his vision he had not yet beheld. But he believed

## THE MIRACLES OF HEALING UNSOLICITED.

in him, for he defended him from the same charge of wickedness from which Jesus had defended him. "Give God the praise," they said; "we know that this man is a sinner." "God heareth not sinners," he replied; "and this man hath opened my eyes." It is no wonder that when Jesus found him and asked him, "Dost thou believe on the Son of God?" he should reply, "Who is he, Lord, that I might believe on him?" He was ready. He had only to know which was he, that he might worship him. Here, at length, was the Light of the world before him—the man who had said, "I am the light of the world," and straightway the world burst upon him in light. Would this man ever need further proof that there was indeed a God of men? I suspect he had a grander idea of the Son of God than any of his disciples as yet. The would-be refutations of experience, for "since the world began was it not heard that any man opened the eyes of one that was born blind;" the objections of the religious authorities, "This man is not of God, because he keepeth not the Sabbath day:" endless possible perplexities of the understanding, and questions of the *how* and the *why*, could never touch that man to the shaking of his confidence: "One thing I know, that whereas I was blind, now I see." The man could not convince the Jews that Jesus must be a good man; neither could he doubt it himself, whose very being, body and soul and spirit, had been enlightened and glorified by him. With light in the eyes, in the brain, in the heart, light permeating and unifying his physical and moral nature, asserting itself in showing the man to himself one whole—how could he doubt!

The miracles were for the persons on whom they passed. To the spectators they were something, it is true; but they were of unspeakable value to, and of endless influence upon their subjects. The true mode in which they reached others was through the healed themselves. And the testimony of their lives would go far beyond the testimony of their tongues. Their tongues could but witness to a fact; their lives could witness to a truth.

In this miracle, as in all the rest, Jesus did in little the great work of the Father; for how many more are they to whom God has given the marvel of vision than those blind whom the Lord enlightened! The remark will sound feeble and far-fetched to the man whose familiar spirit is the Mephistopheles of the commonplace. He who uses his vision only for the care of his body or the indulgence of his mind—how should he understand the gift of God in its marvel? But the man upon whose soul the grandeur and glory of the heavens and the earth and the sea and the fountains of waters have once arisen will understand what a divine *invention*, what a mighty gift of God is this very common thing—these eyes to see with—that light which enlightens the world, this sight which is the result of both. He will understand what a believer the man born blind must have become, yea, how the mighty inburst of splendor might render him so capable of believing that nothing should be too grand and good for him to believe thereafter—not even the doctrine hardest to commonplace humanity, though the most natural and reasonable to those who have beheld it—that the God of the light is a faithful, loving, upright, honest, and self-denying being, yea, utterly devoted to the uttermost good of those whom he has made.

Such is the Father of lights who enlightens the world and every man that cometh into it. Every pulsation of light on every brain is from him. Every feeling of law and order is from him. Every hint of right, every desire after the true, whatever we call aspiration, all longing for the light, every perception that this is true, that that ought to be done, is from the Father of lights. His infinite and varied light gathered into one point—for how shall we speak at all of these things if we do not speak in figures?—concentrated and embodied in Jesus, became *the* light of the world. For the light is no longer only diffused, but in him man "beholds the light *and whence it flows.*" Not merely is our chamber enlightened, but we see the lamp. And so we turn again to God, the Father of lights, yea, even of The Light of the World. Henceforth we know that all the light wherever diffused has its centre in God, as the light that enlightened the blind man flowed from its centre in Jesus. In other words, we have a glimmering, faint, human perception of the absolute glory. We know what God is in recognizing him as our God. Jesus did the works of the Father.

The next miracle—recorded by St. Luke alone—is the cure of the man with the dropsy, wrought also upon the Sabbath, but in the house of one of the chief of the Pharisees. Thither our Lord had gone to an entertainment, apparently large, for the following parable is spoken "to those which were bidden, when he marked how they chose out the best rooms." (Not *rooms*, but *reclining places* at the table.) Hence the possibility at least is suggested, that the man was one of the guests. No doubt their houses were more accessible than ours, and it was not difficult for one uninvited to make his way in, especially upon occasion of such a gathering. But I think the word translated *before him* means *opposite to him* at the table; and that the man was not too ill to appear as a guest. The "took him and healed him and let him go," of our translation, is against the notion rather, but merely from its indefiniteness being capable of meaning that he sent him away; but such is not the meaning of the original. That merely implies that he *took him*, went to him and laid his hands upon him, thus connecting the cure with himself, and then released him, set him free, took his hands off him, turning at once to the other guests and justifying himself by appealing to their own righteous conduct towards the ass and the ox. I think the man remained reclining at the table, to enjoy the appetite of health at a good meal; if, indeed, the gladness of the relieved breath, the sense of lightness and strength, the consciousness of a restored obedience of body, not to speak of the presence of him who had cured him, did not make him too happy to care about his dinner.

I come now to the last of the group, exceptional in its nature, inasmuch as it was not the curing of a disease or natural defect, but the reparation of an injury, or hurt at least, inflicted by one of his own followers. This miracle also is recorded by St. Luke alone. The other evangelists relate the occasion of the miracle, but not the miracle itself; they record the blow, but not the touch. I shall not, therefore, compare their accounts, which have considerable variety, but no inconsistency. I shall confine myself to the story as told by St. Luke.

Peter, intending, doubtless, to cleave the head of a servant of the high priest who had come out to take Jesus, with unaccustomed hand, probably trembling with rage and perhaps with fear, missed his well-meant aim, and only cut off the man's ear. Jesus said, "Suffer ye thus far." I think the words should have a point

## THE MIRACLES OF HEALING UNSOLICITED.

of interrogation after them, to mean, "Is it thus far ye suffer?" "Is this the limit of your patience?" but I do not know. With the words, "he touched his ear and healed him." Hardly had the wound reached the true sting of its pain, before the gentle hand of him whom the servant had come to drag to the torture, dismissed the agony as if it had never been. Whether he restored the ear, or left the loss of it for a reminder to the man of the part he had taken against his Lord, and the return the Lord had made him, we do not know. Neither do we know whether he turned back ashamed and contrite, now that in his own person he had felt the life that dwelt in Jesus, or followed out the capture to the end. Possibly the blow of Peter was the form which the favor of God took, preparing the way, like the blindness from the birth, for the glory that was to be manifested in him. But the Lord would countenance no violence done in his defence. They might do to him as they would. If his Father would not defend him, neither would he defend himself.

Within sight of the fearful death that awaited him, his heart was no whit hardened to the pain of another. Neither did it make any difference that it was the pain of an enemy—even an enemy who was taking him to the cross. There was suffering: here was healing. He came to do the works of him that sent him. He did good to them that hated him, for his Father is the Saviour of men, saving "them out of their distresses."

## XXIII.

## MIRACLES OF HEALING SOLICITED BY THE SUFFERERS.

"According to your faith be it unto you."—Matthew 9: 29.

I come now to the second group of miracles, those granted to the prayers of the sufferers. But before I make any general remarks on the speciality of these, I must speak of one case which appears to lie between the preceding group and this. It is that of the woman who came behind Jesus in the crowd, and involves peculiar difficulties in connection with the facts which render its classification uncertain.

At Capernaum, apparently, our Lord was upon his way with Jairus to visit his daughter, accompanied by a crowd of people who had heard the request of the ruler of the synagogue. A woman who had been ill for twelve years came behind him and touched the hem of his garment. This we may regard as a prayer in so far as she came to him, saying "within herself, if I may but touch his garment I shall be whole." But, on the other hand, it was no true prayer in as far as she expected to be healed without the knowledge and will of the healer. Although she came to him, she did not ask him to heal her. She thought with innocent theft to steal from him a cure. What follows, according to St. Matthew's account, occasions me no difficulty. He does not say that the woman was cured by the touch; he says nothing of her cure until Jesus had turned and

## MIRACLES OF HEALING SOLICITED.

seen her, and spoken the word to her, whereupon he adds: "And the woman was made whole from that hour." But St. Mark and St. Luke represent that the woman was cured upon the touch, and that the cure was only confirmed afterwards by the words of our Lord. They likewise represent Jesus as ignorant of what had taken place, except in so far as he knew that, without his volition, some cure had been wrought by contact with his person, of which he was aware by the passing from him of a saving influence. By this, in the heart of a crowd which pressed upon him so that many must have come into bodily contact with him, he knew that some one had touched him with special intent. No perplexity arises from the difference between the accounts, for there is only difference, not incongruity; the two tell more than the one; it is from the nature of the added circumstances that it springs, for those circumstances necessarily involve inquiries of the most difficult nature. Nor can I in the least pretend to have satisfied myself concerning them. In the first place comes the mode of the cure, which *seems* at first sight (dissociated, observe, from the will of the healer) to partake of the nature of magic—an influence without a sufficient origin. Not for a moment would I therefore yield to an inclination to reject the testimony. I have no right to do so, for it deals with circumstances concerning which my ignorance is all but complete. I cannot rest, however, without seeking to come into some spiritual relation with the narrative—that is, to find some credible supposition upon which, without derogating from the lustre of the object of the whole history, the thing might take place. The difficulty, I repeat, is that the woman could be cured by the garment of Jesus, without (not against) the will of Jesus. I think that the whole difficulty arises from our ignorance—a helpless ignorance—of the relations of thought and matter. I use the word *thought* rather than spirit, because in reflecting upon spirit (which is thought), people generally represent to themselves a vague form of matter. All religion is founded on the belief or instinct—call it what we will—that matter is the result of mind, spirit, thought. The relation between them is therefore simply too close, too near for us to understand. Here is what I am able to suggest concerning the account of the miracle as given by St. Mark and St. Luke.

If even in what we call inanimate things there lies a healing power in various kinds; if, as is not absurd, there may lie in the world absolute cure existing in analysis, that is parted into a thousand kinds and forms, who can tell what cure may lie in a perfect body, informed, yea, caused, by a perfect spirit? If stones and plants can heal by the will of God in them, might there not dwell in the perfect health of a body, in which dwelt the Son of God, a necessarily healing power? It may seem that in the fact of the many crowding about him, concerning whom we have no testimony of influence received, there lies a refutation of this supposition. But who can tell what he may have done even for them without their recognizing it save in conscious well-being? Besides, those who crowded nearest him would mostly be of the strongest who were least in need of a physician, and in whose being consequently there lay not that bare open channel hungering for the precious lief-current. And who can tell how the faith of the heart, calming or arousing the whole nature, may have rendered the very person of the woman more fit than the persons of others in the crowd to receive the sacred

## MIRACLES OF HEALING SOLICITED.

influence? For although she did not pray, she had the faith as alive though as small as the mustard seed. Why might not health from the fountain of health flow then into the empty channel of the woman's weakness? It may have been so. I shrink from the subject, I confess, because of the vulgar forms such speculations have assumed in our days, especially in the hands of those who savor unspeakably more of the charlatan than the prophet. Still, one must be honest and truthful even in regard to what he has to distinguish, as he can, into probable and impossible. Fact is not the sole legitimate object of human inquiry. If it were, farewell to all that elevates and glorifies human nature—farewell to God, to religion, to hope! It is that which lies at the root of fact, yea, at the root of law, after which the human soul hungers and longs.

In the preceding remarks I have anticipated a chapter to follow—a chapter of speculation, which may God make humble and right. But some remark was needful here. What must be to some a far greater difficulty has yet to be considered. It is the representation of the Lord's ignorance of the cure, save from the reaction upon his own person of the influence which went out from him to fill that vacuum of suffering which the divine nature abhors: he did not know that his body was about to radiate health. But this gives me no concern. Our Lord himself tells us in one case, at least, that he did not know, that only his Father knew. He could discern a necessary result in the future, but not the day or the hour thereof. Omniscience is a consequence, not an essential of the divine nature. God knows because he creates. The Father knows because he orders. The Son knows because he obeys. The knowledge of the Father must be perfect; such knowledge the Son neither needs nor desires. His sole care is to do the will of the Father. Herein lies his essential divinity. I do not believe that when he chose Judas he knew that he would betray him. We must take his own words as true. Not only does he not claim perfect knowledge, but he disclaims it. He speaks once, at least, to his Father with an *if it be possible*. Those who believe omniscience essential to divinity, will therefore be driven to say that Christ was not divine. This will be their punishment for placing knowledge on a level with love. No one who does so can worship in spirit and in truth, can lift up his heart in pure adoration. He will suppose he does, but his heaven will be in the clouds, not in the sky.

But now we come to the holy of holies of the story —the divinest of its divinity. Jesus could not leave the woman with the half of a gift. He could not let her away so poor. She had stolen the half: she must fetch the other half—come and take it from his hand. That is, she must know who had healed her. Her will and his must come together; and for this her eyes and his, her voice and his ears, her ears and his voice must meet. It is the only case recorded in which he says *Daughter*. It could not have been because she was younger than himself; there could not have been much difference between their ages in that direction. Let us see what lies in the word.

With the modesty belonging to her as a woman, intensified by the painful shrinking which had its origin in the peculiar nature of her suffering, she dared not present herself to the eyes of the Lord, but thought merely to gather from under his table a crumb unseen. And I do not believe that our Lord in calling her had any desire to make her tell her tale of grief, and, in her

eyes, of shame. It would have been enough to him if
she had come and stood before him, and said nothing.
Nor had she to appear before his face with only that
poor remnant of strength which had sufficed to bring
her to the hem of his garment behind him; for now
she knew in herself that she was healed of her plague,
and the consciousness must have been strength. Yet
she trembled when she came. Filled with awe and
gratitude, she could not stand before him; she fell
down at his feet. There, hiding her face in her hands,
I presume, she forgot the surrounding multitude, and
was alone in the chamber of her consciousness with
the Son of Man. Her love, her gratitude, her holy awe
unite in an impulse to tell him all. When the lower
approaches the higher in love, even between men, the
longing is to be known; the prayer is "Know me."
This was David's prayer to God, " Search me and know
me." There should be no more concealment. Besides,
painful as it was to her to speak, he had a right to know
all, and know it he should. It was her sacrifice offered
unto the Lord. She told him all the truth. To conceal
anything from him now would be greater pain than to
tell all, for the thing concealed would be as a barrier
between him and her; she would be simple—onefold;
her whole being should lie open before him. I do not
for a moment mean that such thoughts, not to say
words, took shape in her mind; but sometimes we can
represent a single consciousness only by analyzing it
into twenty thoughts. And he accepted the offering.
He let her speak, and tell all.

But it was painful. He understood it well. His
heart yearned towards the woman to shield her from
her own innocent shame, to make as it were a heaven
about her whose radiance should render it " by clarity

invisible." Her story appealed to all that was tenderest in humanity; for the secret which her modesty had hidden, her conscience had spoken aloud. Therefore the tenderest word that the language could afford must be hers. "Daughter," he said. It was the fullest reward, the richest acknowledgment he could find of the honor in which he held her, his satisfaction with her conduct, and the perfect love he bore her. The degrading spirit of which I have spoken, the spirit of the commonplace, which lowers everything to the level of its own capacity of belief, will say that the word was an eastern mode in more common use than with us. I say that whatever Jesus did or said, he did and said like other men—he did and said as no other man did or said. If he said *Daughter*, it meant what any man would mean by it; it meant what no man could mean by it—what no man was good enough, great enough, loving enough to mean by it. In him the Father spoke to this one the eternal truth of his relation to all his daughters, to all the women he has made, though individually it can be heard only by those who lift up the filial eyes, lay bare the filial heart. He did the works, he spoke the words of him that sent him. Well might this woman, if she dared not lift the downcast eye before the men present, yet depart in shameless peace: he who had healed her had called her *Daughter*. Everything on earth is paltry before such a word. It was the deepest gift of the divine nature—the recognition of the eternal in her by him who had made it. Between the true father and the true daughter nothing is painful.

I think also that very possibly some compunction arose in her mind, the moment she knew herself healed, at the mode in which she had gained her cure. Hence, when the Lord called her she may have thought he was offended with her because of it. Possibly her contrition for the little fault, if fault indeed it was, may have increased the agony of feeling with which she forced rather than poured out her confession. But he soothes her with gentle, consoling, restoring words: "Be of good comfort." He heels the shy suffering spirit, "wherein old dints of deep wounds did remain." He confirms the cure she feared perhaps might be taken from her again. "Go in peace, and be whole of thy plague." Nay, more, he attributes her cure to her own faith. "Thy faith hath made thee whole." What wealth of tenderness! She must not be left in her ignorance to the danger of associating power with the mere garment of the divine. She must be brought face to face with her healer. She must not be left kneeling on the outer threshold of the temple. She must be taken to the heart of the Saviour, and so redeemed, then only redeemed utterly. There is no word, no backward look of reproach upon the thing she had condemned. If it was evil it was gone from between them forever. Confessed, it vanished. Her faith was an ignorant faith, but, however obscured in her consciousness, it was a true faith. She believed in the man, and our Lord loved the modesty that kept her from pressing into his presence. It may indeed have been the very strength of her faith working in her ignorance that caused her to extend his power even to the skirts of his garments. And there he met the ignorance, not with rebuke, but with the more grace. If even her ignorance was so full of faith, of what mighty confidence was she not capable! Even the skirt of his garment would minister to such a faith. It should be as she would. Through the garment of his Son, the Father would cure her who believed enough to put forth her hand and touch it. The kernel-faith was none the worse that it was closed in the uncomely shell of ignorance and mistake. The Lord was satisfied with it. When did he ever quench the smoking flax? See how he praises her. He is never slow to commend. The first quiver of the upturning eyelid is to him faith. He welcomes the sign, and acknowledges it; commends the feeblest faith in the ignorant soul, rebukes it as little only in apostolic souls where it ought to be greater. "Thy faith hath saved thee." However poor it was, it was enough for that. Between death and the least movement of life there is a gulf wider than that fixed between the gates of heaven and the depths of hell. He said " *Daughter.*"

I come now to the first instance of plain request—that of the leper who fell down before him, saying, "Lord, if thou wilt, thou canst make me clean"—a prayer lovely in the simplicity of its human pleading—an appeal to the power which lay in the man to whom he spoke: his power was the man's claim; the relation between them was of the strongest—that between plenty and need, between strength and weakness, between health and disease—poor bonds comparatively between man and man, for man's plenty, strength, and health can only supplement, not satisfy the need; support the weakness, not change it into strength; mitigate the disease of his fellow, not slay it with invading life; but in regard to God, all whose power is creative, any necessity of his creatures is a perfect bond between them and him; his magnificence must flow into the channels of the indigence he has created.

Observe how Jesus responds in the terms of the man's request. The woman found the healing where she sought it—in the hem of his garment. One man says, "Come with me;" the Lord goes. Another says, "Come not under my roof, I am not worthy;" the Lord remains. Here the man says, "If thou wilt;" the Lord answers, "I will." But he goes far beyond the man's request.

I need say nothing of the grievous complaint under which he labored. It was sore to the mind as well as the body, for it made of the man an outcast and ashamed. No one would come near him lest he should share his condemnation. Physical evil had, as it were, come to the surface in him. He was "full of leprosy." Men shrink more from skin-diseases than from any other. Jesus could have cured him with a word. There was no need he should touch him. *No need* did I say? There was every need. For no one else would touch him. The healthy human hand, always more or less healing, was never laid on him; he was despised and rejected. It was a poor thing for the Lord to cure his body; he must comfort and cure his sore heart. Of all men a leper, I say, needed to be touched with the hand of love. Spenser says, "Entire affection hateth nicer hands." It was not for our master, our brother, our ideal man, to draw around him the skirts of his garments and speak a lofty word of healing, that the man might at least be clean before he touched him. The man was his brother, and an evil disease cleaved fast unto him. Out went the loving hand to the ugly skin, and there was his brother as he should be—with the flesh of a child. I thank God that the touch went before the word. Nor do I think it was the touch of a finger, or of the finger-tips. It was a kindly healing touch in its nature as in its power. O blessed leper! thou knowest henceforth what kind of a God there is in the earth—not the God of the priests, but a God such as himself only can reveal to the hearts of his own. That touch was more than the healing. It was to the leper what the word *Daughter* was to the woman in the crowd, what the *Neither do I* was to the woman in the temple—the sign of the perfect presence. Outer and inner are one with him: the outermost sign is the revelation of the innermost heart.

Let me linger one moment upon this coming together of creative health, and destroying disease. The health must flow forth; the disease could not enter: Jesus was not defiled by the touch. Not that, even if he would have been, he would have shrunk and refrained; he respected the human body in most evil case, and thus he acknowledged it his own. But each one must call up for himself the analogies—only I cannot admit that they are mere analogies—between the cure of the body and the cure of the soul: here they were combined in one act, for that touch went to the man's heart. I can only hint at them here. Hand to hand is enough for the cure of the bodily disease; but heart to heart will Jesus visit the man who, in deepest defilement of evil habits, yet lifts to him a despairing cry. The healthful heart of the Lord will cure the heart spotted with the plague: it will come again as the heart of a child. *Only this kind goeth not out save by prayer and abstinence.*

The Lord gave him something to do at once, and something not to do. He was to go to the priest, and to hold his tongue. It is easier to do than to abstain; he went to the priest; he did not hold his tongue.

That the Lord should send him to the priest requires no explanation. The sacred customs of his country our Lord in his own person constantly recognized. That he saw in them more than the priests themselves was no reason for passing them by. The testimony

## MIRACLES OF HEALING SOLICITED. 271

which he wished the man to bear concerning him lay in the offering of the gift which Moses had commanded. His healing was in harmony with all the forms of the ancient law; for it came from the same source, and would in the lapse of ages complete what the law had but begun. This the man was to manifest for him. The only other thing he required of him—silence—the man would not, at least did not, yield. The probability is that he needed the injunction for his own sake more than for the Master's sake; that he was a talkative, demonstrative man, whose better life was ever in danger of evaporating in words; and that the Lord required silence of him, that he might think, and give the seed time to root itself well before it shot its leaves out into the world. Are there not not some in our own day, who, having had a glimpse of truth across the darkness of a moral leprosy, instantly begin to blaze abroad the matter, as if it were their part at once to call to their fellows, and teach them out of an intellectual twilight, in which they can as yet see men only as trees walking, instead of retiring into the wilderness, for a time at least, to commune with their own hearts, and be still? But he meant well, nor is it any wonder that such a man should be incapable of such a sacrifice. The Lord had touched him. His nature was all in commotion with gratitude. His self-conceit swelled high. His tongue would not be still. Perhaps he judged himself a leper favored above his fellow-lepers. Nothing would more tend to talkativeness than such a selfish mistake. He would be grateful. He would befriend his healer against his will. He would work for him—alas! only to impede the labors of the Wise; for the Lord found his popularity a great obstacle to the only success he sought. "He went out and began to blaze abroad the matter, insomuch that Jesus could no more openly enter into the city." His nature could not yet understand the kingdom that cometh not with observation, and from presumption, mingled with affection, he would serve the Lord after a better fashion than that of doing his will. And he had his reward. He had his share in bringing his healer to the cross.

Obedience is the only service.




O GOD, Maker and Governor of the world, who on the seventh day didst rest from all thy works, and has promised an everlasting rest to all thy faithful servants, make us to rest from our works, that we who are weary and heavy laden with our sins and sorrows may take up the yoke and burden of Jesus Christ, and so find rest unto our souls; for his yoke is easy and his burden is light. A*men.*

## XXIV.

## OTHER MIRACLES SOLICITED BY SUFFERERS.

"AND THEY LIFTED UP THEIR VOICES AND SAID, JESUS, MASTER, HAVE MERCY ON US."
—Luke 17: 13.

I take now the cure of the ten lepers, done apparently in a village of Galilee towards Samaria. They stood afar off in a group, probably afraid of offending him by any nearer approach, and cried aloud, "Jesus, Master, have mercy on us." Instead of at once uttering their cure, he desired them to go and show themselves to the priests. This may have been partly for the sake of the priests, partly perhaps for the justification of his own mission, but more certainly for the sake of the men themselves, that he might, in accordance with his frequent practice, give them something wherein to be obedient. It served also, as the sequel shows, to individualize their relation to him. The relation as a group was not sufficient for the men. Between him and them it must be the relation of man to man. Individual faith must, as it were, break up the group—to favor a far deeper reunion. Its bond was now a common suffering; it must be changed to a common faith in the healer of it. His intention wrought in them—at first with but small apparent result. They obeyed, and went to go to the priests, probably wondering whether they would be healed or not, for the beginnings of faith are so small that they can hardly be recognized as such.

Going, they found themselves cured. Nine of them held on their way, obedient; while the tenth, forgetting for the moment in his gratitude the word of the Master, turned back and fell at his feet. A moral martinet, a scribe, or a pharisee, might have said, "The nine were right, the tenth was wrong: he ought to have kept to the letter of the command." Not so the Master: he accepted the gratitude as the germ of an infinite obedience. Real love is obedience and all things beside. The Lord's own devotion was that which burns up the letter with the consuming fire of love, fulfilling and setting it aside. High love needs no letter to guide it. Doubtless the letter is all that weak faith is capable of, and it is well for those who keep it! But it is ill for those who do not outgrow and forget it! Forget it, I say, *by outgrowing it*. The Lord cared little for the letter of his own commands; he cared all for the spirit, for that was life.

This man was a stranger, as the Jews called him, a Samaritan. Therefore the Lord praised him to his followers. It was as if he had said, "See, Jews, who think yourselves the great praisers of God! here are ten lepers cleansed: where are the nine? One comes back to glorify God—a Samaritan!" To the man himself he says, "Arise, go thy way; thy faith hath made thee whole." Again this commending of individual faith! "Was it not the faith of the others too that had healed them?" Doubtless. If they had had enough to bring them back, he would have told them that their faith had saved them. But they were content to be healed, and until their love, which is the deeper faith, brought them to the Master's feet, their faith was not ripe for praise. But it was not for their blame, it was for the Samaritan's praise that he spoke. Probably this man's faith

## OTHER MIRACLES SOLICITED BY SUFFERERS. 275

had caused the cry of all the ten; probably he was the salt of the little group of outcasts—the tenth, the righteous man. Hence they were contented, for the time, with their cure: he forgot the cure itself in his gratitude. A moment more, and with obedient feet he would overtake them on their way to the priest.

I may not find a better place for remarking on the variety of our Lord's treatment of those whom he cured; that is, the variety of the form in which he conveyed the cure. In the record I do not think we find two cases treated in the same manner. There is no massing of the people with him. In his behavior to men, just as in their relation to his Father, every man is alone with him. In this case of the ten, as I have said, I think he sent them away, partly that this individuality might have an opportunity of asserting itself. They had stood afar off, therefore he could not lay the hand of love on each. But now one left the group and brought his gratitude to the Master's feet, and with a loud voice glorified God the Healer.

In reflecting then on the details of the various cures we must seek the causes of their diversity mainly in the individual differences of the persons cured, not forgetting, at the same time, that all the accounts are brief, and that our capacity is poor for the task. The whole divine treatment of man is that of a father to his children—only a father infinitely more a father than any man can be. Before him stands each, as much an individual child as if there were no one but him. The relation is awful in its singleness. Even when God deals with a nation as a nation, it is only as by this dealing the individual is aroused to a sense of his own wrong, that he can understand how the nation had sinned, or can turn himself to work a change. The nation cannot change save as its members change; and the few who begin the change are the elect of that nation. Ten righteous individuals would have been just enough to restore life to the festering masses of Sodom—festering masses because individual life had ceased, and the nation or community was nowhere. Even nine could not do it: Sodom must perish. The individuals must perish now; the nation had perished long since. All communities are for the divine sake of individual life, for the sake of the love and truth that is in each heart, and is not cumulative—cannot be in two as one result. But all that is precious in the individual heart depends for existence on the relation the individual bears to other individuals: alone—how can he love? alone—where is his truth? It is for and by the individuals that the individual lives. A community is the true development of individual relations. Its very possibility lies in the conscience of its men and women. No setting right can be done in the *mass*. There are no masses save in corruption. Vital organizations result alone from individualities and consequent necessities, which, fitting the one into the other, and working for each other, make combination not only possible but unavoidable. Then the truth which has *informed* in the community reacts on the individual to perfect his individuality. In a word, the man, in virtue of standing alone in God, stands *with* his fellows, and receives from them divine influences without which he cannot be made perfect. It is in virtue of the living consciences of its individuals that a common conscience is possible to a nation.

I cannot work this out here, but I would avoid being misunderstood. Although, I say, every man stands alone in God, I yet say two or many can meet in God as they cannot meet save in God; nay, that only in God can two or many truly meet; only as they recognize their oneness with God can they become one with each other.

In the variety then of his individual treatment of the sick, Jesus did the works of his Father *as* his Father does them. For the Spirit of God speaks to the spirit of the man, and the Providence of God arranges everything for the best good of the individual—counting the very hairs of his head. Every man had a cure of his own; every woman had a cure of her own—all one and the same in principle, each individual in the application of the principle. This was the foundation of the true church. And yet the members of that church will try to separate upon individual and unavoidable differences!

But once more the question recurs: Why say so often that this and that one's faith had saved him? Was it not enough that he had saved them?—Our Lord would knit the bond between him and each man by arousing the man's individuality, which is, in deepest fact, his conscience. The cure of a man depended upon no uncertain or arbitrary movement of the feelings of Jesus. He was always ready to heal. No one was ever refused who asked him. It rested with the man: the healing could not have its way and enter in, save the man would open his door. It was there for him if he would take it, or rather when he would allow him to bestow it. Hence the question and the praise of the patient's faith. There was no danger then of that diseased self-consciousness which nowadays is always asking, "Have I faith? Have I faith?" searching, in fact, for grounds of self-confidence, and turning away the eyes in the search from the only source whence confidence can flow—the natal home of power and love. How shall faith be born but of the beholding of the faithful? This diseased self-contemplation was not indeed a Jewish complaint at all, nor possible in the bodily presence of the Master. Hence the praise given to a man's faith could not hurt him; it only made him glad and more faithful still. This disease itself is in more need of his curing hand than all the leprosies of Judæa and Samaria.

The cases which remain of this group are of blind men—the first, that recorded by St. Matthew of the two who followed Jesus, crying, "Thou Son of David, have mercy on us." He asked them if they believed that he was able to do the thing for them, drawing, I say, the bond between them closer thereby. They said they did believe it, and at once he touched their eyes —again the bodily contact, as in the case of the blind man already considered—especially needful in the case of the blind, to associate the healing with the healer. But there are differences between the cases. The man who had not asked to be healed was, as it were, put through a longer process of cure—I think, that his faith and his will might be called into exercise; and the bodily contact was made closer to help the development of his faith and will: he made clay and put it on his eyes, and the man had to go and wash. Where the prayer and the confession of faith reveal the spiritual contact already effected, the cure is immediate. "According to your faith," the Lord said, "be it unto you."

On these men, as on the leper, he laid the charge of silence, by them, as by him, sadly disregarded. The fact that he went into the house, and allowed them to follow him there before he cured them, also shows that he desired in their case, doubtless because of circumstances, to avoid publicity, a desire which they foiled. Their gladness overcame, if not their gratitude, yet the higher faith that is one with obedience. When the other leper turned back to speak his gratitude, it was but the delay of a moment in the fulfilling of the command. But the gratitude that disobeys an injunction, that does what the man is told not to do, and so plunges into the irretrievable, is a virtue that needs a development amounting almost to a metamorphosis.

In the one remaining case there is a slight confusion in the records. St. Luke says that it was performed as Jesus entered into Jericho; St. Mark says it was as he went out of Jericho, and gives the name and parent, age of the blind beggar; indeed his account is considerably more minute than that of the others. St. Matthew agrees with St. Mark as to the occasion, but says there were two blind men. We shall follow the account of St. Mark.

Bartimæus, having learned the cause of the tumultuous passing of feet, calls, like those former two blind men, upon the Son of David to have mercy on him. The multitude finds fault with his crying and calling. I presume he was noisy in his eagerness after his vanished vision, and the multitude considered it indecorous. Or, perhaps the rebuke arose from that common resentment of a crowd against any one who makes himself what they consider unreasonably conspicuous, claiming a share in the attention of the potentate to which they cannot themselves pretend. But the Lord stops, and tells them to call the man; and some of them—either being his friends, or changing their tone when the great man takes notice of him, begin to congratulate and comfort him. He, casting away his garment in his eagerness, rises and is lead through the yielding crowd to the presence of the Lord. To enter in some degree into the personal knowledge of the man before curing him, and to consolidate his faith, Jesus, the tones of whose voice, full of the life of God, the cultivated hearing of a blind man would be best able to interpret, began to talk a little with him.

"What wilt thou that I should do unto thee?"

"Lord, that I might receive my sight."

"Go thy way; thy faith hath made thee whole."

Immediately he saw; and the first use he made of his sight was to follow him who had given it.

Neither St. Mark nor St. Luke, whose accounts are almost exactly the same, says that he touched the man's eyes. St. Matthew says he touched the eyes of the *two* blind men whom his account places in otherwise identical circumstances. With a surrounding crowd who knew them, I think the touching was less necessary than in private; but there is no need to inquire which is the more correct account. The former two may have omitted a fact, or St. Matthew *may* have combined the story with that of the two blind men already noticed, of which he is the sole narrator. But in any case there are, I think, but two recorded instances of the blind praying for cure. Most likely there were more, perhaps there were many such.

I have now to consider, as suggested by the idea of this group, the question of prayer generally; for Jesus did the works of him who sent him: as Jesus did, so God does.

I have not seen an argument against what is called the efficacy of prayer which appears to me to have any force but what is derived from some narrow conception of the divine nature. If there be a God at all, it is absurd to suppose that his ways of working should be

## OTHER MIRACLES SOLICITED BY SUFFERERS. 281

such as to destroy his side of the highest relation that can exist between him and those whom he has cared to make—to destroy, I mean, the relation of the will of the creator to the individual will of his creature. That God should bind himself in an iron net of his own laws—that his laws should bind him in any way, seeing they are just his nature in action—is sufficiently absurd; but that such laws should interfere with his deepest relation to his creatures, should be inconsistent with the highest consequences of that creation which alone gives occasion for those laws—that, in fact, the will of God should be at strife with the foregoing action of God, not to say with the very nature of God —that he should, with an unchangeable order of material causes and effects, cage in forever the winged aspirations of the human will which he has made in the image of his own will, towards its natural air of freedom in his will, would be pronounced inconceivable, were it not that it has been conceived and uttered— conceived and uttered, however, only by minds to which the fact of this relation was, if at all present, then only in the vaguest and most incomplete form. That he should not leave himself any *willing* room towards those to whom he gave need, room to go wrong, will to turn and look up and pray and hope, is to me grotesquely absurd. It is far easier to believe that as both—the laws of nature, namely, and the human will —proceed from the same eternally harmonious thought, they too are so in harmony, that for the perfect operation of either no infringement upon the other is needful; and that what seems to be such infringement would show itself to a deeper knowledge of both as a perfectly harmonious co-operation. Nor would it matter that we know so little, were it not that with each fresh discovery we are so ready to fancy anew that now, at last, we know all about it. We have neither humility enough to be faithful, nor faith enough to be humble. Unfit to grasp any whole, yet with an inborn idea of wholeness which ought to be our safety in urging us ever on towards the Unity, we are constantly calling each new part the whole, saying we have found the idea, and casting ourselves on the couch of self-glorification. Thus the very need of unity is by our pride perverted to our ruin. We say we have found it when we have it not. Hence, also, it becomes easy to refuse certain considerations, yea, certain facts, a place in our system—for the system will cease to be a system at all the moment they are acknowledged. They may have in them the very germ of life and truth; but what is that, if they destroy this Babylon that we have built? Are not its forms stately and fair? Yea, *can* there be statelier and fairer?

The main point is simply this, that what it would not be well for God to give before a man had asked for it, it may be not only well, but best, to give when he has asked. I believe that the first half of our training is up to the asking point; after that the treatment has a grand new element in it. For God can give when a man is in the fit condition to receive it, what he cannot give before because the man cannot receive it. How give instruction in the harmony of colors or tones to a man who cannot yet distinguish between shade and shade or tone and tone, upon which distinction all harmony depends? A man cannot receive except another will give; no more can a man give if another will not receive; he can only offer. Doubtless, God works on every man, else he *could* have no divine tendency at all; there would be no *thither* for him to turn his face to-

## OTHER MIRACLES SOLICITED BY SUFFERERS.

wards; there could be at best but a sense of want. But the moment the man has given in to God—to use a homely phrase—the spirit for which he prays can work in him all *with* him, not now (as it *appeared* then) *against* him. Every parent at all worthy of the relation must know that occasions occur in which the asking of the child makes the giving of the parent the natural correlative. In a way infinitely higher, yet the same at the root, for all is of God, he can give when the man asks what he could not give without, because, in the latter case, the man would take only the husk of the gift, and cast the kernel away—a husk poisonous without the kernel, although wholesome and comforting with it.

But some will say, "We may ask, but it is certain we shall not have everything we ask for."

No, thank God, certainly not; we shall have nothing which we ourselves, when capable of judging and choosing with eyes open to its true relation to ourselves, would not wish and choose to have. If God should give otherwise, it must be as a healing punishment of inordinate and hurtful desire. The parable of the father dividing his living at the prayer of the younger son, must be true of God's individual sons, else it could not have been true of the Jews on the one hand and the Gentiles on the other. He will grant some such prayers because he knows that the swine and their husks will send back his son with quite another prayer on his lips. If my supposed interlocutor answers, "What then is the good of praying, if it is not to go by what I want?" I can only answer, "You have to learn, and it may be by a hard road." In the kinds of things which men desire, there are essential differences. In physical well-being, there is a divine good. In sufficient food and raiment, there is a divine fitness. In wealth, as such, there is *none*. A man may pray for money to pay his debts, for healing of the sickness which incapacitates him for labor or good work, for just judgment in the eyes of his fellow-men, with an altogether different confidence from that with which he could pray for wealth or for bodily might to surpass his fellows, or for vengeance upon those whose judgment of his merits differed from his own; although even then the divine soul will with his Saviour say, "If it be possible: not my will but thine." For he will know that God gives only the best.

"But God does not even cure every one who asks him. And so with the other things you say are good to pray for."

Jesus did not cure all the ills in Judæa. But those he did cure were at least real ills and real needs. There was a fitness in the condition of some, a fitness favored by his own bodily presence amongst them, which met the virtue ready to go out from him. But God is ever present, and I have yet to learn that any man prayed for money to be honest with and to meet the necessities of his family, and did the work of him who had called him from the market-place of the nation, who did not receive his penny a-day. If to any one it seems otherwise, I believe the apparent contradiction will one day be cleared up to his satisfaction. God has not to satisfy the judgment of men as they are, but as they will be and must be, having learned the high and perfectly honest and grand way of things which is his will. For God to give men just what they want would often be the same as for a man to give gin to the night-wanderer whom he had it in his power to take home and set to work for wages. But I must believe that many of the ills of which men complain would be speedily cured if they would work in the strength of prayer. If the man had not taken up his bed when Christ bade him, he would have been a great authority with the scribes and chief priests against the divine mission of Jesus. The power to work is a diviner gift than a great legacy. But these are individual affairs to be settled individually between God and his child. They cannot be pronounced upon generally because of individual differences. But here as there, now as then, the lack is *faith*. A man may say, "How can I have faith?" I answer, "How can you indeed, who do the thing you know you ought not to do, and have not begun to do the thing you know you ought to do? How should you have faith? It is not well that you should be cured yet. It would have hurt these men to cure them if they would not ask. And you do not pray." The man who has prayed most is, I suspect, the least doubtful whether God hears prayer now as Jesus heard it then. That we doubt is well, for we are not yet in the empyrean of simple faith. But I think the man who believes and prays now, has answers to his prayers even better than those which came to the sick in Judæa; for although the bodily presence of Jesus made a difference in their favor, I do believe that the Spirit of God, after widening its channels for nearly nineteen hundred years, can flow in greater plenty and richness now. Hence the answers to prayer must not only not be of quite the same character as then, but they must be better, coming yet closer to the heart of the need, whether known as such by him who prays, or not. But the change lies in man's power of reception, for God is always the same to his children. Only, being infinite, he must speak to them and act for them in the endless diversity which their growth and change render necessary. Thus only they can receive of his fulness who is all in all and unchangeable.

In our imperfect condition both of faith and of understanding, the whole question of asking and receiving must necessarily be surrounded with mist and the possibility of mistake. It can be successfully encountered only by the man who for himself asks and hopes. It lies in too lofty regions and involves too many unknown conditions to be reduced to formulas of ours; for God must do only the best, and man is greater and more needy than himself can know.

Yet he who asks *shall* receive—of the very best. One promise without reserve, and only one, because it includes all, remains: the promise of the Holy Spirit to them who ask it. He who has the Spirit of God, God himself, in him, has the Life in him, possesses the final cure of all ill, has in himself the answer to all possible prayer.

www.ingramcontent.com/pod-product-compliance
Lightning Source LLC
Chambersburg PA
CBHW022106150426
43195CB00008B/288